# BRITISH FRESH-WATER
# FISHES

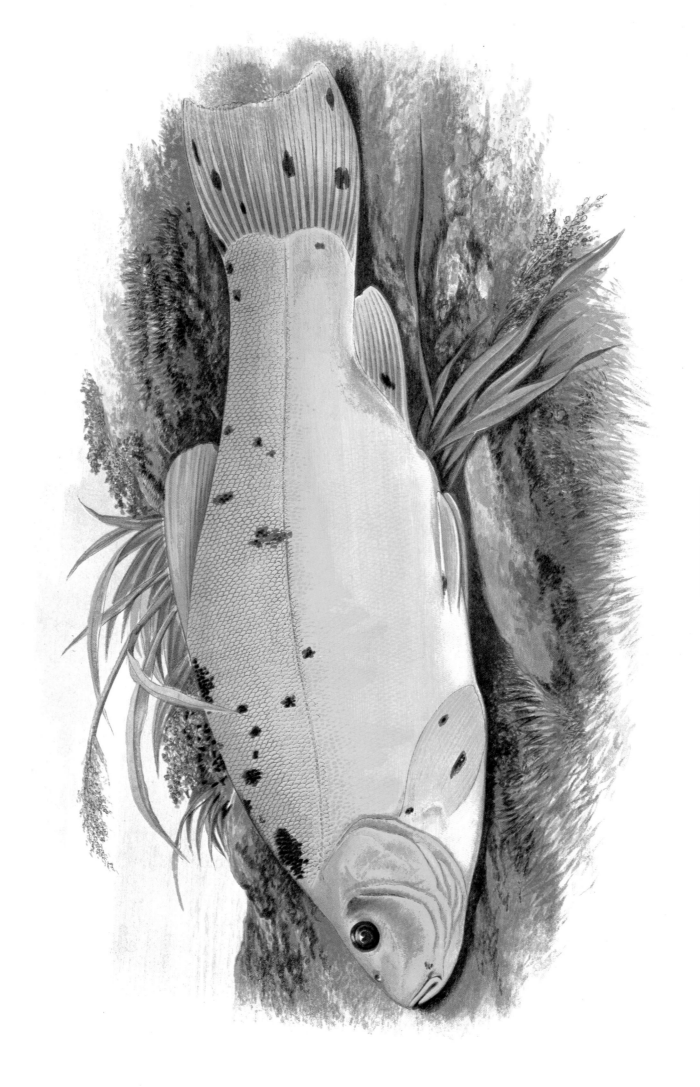

GOLDEN TENCH

# BRITISH FRESH-WATER
# FISHES

## The Rev. W. Houghton

Foreword by Lord Hardinge of Penshurst

Illustrated by A.F. Lydon    Engraved by Benjamin Fawcett

PEERAGE BOOKS

*British Fresh-water Fishes* first published 1879

This redesigned one-volume edition with additional material first published in Great Britain in 1981 by Webb & Bower (Publishers) Ltd

Designed by Malcolm Couch

This edition published in 1984 by Peerage Books
59 Grosvenor Street
London W1

© 1981 Webb & Bower (Publishers) Ltd

ISBN 0 907408 77 X

Printed in Hong Kong

# Foreword

## Lord Hardinge of Penshurst

Although I had heard about this marvellous book, I had never read, held or even seen it until the publishers asked me to write a foreword to their facsimile reproduction. The comprehensive scholarship of the Reverend Houghton's text and the beauty of A. F. Lydon's illustrations, have come to me as a revelation.

Perhaps only a clergyman in Victorian England could have found the time and energy and sheer dedication that enabled an amateur enquiry to result in a scholarly compendium. But the Rev. Houghton was no ordinary man; among many other talents, he has at his disposal a vocabulary of a Shakespearian scope. 'The *Anabas*, or Climbing Perch of the tropics, has receptacles in which it can retain water, as in reservoirs, wherewith to moisten the folded branchial laminae. Besides the branchiae, most osseous fishes possess certain vascular bodies called "pseodobranchiae."' Or again: 'The term grilse or Salmon-peal denotes a fish on its first return from the sea; the former word is probably a corruption of the Swedish *graelax* " a grey lax," *i.e.* "a grey salmon." *Kelt* applies to a salmon whether male or female, after spawning, but the male is also specially distinguished by the term *kipper*; the female is called *shedder* or *baggit*.'

The Rev. Houghton, though an enthusiastic angler with some splendid anecdotes to recount, firmly repudiates any intention to instruct in the art of angling. 'For such information the reader will find all, and perhaps even more than he wants, in the various numerous handbooks which have been published on this subject.' As far as that goes, nothing much has changed since 1879. But he is human, like the rest of us anglers, and his enthusiasm occasionally leads him to give advice, especially when he is fishing for sea-trout and *Salmo ferox*.

His account of these two species is interesting in itself, even controversial. I had thought that the salmon-trout was a fish that had its being only on restaurant menus, and there is not a great difference of opinion between Mr Houghton and me about that; it is just that he regards salmon-trout as an alternative nomenclature for sea-trout—he keeps it strictly within those limits. I had also thought—though from an ignorance that compares ill with the Rev. Houghton's scholarship, so I would not press the point—that *Salmo ferox* was a migratory salmon that had accidentally become landlocked. The author describes it as 'non-migratory'.

I will stay with salmon since my only standing in the matter is as an occasional holiday angler—and for salmon if I have the choice. It is fascinating to note that the Rev. Houghton gave quite serious consideration to a theory then current that 'parr' were not salmon at all, but an entirely different species of small fresh-water fish, a theory that must have assumed that the young salmon went from egg to fry and then direct to smolt. With characteristic persistence and thoroughness he proved to his own satisfaction that the beautifully coloured little parr that abound in salmon rivers are indeed 'salmon parr', the stage of development between fry and smolt.

He describes the disease that plagued salmon in his own time, and, although it bears a different name from the one applied to the outbreak of disease in our own time, many of the symptoms sound the same. He believed, however, that cold conditions and cold water would stem its virulence and spread, whereas it has been a feature of the recent outbreak that it flourished strongly in freezing waters and among early springers, and that it arrived later and weaker in warmer streams, such as those summer rivers on the west coast of Ireland where there is not a salmon to be seen before May.

It is a strange but well-known fact that salmon do not feed in fresh water after they have returned from their sojourn in the oceans, where they have fed hugely and grown sleek and strong. The Rev. Houghton, however, took nothing on trust, and examined personally the contents of the stomachs of many mature fish caught in rivers, all of which he found empty. This is characteristic of his thoroughness, amounting—in the sense of any infinite capacity for taking pains—to genius. He offers the suggestion that the fasting salmon in the river, between the sea and the spawning beds, is in a state of 'quasi-hybernation'. This is a most intriguing notion, and might go some way to explaining the extraordinary capriciousness of 'the King of Fresh-water Fish'. And yet the salmon, leaping falls of twelve feet high or more, or fighting for its life on the end of an angler's line, does not convey any sense of remoteness or sleepiness, but rather of indomitable alertness and vitality.

He is not without humour, as will have been noted from his dry reference to the superfluity in his time of instructional fishing books. Whether the intention of the following passage is humorous I would not care to say. 'Everyone who happens to be in London in the month of November must have viewed with wonder the magnificent Salmon of many pounds weight and of bright silvery hue, exposed for sale on the slabs of the fishmongers' shops. According to our salmon laws it is illegal to take or expose for sale any Salmon between the 2nd of November and the 1st of February. Of course, therefore, these must be foreign fish; they come from the Rhine, not a great way from Rotterdam.' How many images this passage conjures up! The fishmongers' shops of London—the salmon from the Rhine near Rotterdam. We cannot visualize them in these terms, especially the latter, since there are few salmon in the Rhine these days. But it is the words 'Of course, therefore' that catch the eye. No Briton would dream of taking a salmon after the 2nd November, would he, when the law forbade it? Tut tut, perish the thought. Yet it is clear enough that the Rev. Houghton is no common Victorian prig.

To the exquisite illustrations I can only bring a fisherman's eye, not an artist's. But that is Salar the Salmon all right with his gleaming silver hue and just a suggestion of the delicate purple tint he bears when he is fresh and new from the sea and when we are lucky enough to catch him with the tiny sea-lice still on his body. He is not so gaudy as some of his inferiors, but if he cannot compete in decoration with the carp or the golden tench (which offer the artist greater opportunity) he remains the undisputed king. It is a minor sadness to me that an artist so precise and delicate was denied the opportunity to exercise his talent on the climbing perch of the tropics but there is enough joy and beauty here to compensate for the loss.

It is an honour to be associated in even the humblest way with the facsimile reissue of this superb treasury of a book.

# Publisher's Note

BRITISH FRESH-WATER FISHES is a particularly fine example of classic English works of natural history illustrated with coloured lithographs. One of the leading engravers of the time was Benjamin Fawcett, who worked closely with such well-known naturalists as the Rev. W. Houghton, the Rev. F. O. Morris and his brother, Dr B. R. Morris. In many of these works the artist was A. F. Lydon, but Fawcett did use his own paintings, particularly for his early work, to produce his wood-engravings and lithographs.

Benjamin Fawcett, born in 1808 in Bridlington, Yorkshire, was the third person to make his name as a wood-engraver with a book about British birds. Bewick, one of his contemporaries, had used monochrome wood-engraved illustrations to delineate birds; Baxter, another contemporary, had demonstrated the attractiveness of colour printing from engraved wood blocks and was able to produce reasonably accurate colours. Fawcett, a keen naturalist, illustrated his first bird book with hand-coloured wood-engravings and invented his own technique when he turned to colour printing, by using only wood blocks and ordinary inks, unlike Baxter who used both wood and metal plates and oily inks. Fawcett copied his illustrations from watercolours, many of which he produced himself and he accurately imitated the body tones.

An industrious worker, he soon set up business for himself as a bookseller, stationer and printer in the market town of Driffield, near Bridlington, where he printed and bound his own books. This was an immediate success, particularly with the publication of a series of children's copy books with illustrations drawn and engraved by himself. He became acquainted with the Rev. Francis Orpen Morris when he was appointed to a nearby vicarage and they soon formed a literary association that lasted for over forty years. *Bible Natural History*, the result of their first collaboration, appeared in 1849, the text being written by Morris and the hand-coloured engravings produced by Fawcett. They followed the success of this and another publication, *A Book of Natural History*, with work on their first large undertaking, *A History of British Birds*. It took over seven years to complete the vast undertaking of preparing the text and the 357 hand-coloured wood-engravings for the six volumes. Each month they issued one part of four plates and twenty-four pages of letterpress and, on completion, they had sold fifty times more copies than their original estimate.

Fawcett's individual technique for printing in colour was a remarkable breakthrough in this field. Using extremely fine lines he engraved on Turkish boxwood for the key and colour blocks; only hand-presses were used and every plate when printed was always inspected by Fawcett.

Alexander Francis Lydon, who came to Fawcett in the 1850s to learn wood-engraving, became the craftsman's most outstanding pupil. When his skill at watercolour drawings was discovered, however, Lydon became Fawcett's resident artist and had produced drawings for over 1,500 colour wood blocks and innumerable black and white engravings before he left in 1883. Some of his best work appeared in F. O. Morris's *County Seats* which used an average of eight separate blocks for each of the 240 plates.

Lydon then established himself as an illustrator in London, working for another thirty years. Apart from designing plates for books, he drew and exhibited numerous pictures and many of his illustrations appeared in periodicals including *Animal World* and *Illustrated London News*.

Lydon, Morris and other well-known contemporary writers and illustrators liked and respected Fawcett and worked with him for a long period. Between them they produced many beautifully illustrated titles and succeeded in maintaining a high standard of production, despite their vast output. While aiming to produce books which the poorer members of society could afford, excellence was their objective, and their remarkable achievement.

# BRITISH FRESH-WATER FISHES.

GALWAY SEA TROUT

# CONTENTS.

# PREFACE.

IT is hoped that this Work on the Fresh-water Fishes of the British Isles will be found acceptable, and prove generally useful. A description and a coloured drawing of every fresh-water species will, it is believed, enable any one to identify any fish that may be met with. Several species of *Salmonidæ* are now here for the first time illustrated by coloured drawings; the illustrations, in every case where possible, having been made from specimens of the fish themselves.

It only remains for me to express my thanks to those gentlemen who have rendered me assistance in procuring specimens, or otherwise helping me. I must especially thank Dr. A. Günther, of the British Museum—the highest living ichthyological authority*—for permission to make use of the Plates in *The Proceedings of the Zoological Society of London*, (1862, 1863, 1865,) illustrating his papers on the British species of Charr; I have also to thank the Council of that Society for granting me the same permission. I have been fortunate enough to see and handle all the British Charrs, and specimens of all the species have been before the artist engaged in this work, but the Plates above named were found most useful in giving the characteristic colouration which specimens some days out of the water, or specimens preserved in spirits, almost invariably lose. I have also, through the kindness of Dr. Günther, had opportunities of examining specimens of various fish in the British Museum; and the artist has been able to take figures of some species which are either rare, or which I failed to procure for myself.

To Mr. Masefield, of Ellerton Hall, Shropshire, a most successful pisciculturist, I am indebted for specimens of several species, one of the most interesting of which is the Golden Tench. I have also to express my thanks to my brother-in-law, Lieutenant-Colonel Masefield, and to my brother, Major Henry Houghton, for assistance and information. I am greatly obliged to Mr. Thomas Brooke, of the Castle, Lough Esk, and to Mr. Arthur R. Wallace, of Dublin, for several specimens of that very local species, Cole's Charr *(Salmo colii)*. I owe many thanks to Mr. Alexander Scott, of the Garrison Hotel, Lough Melvin, for specimens of Gray's Charr *(S. grayi)*, and the Great Lake Trout *(S. ferox)*. To Mr.

---

* In acknowledgment of Dr. Günther's services the Council of the Royal Society has lately presented this distinguished Naturalist with one of their medals.

John Parnaby, of Troutdale, Keswick, Cumberland, I am indebted for specimens of Windermere Charr, and of the American Trout, *(Salmo fontinalis)*. To Mr. T. J. Moore, the ever obliging Curator of the Liverpool Museum, I owe many thanks for opportunities of examining the fresh-water fishes in that collection; especially for some specimens of the so-called Azurine, taken many years ago from some of the ponds on the Earl of Derby's estate at Knowsley. Mr. Frank Buckland obligingly sent me a few specimens of the young of the Bull Trout of the Coquet; for several large specimens (male and female) of this fish I have to thank Sir Walter B. Riddell, Bart., of Hepple, Northumberland, and Mr. Pape, of Newcastle. Mr. William Dunbar has given me his opinion as to the Coquet Bull Trout, and his remarks will be found in their place. The Earl of Enniskillen was kind enough to write me a letter containing information which proved useful during my visit to Ireland in the summer of 1878. I must not forget to thank Mr. William Haynes, of Patrick Street, Cork, for specimens of the Galway Sea Trout, and for his opinion and experiences of the Slob or Tidal Trout of the Lee and Bandon rivers. To Mr. Charles Selby Bigge, one of the Conservators of the Dee Fishery Board, I must express my best thanks for assistance and information. Sir Watkin Williams Wynn, Bart., most kindly placed his little steam-launch, men, and nets at my disposal in Bala Lake, in September, 1878, for the purpose of procuring Gwyniad; I beg to express my best thanks to the worthy Baronet, as well as to Mr. Owen Wynne and Mr. Bigge, for accompanying me and superintending the fishing. Lastly, I have to thank the artist for the care he has bestowed on the drawings, which I think cannot fail to give satisfaction both as regards accuracy and artistic effect.

Although some additional knowledge on the subject of the British fresh-water fishes has been gained since the publication of the works of Yarrell and Couch,—excellent as those works are,—yet much remains at present obscure. It is not often we know the whole life-history of a fish; this is especially the case with many of the *Salmonidæ*. The solution of various questions relating to this exceedingly difficult family, can, I think, only be successfully made by persons trained more or less in scientific subjects, who have almost unlimited time and ample pecuniary resources at their command, and of course permission from the various Boards of Conservators throughout the country to take from time to time during the whole year, even with nets of very small meshes, such fish, whether small or large, as they may wish to examine. In this way it would be possible to clear away much of the obscurity that at present exists.

This book treats of the natural history of the various species of fishes that are known to occur in the rivers, lakes, and ponds of the British Isles; it is not intended to supply information as to the various modes of angling, whether trolling, spinning, bottom-fishing, fly-fishing, etc., adopted in this country. For such information the reader will find all, and perhaps even more than he wants, in the various numerous handbooks which have been published on this subject.

*Preston-on-the-Weald Moors Rectory, Shropshire,*
*March 1st., 1879.*

# INTRODUCTION.

---

FISHES form the fourth class of vertebrate animals; they are provided either with gills (*branchiæ*), or gill-sacs (*marsipobranchiæ*), by means of which they are enabled to breathe the air contained in the water in which they live; the heart, which consists of a single auricle and ventricle, is present in almost all fish except in the sub-class *Leptocardii*, where certain pulsating sinuses perform the functions of a heart, as in the curious little marine fish the Lancelet *(Branchiostomi lanceolatum)*. The limbs in fishes, corresponding to those organs in other vertebrates, occur, when present, in the form of fins. These fins are generally arranged in pairs at the sides, when they represent the limbs of other vertebrata, or they may occur singly on the back and abdomen; the paired fins are the pectoral and the ventral; the dorsal, anal, and caudal fins are unpaired or asymmetrical.

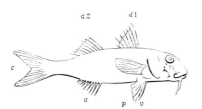

The arrangement of the fins will be readily seen in the accompanying woodcut of the Bearded Mullet (*Mullus barbatus*), d1 is the first dorsal fin; d2 the second dorsal; v one of the paired ventrals; p one of the paired pectorals; a the anal fin, and c the caudal fin or tail. For the most part these fins are structurally similar; they consist of a fold of the skin, or expansions of the integument, and are supported by bony or cartilaginous rays, pretty much in the way, as Milne Edwards says, "that the wings of bats are supported by the fingers and ribs." The pectoral fins, which are analogous to the fore-limbs of other vertebrates, are attached by their base to a strong bony arch, which is itself fixed to the back of the skull, or to the anterior part of the spinal column; this arrangement may be readily seen by any one who carves a Cod's head and shoulders at dinner; the ventrals, or the hind-limbs of fishes, are fixed to an arch of bone—the representation of the pelvic arch of the higher vertebrates—which is sometimes merely supported by the muscles, in cases where these organs are placed far back as in the Pike, a complete skeleton of which is before me as I write; but where the ventral fins are situated not far back, but in the vicinity of the pectoral, the pelvic arch is united to the pectoral arch; the unpaired or *median* fins, as they are sometimes called, are strengthened by osseous or cartilaginous rays, and are supported upon "interspinous bones" imbedded in the flesh of the fish; the points of the interspinous bones are attached to the spinous processes of the vertebræ, each by a ligament, their heads are firmly united to the bases of the fin rays; this arrangement between the median fins, the interspinous bones, and the vertebral spinous processes, may easily be seen by anyone, who will take the trouble to look out for it, when he is eating a fried Perch for breakfast or dinner.

The caudal fin or tail is the chief organ of motion in a fish; by a rapid succession of oblique lateral impulses the fish is enabled to dart through the water at a very quick pace. There are two distinct types of tail in fishes, one being much more common than the other: in one type this organ consists of two equal or nearly equal lobes, which are attached to the spinous processes of the posterior part of the vertebral column; as is the case in all the British fresh-water species of fish, with the exception of the Sturgeon. This symmetrical tail is said to be *homocercal;* from ομος, "the same," and κερκος, "the tail." The other type of tail, which occurs in the Sturgeon, Sharks, Dog-fishes, &c., exhibits an unsymmetrical form, for the lobes are unequal, while the vertebral column runs right into the upper portion of the tail; this structural arrangement is designated by the term *heterocercal;* from ετερος, "different," and κερκος, "the tail" (See this form of tail in the plate of the Sturgeon.)

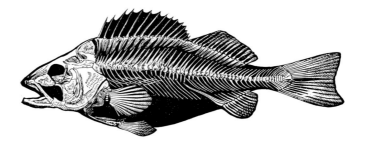

Skeleton of Perch.
The interspinous bones are seen between the vertebral column and the dorsal fins.

The skeleton is either osseous or cartilaginous. Most of the British fresh-water species have osseous skeletons, and belong to the sub-class TELEOSTEI; others, as the Lampreys, have cartilaginous skeletons throughout life; in some fishes, as in the Sturgeon, the skeleton is partly cartilaginous; in the Lancelet, a salt-water fish of the lowest type, there is no true skeleton, the vertebral column being merely a gelatinous notochord. The vertebra of a bony fish is cup-shaped at both ends, the margins being attached by ligaments. In the cavities formed by the junction of the vertebræ there is a quantity of jelly-like substance, imparting to the spine great flexibility: this lubricating gelatinous substance passes from one intervertebral cavity into another through minute pores which perforate their centres. The spinal column consists of two parts, an abdominal, and a caudal. The spinal cord passes through the upper or *neural* arch of the vertebræ for the whole length of the body of the fish: the abdominal vertebræ possess also a superior spinous process, and two transverse processes for the attachment of the ribs. In the caudal vertebræ there are no transverse processes, but this portion of the column possesses an inferior or *hæmal* arch, as well as inferior spinous processes.

The bones of a fish's skull are numerous, and the structure of the head is very complex; the cranium of osseous fishes, when its parts are complete, is made up of no fewer than twenty-six bones. In the median portion of the cranium there is a cavity which contains the brain and the auditory apparatus. The other parts necessary to be noticed for the discrimination of species are:—(1) The gill-cover, consisting of the operculum, præoperculum, suboperculum, and interoperculum. (2) The upper portion of the jaw, called the maxillary. (3) The præ-

or intermaxillary. (4) The palatine bones. (5) The vomer. (6) The hyoid bones. (7) The mandible or lower jaw. (8) The branchiostegal rays.

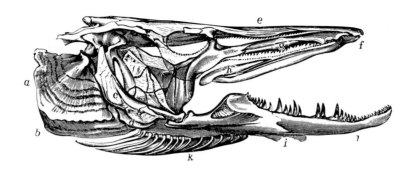

Head of Pike.

*a*, operculum.   *b*, suboperculum.   *c*, preoperculum.   *d*, interoperculum.   *e*, vomer.   *f*, præmaxillary.   *g*, palatine.   *h*, maxillary.   *i*, hyoid.
*k*, branchiostegal rays hyoid.   *l*, mandible.

Fish as a rule have their external integuments covered with scales, though there are fish quite destitute of scales; amongst the scaleless fresh-water fish may be mentioned the Miller's Thumb and the Lampreys.    Important characters may sometimes be drawn from the form of the scales.    Agassiz enumerates four kinds of scales, which he termed *cycloid, ctenoid, placoid,* and *ganoid.*

(1.) *Cycloid* scales (from κυκλος, "a circle,") are thin scales more or less circular, with a smooth margin; they occur in most of our fishes.

(2.) *Ctenoid* scales (from κτεις, κτενος, "a comb,") have their hinder margins cut into comb-like spines, as in the Perch.

(3.) *Placoid* scales (from πλαξ, πλακος, "anything flat and broad,") consist of detached bony plates scattered through the skin; these scales are not unfrequently armed with projecting spines, as in the common Thornback Ray.

(4.) *Ganoid* scales (from γανος, "brightness," "polish,") are generally much thicker than other scales; they are often oblong or rhomboidal, or lozenge-shaped in form, and seldom overlap one another, as in *Lepidosteus,* or Bony Pike of North America.

In nearly all fish a peculiar line, called "the lateral line," is to be seen; this line consists of a number of perforations in the scales, each scale having a pore with a minute tube leading into a longitudinal canal, which has the power of secreting a mucus to lubricate the surface of the whole body; a very desirable object, whereby the fish is enabled to dart through the watery medium in which it passes its life.

The digestive system in fishes consists of an œsophagus, a stomach, and an intestine. The mouth is usually furnished with teeth, which present greater diversity in their mode, as well as in their place of attachment, than is observable in any other class of animals.    In some fishes almost every bone of the mouth is provided with teeth, and even the tongue is armed with these weapons; notably I may instance the teeth in the genus *Esox* (Pike), and in that of *Salmo.*    Everyone knows what a formidable dental armature the Pike possesses; there are large and strong teeth of unequal size on the mandible, the maxillary is destitute of teeth, but the premaxillary, the vomer, the palatine, and the hyoid bones are thickly studded with cardiform* teeth, of which those of the palatines are the largest and disposed most irregularly.    So again, what an effective apparatus for seizing and retaining hold of a

---

* *Cardiform* is from *carduus,* "a thistle;" or more directly from the brush set with wire-teeth for "carding" wool, cotton, etc.

slippery prey is possessed by the Common Trout! the vomer, palantines, intermaxillary, maxillary, the mandible, and the tongue are all furnished with sharp conical teeth. Some fish are entirely destitute of teeth in the mouth, others possess them in a very rudimentary form. In the family of the *Cyprinidæ*, as the Carp, Tench, Roach, etc., the mouth is utterly toothless, hence these fishes are popularly designated by anglers as "leather-mouthed" fishes; but he would make a very great mistake who would assert that these fish are altogether devoid of a dental apparatus. The teeth of the *Cyprinidæ* are situated in the throat, on the pharyngeal bones; though formed on one general type these bones and teeth present differences of form in different species, and this difference of form often possesses high value in the determination of closely allied species or of hybrids. I have dissected out these pharyngeal teeth from all the species of our *Cyprinidæ*, figures of some of which are given on page xvi. Let us notice the form and position of the dental apparatus in one of these fishes, and from thence deduce the functions thereof.

Dental apparatus of Tench.

The figure represents the dental apparatus of the Common Tench; *a* is the roof of the mouth, *b* is the œsophagus, *c* is a hardened and dilated projection from the basilar bone of the cranium; at *d, d* are seen the pharyngeal teeth. By means of strong muscles these

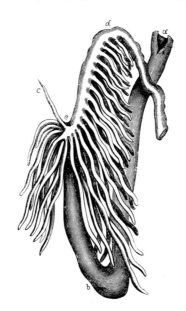

Portion of alimentary canal of Salmon.

*a*, cardia.   *b*, pylorus.   *d*, duodenum, or intestine, with numerous pyloric cæca at *c*.   *e*, bile-duct.

teeth are worked upon the hardened body *c*, which forms a kind of anvil upon which the bruising throat teeth work, and thus whatever food—which in the *Cyprinidæ* is frequently of a vegetable nature—passes into the œsophagus undergoes a triturating process whereby it is more readily rendered digestible.

The stomach of a fish is usually of a large size; it varies, however, both in size and shape; generally it forms a curved tube, like a siphon; the descending portion is called the *cardia*, the ascending part is the *pylorus*, which is generally provided with a valve. Sometimes the pyloric portion has its walls very much thickened, as in the *Salmo stomachicus*, or Gillaroo* Trout of the lakes of Ireland. Behind the pyloric opening of the stomach there are in many fish a number of blind tubes called the *appendices pyloricæ*, or "pyloric cæca;" they vary in number as well as in structure; there may be only two or three of these cæca, or there may be as many as two hundred; in form they may be simple short tubes, sometimes mere cylindrical capsules, as in Cole's Charr (*Salmo colii*), or they may consist of elaborate branches. It is supposed these appendages perform the function of the pancreas; in many fish they are altogether absent. Attention should always be given to these *pyloric cæca*, as they are sometimes of value in determining a species; the Galway Sea Trout (*Salmo gallivensis*), for instance, is at once recognised from the Common Sea or Salmon Trout (*S. trutta*) by the excessive shortness of these blind tubes.

Some fish are entirely carnivorous in their habits, others are to a great extent herbivorous; the solvent power in a voracious species of fish is most conspicuously exemplified; if, for instance, a Pike be captured soon after it has swallowed its prey, the head portion of the same, which is the part that generally first reaches the stomach, will be found more or less digested and dissolved, whilst that part which still remains in the gullet may remain entire. It is mentioned by Aristotle and other ancient writers as a curious fact, that the only fish known to ruminate is the Scarus.†

It appears, however, that amongst the *Cyprinidæ*, as the Carp, Tench, Roach, &c., and other herbivorous fishes, rumination is quite a normal process, and here the curious throat-teeth play a most important part. "The muscular action of a fish's stomach," says Professor Owen, "consists of vermicular contractions, creeping slowly in continuous succession from the cardia to the pylorus, and impressing a two-fold gyratory motion on the contents: so that, while some portions are proceeding to the pylorus, other portions are returning towards the cardia. More direct constrictive and dilative movements occur, with intervals of repose, at both the orifices, the vital contraction being antagonized by pressure from within. The pylorus has the power, very evidently, of controlling that pressure, and only portions of completely comminuted and digested food (chyme) are permitted to pass into the intestine. The cardiac orifice appears to have less control over the contents of the stomach; *coarser portions of the food from time to time return into the œsophagus, and are brought again within the sphere of the pharyngeal jaws, and subjected to their masticatory and comminuting operations.* The fishes which afford the best evidence of this ruminating action are the Cyprinoids (Carp, Tench, Bream,) caught after they have fed voraciously on the ground-bait, previously laid in their feeding haunts to insure the angler good sport. A Carp in this predicament, laid open, shows well

---

* The name of Gillaroo is a corruption of the Irish words *gilla, gille,* "a boy," "an attendant," and *ruadh,* "red;" "the red fellow," in allusion to the bright large red spots on this fish. Gill is the root of the word "gillie," the Salmon Fisher's *gillie* or attendant. Compare the Anglo-Saxon *gilda,* "a companion."

† The Scarus of the Ancients is doubtless the *Scarus cretensis* of Aldrovandi, a Mediterranean species noticed by Spratt and Forbes, still abundant on the Lycian shores; by means of its parrot-shaped mouth, it bites off and feeds on the stony corallines, nullipores, &c., its chief food. It is probable that the Scarus returns portions of the hard coralline contents of the stomach for trituration. Oppian has most clearly expressed the ruminating process in this fish in the following words—

και μουνος εδητυν
αψορρον προιησιν ανα στομα. δευτερον αυτις
δαινυμενος, μηλοισιν αναπτυσσων ισα φοσβην.
(HAL. i. 2.)

and long the peristaltic movements of the alimentary canal; and the successive regurgitations of the gastric contents produce actions of the pharyngeal jaws, as the half bruised grains come into contact with them, and excite the singular tumefaction and subsidence of the irritable palate, as portions of the regurgitated food are pressed upon it. The shortness and width of the œsophagus, the masticatory mechanism at its commencement, and its direct terminal continuation with the cardiac portion of the stomach, relate to the combination of an act analogous to rumination, with the ordinary process of digestion, in all fishes possessing these concatenated and peculiar structures."—(*Anat. of Verteb.*, i. p. 419.)

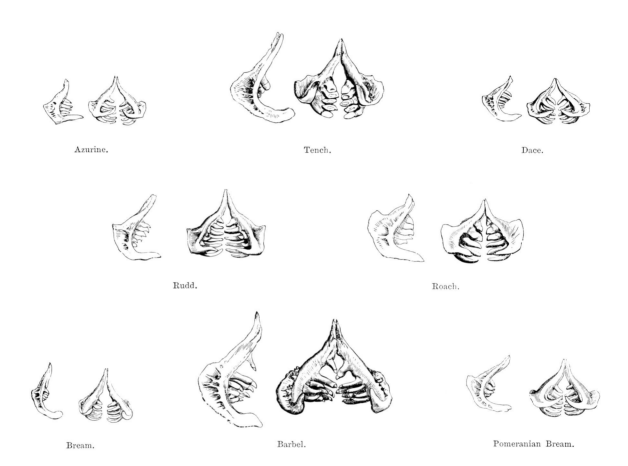

Azurine.　　　　　　　　　Tench.　　　　　　　　　Dace.

Rudd.　　　　　　　　　Roach.

Bream.　　　　　　　　　Barbel.　　　　　　　　　Pomeranian Bream.

In a letter with which Professor Owen, with his characteristic kindness, some few years ago favoured me, he says, "Continued observations under the rare and difficult circumstances according to which they can be made, have now convinced me, that matters for mastication by throat-chewers come *from behind*, as those by mouth-chewers *from before*. And indeed when one comes to consider how thoroughly and regularly the mouth of a fish is washed out by the branchial streams, there needs must be some special arrangement for the masticating machinery in lithophagus and phytophagous fishes. Consider what would be the consequence to the partially broken up coral and pulp, if retained at the back of the mouth, to be pounded piecemeal by the pharyngeals, the rush of two diverging streams through that faucial area going on the while like clockwork. No! the food, reduced if needful to a size swallowable, is bolted, and the branchial way speedily cleared. Then comes into play that anti-peristaltic rotation of the short gullet, and bit by bit the contents are shed in *a tergo* between the grinders till all is pulped."

A fish's intestine is usually short and wide, and more or less convoluted; the mucous membrane presents numerous modifications; it has often a spiral folding (as in the Sharks), which winds in a corkscrew fashion from the pylorus to the anus; by these means of course the absorbing surface is considerably increased; it is generally thick and glandular, always vascular; it is reticulate in many fishes, as in the Muræna and the Sturgeon; in the Salmon the mucous membrane is more or less rugose.

The liver in fishes is generally of a large size and well developed, and frequently contains an enormous quantity of oil, this alone forming an important article of commerce; its texture is usually very soft; the lobes are often numerous; a gall-bladder, from which the bile is poured into the intestine through a single duct, which terminates near the pylorus (see fig. *c*), is, as a rule, present, though there are a few exceptions. Among fresh-water fishes, the gall-bladder is absent in the Lampreys.

In fishes the kidneys consist of two lengthened dark red-brown bodies, on each side of the median line of the body, beneath the vertebræ, extending through the whole or the greater part of the dorsal region of the abdomen. The kidneys of a fish are readily discernible; they form that long red band which lies adjacent to the backbone, easily seen after the extraction of the other viscera; it is that part of a fish which a careless cook fails to clean out thoroughly, which can only be done by means of several scrapings with the sharp point of a knife and copious ablutions of pure cold water.

The respiration of all fishes is purely aquatic; it is beautifully effected in all osseous fishes, with the exception of the *Lophobranchii*,—as the Pipe-fishes (*Syngnathus*), and the Sea-horses (*Hippocampus*),—by means of gills or *branchiæ*. These organs consist of a single or double series of flat cartilaginous bodies which support delicate fringes richly supplied with blood; above, the gills are united to the under side of the head; below, they are connected with the tongue or hyoid bone. The mechanism of the respiratory process is simple in nearly all osseous fishes. The water is taken in at the mouth, and bathes the branchial fissures; having lost its oxygen, the water is forcibly driven through the wide opening on each side of the neck called the gill-fissure, which fissure is closed in front by a series of flat bony scales called the gill-cover or "operculum." The normal number of these vascular branchial arches is four on each side of the hyoid bone in osseous fishes; in cartilaginous fishes the usual number is five; in the *Cyclostomata*, as in the Lampreys, it is seven; in these last-named fish the oxygenating water does not reach the branchial sacs through the mouth; it passes through the gill-sac openings by a tube leading into the pharynx, from whence it passes into the gill-sacs, these gill-sacs freely communicating with each other through the pharynx.

The smaller the external orifice of the gills, and the closer the gill-cover fits on these organs, the greater is the power in the fish to bear exposure to the outward air; so long as the branchial laminæ are kept moist, they can, to some extent, perform their function of appropriating to themselves the oxygen of the water retained within the branchial chamber; but when the external aperture of the gills is large, desiccation by the atmospheric air takes place, and the delicate branchial laminæ collapse, and death speedily ensues, for the blood can no longer effect a passage through them. Perhaps of all fresh-water fishes the Eel is best able to survive a lengthened period out of its watery element. In the Eels the gill-opening is a mere external fissure, a small vertical slit, and is removed very far back; so that the cavity, which lodges the branchiæ, is converted into a long chamber wherein can be retained a considerable quantity of water; so that in early summer mornings, when the dew is on the grass, Eels are able to make their overland-way to some distance from one piece of water to another.

The *Anabas*, or Climbing Perch of the tropics, has receptacles in which it can retain water, as in reservoirs, wherewith to moisten the folded branchial laminæ. Besides the branchiæ, most osseous fishes possess certain vascular bodies called "pseudobranchiæ." There are genera in which these organs have not been detected; they are situated on each side of the head at the dorsal end of the first gill; each pseudobranch consists of a small exposed row of vascular filaments, or as "a vaso-ganglionic body, composed of parallel vascular lobes, and covered by the membrane of the branchial chamber, as in *Esox, Cyprinus, Gadus.* In both cases the vein or efferent vessel of the pseudobranchia becomes the ophthalmic artery."—(Owen.) This organ is small, but can be made out, where present, by the expenditure of a little patience in dissection.

The heart of a fish may almost be said to be in its mouth, so high up in the cavity of the body is it situated. Its situation is in the throat behind the last branchial arch; it is separated from the abdominal cavity by a strong septum. A fish's heart differs from the heart of another vertebrate animal by possessing only one ventricle and one auricle; the latter receives the venous blood from all parts of the body, while the former propels it through the branchial surfaces. From the ventricle there springs a large vessel called the branchial artery, the base of which in most fishes is developed into a strong muscular cavity, the *bulbus arteriosus,* which seems to serve as a kind of second ventricle. This branchial artery carries the venous blood to the gills, where it is oxygenated by the water. From the gills the blood is driven to a single dorsal artery (*aorta*), by whose branches it is conveyed to all parts of the body, returning by the veins to the auricle from which it originally started.

That curious piscine creature, the Lancelet, has no true heart; the circulation is effected by certain pulsating sinuses. In all fishes, except in the Lancelet, the blood is red and cold, that is, it has a temperature equal to that of the medium in which the fish dwells. In the Lepidosiren the heart possesses two auricles and one ventricle. The mention of this strange amphibian-like fish leads me to mention an organ that exists in many fishes, called the "swim-bladder," or "air-bladder," with which every fisherman is familiar. This air-bladder, which is very variable in form according to the species of fish, is a sac filled with gas; it extends along the back of the abdomen, between the kidneys and the intestinal canal. Sometimes, as in the Perch, it is a simple elongated cylinder closed at both ends; sometimes, as in the Carp, Tench, Roach, and other *Cyprinidæ,* this organ is divided crosswise into two portions by a deep constriction, with a minute orifice leading from the one portion to the other. Now this air-bladder is sometimes, and often, simply a closed sac; but in some fishes it opens into the œsophagus by a narrow channel or duct, called the *ductus pneumaticus.* How does the gas or air gain admittance into the bladder? In the case of those fish whose air-bladders possess no *ductus pneumaticus* it seems that the gas must be secreted by the inner membrane of the bladder from the blood; but in fishes which are provided with a *ductus pneumaticus,* so as to lead to a communication with the gullet, the air generated within may be in a great measure derived from the atmosphere. The contained gas of the air-bladder of fishes consists of a mixture of nitrogen and oxygen with traces of carbonic acid; in fresh-water fishes the largest percentage of nitrogen occurs; in salt-water fishes oxygen is said to occur in the largest proportion. Some, I believe, have maintained that the gas of the swim-bladder of Carps consists of pure nitrogen. Humboldt, who experimented on the Electric Eel, (*Gymnotus electricus*), found the gas of its air-bladder to consist of ninety-six per cent. of nitrogen and four of oxygen. Biot, on the other hand, experimenting on some deep-sea Mediterranean fishes, discovered eighty-seven per cent. of oxygen, the rest nitrogen with a trace of carbonic acid.*

---

* The late Dr. Davy was rather doubtful as to the accuracy of these experiments. He remarks, "That the same organ should secrete two gases so very different in their nature appears anomalous and deserving of further enquiry. Indeed does not the entire subject need more minute enquiry? At present the facts relating to it are few, and seem far from adequate to allow of very satisfactory conclusions being drawn as to the use of the bladder and its secretion in the animal economy, except of a mechanical kind as affecting the specific gravity of the fish. Were the gas uniformly of one kind, were it constantly azote, it might be easy to assign it a plausible end; the function of the air-bladder might be inferred to be auxiliary to that of the kidneys. The secretion of oxygen is the anomalous fact, so contrary is it to the ordinary changes in living animals, in which the general tendency is to the consumption of

The swim-bladder does not exist in all fishes; in the Lampreys it is entirely absent; it does not exist in the Sharks, Dog-fish, Rays, and the Chimera. There is a swim-bladder and an air-duct in the Eel, Herring, Salmon, Pike, Carp, Silurus, with their allies; in the order *Anacanthini*, as in the Ophidium, Cod, and Plaice, the air-bladder when present has no pneumatic duct; in the *Acanthopterygii* or spiny-finned Fishes, as in the Perch and Miller's Thumb amongst fresh-water species, the air-bladder, where it exists, is without a pneumatic duct, the same is the case with the orders *Plectognathi*, File-fish, Trunk-fish, Globe-fish, and *Lophobranchii*, Pipe-fishes and Sea-horses. In the sub-class *Dipnoi*, or "Double-breathers," as in the *Protopterus annectens* of Tropical Africa, and the *Lepidosiren paradoxa* of Brazil, we meet with a most interesting form of air-bladder: it is double, cellular, and lung-like, and is provided with an air-duct, glottis, and pulmonary vein.

What then are the functions of the swim-bladder and air-duct, when present? What does their presence appear to indicate? Will it serve to throw any gleam of light on that most interesting subject, the origin of species? There can be no doubt that "under all its diversities of structure and function, the homology of the swim-bladder with the lungs is clearly traceable." True, there is nothing at all in the simple cylindrical closed air-bladder of a Perch, with its shining silvery fibrous tunic, to remind one of the cellular structure of the lung of an amphibian; but it must be remembered that there are numerous gradations, leading by various transitions, from a single cavity up to a highly complex cellular organ, which both in structure and function is indisputably a lung. The fishes which most closely resemble the amphibians are the *Protopterus annectens*, or Mud-fish of Tropical Africa, and the *Lepidosiren paradoxa*, of the river Amazon and its tributaries. In *Protopterus*, we find these traditions complete, for here we see a double lung-like air-bladder, with air-duct, glottis and pulmonary vein, and this respiratory apparatus, be it remembered, is at certain periods functionally identical with the lungs of air-breathing vertebrates; for *Protopterus*, after the rains have ceased to flood the river Gambia, finds itself left behind in the mud of the retreating waters; the scorching rays of a tropical sun compel the fish to burrow in the mud, in which it forms a kind of cocoon of hard-baked clay. How is the fish to live in this changed locality? As an inhabitant of the water, the respiration was effected by means of gills alone, as in ordinary fishes; but how is the circulation to be maintained now that it is a terrestrial animal; Professor Owen tells us in clear and distinct terms. "Whatever amount of respiration was requisite to maintain life during the dry months is effected in the pulmonary air-bladders; its short and wide duct or trachea, the œsophageal origin of which is kept open by a laryngeal cartilage, introduces the air directly into the bladders; the blood transmitted through the branchial arches to the pulmonary arteries, is distributed by their ramifications over the cellular surface of the air-bladders, and is returned arterialised by the pulmonary veins. A mixed venous and arterial blood is thence distributed to the system and again to the air-bladders." —(*Anat. of Vert.*, i. p. 498.) When the *Protopterus* resumes its piscine nature on the return of the water, the branchial circulation again comes into play. In this fish, therefore, we have an instance of an animal which is a fish at certain periods of its existence, and an amphibian at others; and I believe with Darwin that natural selection has operated "in converting a swim-bladder into a true lung, used exclusively for respiration."

It surely is quite conceivable that under changed conditions, acting for a lengthened period, the Salamandroid Protopterus—which some naturalists of note maintain to be more allied to amphibia than to fish—might gradually convert its ichthyic characters into amphibian ones, just as I believe it has converted, not only the swim-bladder and pneumatic duct into an air-breathing lung, trachea and glottis, but also two pairs of the gills of the branchial

oxygen. *A priori*, one might almost as much expect oxygen to be exhaled from the lungs, in respiration, as to be separated from the blood by secretion in the air-bladder; and had we not the authority of so accurate an observer as M. Biot, we might be led to suspect that the statement of its being so was founded on error."—(*Physiol. Res.* p. 271.)

arches into vascular channels, in order that it should be able to maintain a slow circulation as a terrestrial animal, when encased in its cocoon of mud. I see nothing improbable in the supposition that in *Protopterus* we have a living witness of a fish in a transition stage towards becoming, in course of time, under favourable conditions, a true amphibian; and I do believe that amphibia are altered forms of fish, to which in some cases, they bear a considerable resemblance; and I think it probable that one of the steps in the transition—and a most interesting and important step it is—is made by the gradual conversion of the swim-bladder and pneumatic duct, into a lung, trachea, and glottis.

Generally speaking, the function of a fish's swim-bladder is no doubt merely a mechanical one; but this organ cannot be of much importance, nor does it exhibit "such a plain and direct instance of mechanical contrivance" as was maintained by Paley, Roget, Cuvier, and others. For how is it that in different genera of fishes, of precisely similar habits, some have an air-bladder, others have not? One can at once understand why such an organ should be absent in the *Pleuronectidæ* (Soles, Turbots, Flounders, etc.), whose habits confine them to the bottom of the water, and which do not, therefore, require the mechanical upward lift afforded by an air-bladder; but when we find that one surface-swimming Mackerel (*Scomber colias*) has a swim-bladder, and another (*S. vulgaris*), of precisely similar habits, is devoid of one, it is obvious, notwithstanding the general function of the organ when present, that it is by no means an essential adjunct to swimming. Many of the *Siluridæ* possess a large and sometimes complex swim-bladder, but genera occur in which there is no swim-bladder at all. The air-bladder in the *Siluridæ*, and in some of the *Cyprinidæ*, communicates with the organ of hearing by means of the ear-bones, or auditory ossicles, and doubtless serves to intensify the sound. Fish that keep to the bottom, are, as a rule, devoid of this organ, but in the mud-loving Eel we meet with swim-bladder and pneumatic duct.

With respect to the reproductive system, fishes are generally *oviparous*. In osseous fishes, as a rule, the ova are deposited and impregnated by the milt of the male externally. This is the case with all our fresh-water species. Rare instances are met with, as in the marine viviparous Blenny, in which the females produce offspring already somewhat advanced in growth. In such cases impregnation must occur internally, though no structural peculiarity is to be detected in the male or female organs. In the cartilaginous Sharks and Dogfish the generative apparatus is different, and approximates to a certain extent that type of structure observable in reptiles and birds. The ova of the female fish is familiarly known as the "roe;" the milt of the male is spoken of as the "soft roe."

In the construction of their nervous and cerebral system fishes stand the lowest in the vertebrate scale. I cannot do better than quote the remarks of Cuvier on the general attributes of fishes, and their relative position in the animal scale.

"Breathing by the medium of water, that is to say, only profiting by the small quantity of oxygen contained in the air mixed with the water, their blood remains cold; their vitality, the energy of their senses and movements, are less than in mammalia and birds. Thus their brain, although similar in composition, is proportionally much smaller, and their external organs of sense not calculated to impress upon it powerful sensations. Fishes are in fact, of all the vertebrata, those which give the least apparent evidence of sensibility. Having no elastic air at their disposal, they are dumb, or nearly so, and to all the sentiments which voice awakens or entertains they are strangers. Their eyes are, as it were, motionless, their face bony and fixed, their limbs incapable of flexion and moving as one piece, leaving no play to their physiognomy, no expression to their feelings. Their ear, enclosed entirely in the cranium, without external concha, or internal cochlea, composed only of some sacs and membranous canals, can hardly suffice to distinguish the most striking sounds, and, moreover, they have little use for the sense of hearing, condemned to live in the empire of silence, where everything around is mute.

Even their sight in the depths which they frequent could have little exercise, if most of them had not, in the size of their eyes, a means of compensation for the feebleness of the light; but even in these the eye hardly changes its direction, still less by altering its dimensions can it accommodate itself to the distances of objects. The iris never dilates or contracts, and the pupil remains the same in all intensities of illumination. No tear ever waters the eye—no eyelid wipes or protects it—it is in the fish but a feeble representative of this organ, so beautiful, so lively, and so animated in the higher classes of animals.

Being only able to support itself by pursuing a prey, which itself swims more or less rapidly, having no means of seizing it but by swallowing, a delicate perception of savours would have been useless if nature had bestowed it; but their tongue, almost motionless, often entirely bony or coated with dental plates, and only furnished with slender nerves, and these few in number, shows us that this organ also is as obtuse as its little use would lead us to imagine. Their smell even cannot be exercised so continually as in animals which respire air and have their nostrils constantly traversed by odorous vapours.

Lastly, their touch, almost annihilated at the surface of their body by the scales which clothe them, and in their limbs by the want of flexibility in their rays, and the nature of the membranes investing them, is confined to the ends of their lips, and even these in some are osseous and insensible.

Thus, the external senses of fishes give them few lively and distinct impressions. Surrounding nature cannot affect them, but in a confused manner; their pleasures are little varied, and they have no painful impressions from without but such as are produced by wounds.

Their continual need, which, except in the breeding season, alone occupies and guides them, is to assuage the internal feeling of hunger, to devour almost all that they can. To pursue a prey or to escape from a pursuer makes the occupation of their life; it is this which determines their choice of the different situations which they inhabit; it is the principal cause of the variety of their forms, and of the special instincts or artifices which nature has granted to some of the species.

Vicissitudes of temperature affect them little, not only because these are less in the element which they inhabit than in our atmosphere, but because their bodies taking the surrounding temperature, the contrast of external cold and internal heat scarcely exists in their case.* Thus the seasons are not so exclusively the regulators of their migration and propagation as amongst quadrupeds, or more especially birds. Many fishes spawn in winter; it is towards autumn that Herrings come out of the north to shed upon our coast their spawn and milt. It is in the north that the most astonishing fecundity is witnessed, if not in variety of species, at least in individuals; and in no other seas do we find anything approaching to the countless myriads of Herrings and Cod which attract whole fleets to the northern fisheries.

The loves of fishes are cold as themselves; they only indicate individual need. Scarcely is it permitted to a few species that the two sexes should pair, and enjoy pleasure together; in the rest the males pursue the eggs rather than seek the females; they are reduced to impregnate eggs, the mother of which is unknown, and whose produce they will never see. The pleasures of maternity are equally unknown to most species; a small number only carry their eggs with them for a short time; with few exceptions fishes have no nest to build and no young to nourish; in a word, even to the last details, their economy contrasts diametrically with that of birds."†

---

* Sudden change of temperature, however, does affect some kinds of fish in a most marked manner. When placed at once into very cold water, at a temperature considerably lower than the water from which they have been taken, fish will often turn on their backs, become apparently paralyzed and die. The reader will find some interesting experiments on "The Degree of Temperature fatal to Fishes,"—the temperature in these cases being that of warm or hot water—in Dr. J. Davy's *Physiological Researches*, p. 297-305. The experiments were made at Oxford some years ago in conjunction with Mr. Robertson, Demonstrator at the Museum, Oxford, and my valued friend, Professor Rolleston.

† *Cyclop. Anat. & Phys.*, iii. p. 955-6.

The great class of Fishes (Pisces,) is by some naturalists divided into the following six sub-classes, (1) *Teleostei*, (2) *Dipnoi*, (3) *Ganoidei*, (4) *Chondropterygii*, (5) *Cyclostomata*, (6) *Leptocardii*. I follow Dr. Günther in the following classification:—

The first sub-class of TELEOSTEI contains all those fishes which have a complete bony skeleton; this sub-class comprehends more species than all the other sub-classes put together, and nearly all our British fresh-water species belong to this great sub-class. It contains the following orders, which are again themselves divided into different families, the families into genera, and the genera into species.

Order I.—Acanthopterygii, from ακανθος, "a spine," and πτερυξ, "a wing," or "fin," contains those fishes whose fin rays form spines, as in the Common Perch. The air-bladder, when present, has no pneumatic duct.

Order II.—Acanthopterygii-Pharyngognathi, contains those species in which the inferior pharyngeal bones coalesce, as in the marine *Labridæ* or Wrasses; air-bladder without pneumatic duct. There is no British fresh-water species belonging to this order.

Order III.—Anacanthini, in which, excepting in one genus, the vertical and ventral fins are without spinous rays; from α, "not," and ακανθος, "a spine." Air-bladder, when present, without pneumatic duct. This order contains two sub-orders, (*a*) Gadoidei (Codfish families), and (*b*) Pleuronectoidei (Flat-fish, Soles, Turbots, etc.) We have a single fresh-water representative of sub-order (*a*) in the Eel-pout, or Burbot, *(Lota vulgaris)*: and of sub-order (*b*) in the Flounder *(Pleuronectes flesus)*, which is known to ascend our rivers to a considerable distance; some years ago Flounders were common in the Severn as high up as Shrewsbury.

Order IV.—Physostomi. This is an extensive order, and comprises several families, as the *Cyprinidæ*, *Clupeidæ*, *Esocidæ*, *Salmonidæ*, and *Murænidæ*, all of which have British fresh-water representatives. The fin rays are articulated; the first of the dorsal and pectoral being sometimes more or less bony; the spineless ventral fins, when present, are not situated near the pectorals, but on the abdomen. The word *Physostomi* is from the Greek φυσα, "a bladder," and στομα, "a mouth," in allusion to the air-bladder, when present, being connected with the mouth or gullet by means of the pneumatic duct, which is the invariable accompaniment of the air-bladder in this order. Carp, Shad, Pike, Salmon, and Eel are fresh-water representatives of this order.

Order V.—Lophobranchii, from λοφος, "a tuft," and βραγχια, "the gills." In this order the gills are formed of small rounded lobes, and are not laminated. The air-bladder has no pneumatic duct. Marine examples are Sea-horses (*Hippocampus*), and Pipe-fishes (*Syngnathus*). There is no fresh-water representative.

Order VI.—Plectognathi, from πλεκτος, "twisted," or "fastened together," and γναθος, "the jaw," because generally the maxillary and præmaxillary bones of the mouth are immovably connected on each side of the mouth, as in the genera *Ostracion* (Trunkfish), *Balistes* (Filefish), and *Orthagoriscus* (Sunfish). Of this order there is no British fresh-water representative; indeed Günther tells us that nearly all are marine fishes. The air-bladder has no pneumatic duct.

Sub-class II.—DIPNOI is one of the most interesting of all the sub-classes; the word means "double breathers." This has already been explained on pages xix-xx, to which the reader is referred. Two genera and two species only are known, the *Protopterus annectens* of tropical Africa, which has three external branchial appendages, and the *Lepidosiren paradoxa* of Brazil, which is destitute of external appendages.

Sub-class III.—GANOIDEI has the skeleton more or less ossified; the scales often are hard and polished (γανος, "brightness"); ventral fins, when present, are abdominal; the intestine has a spiral valve. It is divided into two orders:

I.—Holostei. Body covered with scales; skeleton bony.

*A.* Scales cycloid. 1. *Amiidæ* (Bowfin or Mudfish of the fresh waters of North America).

*B.* Scales ganoid.

(*a*) Fins without fulcra. 2. *Polypteridæ.* Fresh waters of Central and Western Africa.

(*b*) Fins with fulcra. 3. *Lepidosteidæ,* as the Bony Pike *(L. osseus)* of North America.

II.—CHONDROSTEI. Skin naked, or with osseous bucklers; skeleton partly cartilaginous.

*A.* Mouth small, transverse, inferior. *Acipenseridæ* (Sturgeons).

*B.* Mouth lateral, very wide. *Polyodontidæ* (Spoonbill Sturgeon of the Mississippi .and tributaries).

Fresh-water representative of *A* is met with in the Sturgeon.

Sub-class IV.—CHONDROPTERYGII. In this sub-class the fish have a cartilaginous skeleton, and the skull is without sutures; the tail has a produced upper lobe; the gills are attached to the skin by the outer margin, with several intervening gill-openings; rarely with one gill-opening only; no gill-cover; no air-bladder; intestine with a spiral valve; ovaries with few and large ova impregnated internally, and in some cases developed internally. Males with prehensile organs attached to the ventral fins. Contains two orders.

I.—HOLOCEPHALA. One external gill-opening only,' as in the *Chimæra monstrosa* (Arctic Chimæra).

II.—PLAGIOSTOMATA. From five to seven gill-openings.

Sub-order 1.—*Selachoidei.* Gill-openings lateral (Sharks and Dog-fish).

Sub-order 2.—*Batoidei.* Gill-openings ventral (Rays).

Of this sub-class there is no British fresh-water representative.

Sub-class V.—CYCLOSTOMATA, contains fishes whose skeletons are cartilaginous, and notochordal, which have no ribs, no real jaws; whose skull is not separate from the vertebral column, and which are limbless; the gills have no branchial arches, but are in the form of pouches or sacs, generally seven in number on each side of the neck; there is only one nasal aperture; and the heart has no bulbus arteriosus. The mouth is suctorial in the mature form, or crescent-shaped in the larval form. The alimentary canal is simple, straight, without cæcal appendages, pancreas, or spleen.

There are two families, viz:

1.—*Petromyzontidæ,* in which the nasal duct terminates blind, not penetrating the palate; as in the Lampreys.

2.—*Myxinidæ,* in which the nasal duct penetrates the palate, (Glutinous Hag):

In the sub-class VI.—LEPTOCARDII, the only representative, I believe, is the Lancelet (*Branchiostoma lanceolatum,*) occasionally found on the English southern coasts. This fish occupies the lowest scale amongst vertebrate animals; its skeleton is membrano-cartilaginous and notochordal; it has no ribs, no brain, pulsating sinuses in place of a heart; the blood is colourless; the respiratory cavity is confluent with the abdominal cavity, the branchial clefts are numerous, and the water is expelled by an opening in front of the vent. There are no jaws.

The British ichthyological fauna numbers about two hundred and fifty species, of which about fifty-five are either permanently or periodically inhabitants of fresh water. With the exception of the Sturgeon and the Lampreys, all the fresh-water fishes of the British Isles belong to the great sub-class TELEOSTEI, and to the orders, I. *Acanthopterygii,* which contains six species; III. *Anacanthini,* two species; and IV. *Physostomi,* all the remaining species, represented by the families *Cyprinidæ, Clupeidæ, Esocidæ, Salmonidæ,* and *Murænidæ.*

Fish, like other creatures, are subject to diseases. Various parasites, either in the form of *Entozoa* or *Epizoa,* find a lodgment within or upon their bodies. The internal parasitic hosts are very numerous; they occur generally in the stomach, pyloric appendages, and intestine, in the form of various kinds of tapeworm (*tænia*), or small filamentous annelids (*ascaris*).

Sometimes intermuscular parasites are found, but this is less common, I believe, in fish belonging to this country than in some foreign species. The *Epizoa* are found on the surface of the bodies of fishes; various forms of *Crustacea*, such as *Lernœa*, *Lepeophtharies*, *Argulus foliaceus*, attack them; the curious little *Gyrodactylus elegans* I have found inside the gills of the Three-spined Stickleback; the young fry of the fresh-water swan mussel (*Anodonta cygnea*), I have detected on the fins of the Perch, Stickleback, and a few other fishes; Pike are sometimes, when in a weak and unhealthy state, covered with that curious little discophorous annelid, *Piscicola*. As a rule, however, I do not think that parasitic guests affect fish very seriously. When *epizoa*, or external parasites, abound to a great extent, the fish is, no doubt, injured by them, and a weakly condition of the fish may be to some extent the cause of their attacks. But although the presence of animal parasites, whether external on the skin or internal within the viscera, may be unproductive of much serious mischief, it is quite different with certain subtle forms of vegetable growth, which often occasion fearful destruction, like some epidemic amongst the higher animals.

One essential condition for health in a fish is undoubtedly pure water; this is specially the case in the *Salmonidœ*. Some fish, however, will certainly exist, and apparently thrive, in water which can by no means be called pure. I have taken the Three-spined Stickleback from very foul ditches indeed. Carp and Tench will do fairly well in muddy pools, but they will do better still, and prove more fitted for the table, if kept in ponds supplied by bubbling springs, and containing aquatic plants of various kinds, with a muddy bottom in which they can hybernate in the cold winter. As a rule salt-water fishes are much less liable to suffer from parasitic attacks than fresh-water species. Mr. Jackson, the able Curator of the Southport Aquarium, tells me that fresh-water fish do not thrive in confinement; that they are extremely liable to be attacked, to an injurious extent, by parasites, but that this is not the case with fish in the salt-water tanks. One of the most dreaded and fatal of all the diseases to which piscine nature is subject, occurs in the form of white flocculent patches on the tail, head, or other parts of a fish's body. Everyone, with the slightest experience, must have observed what I am alluding to, if he has merely kept Goldfish in glass globes. This white filamentous growth is either a fungus, or some plant related to a fungus; it is known by the name of *Saprolegnia ferax*, and sometimes does incalculable mischief in some of our Salmon rivers. In ponds or tanks where young Trout are artificially cultivated, thousands often die from the attacks of *Saprolegnia ferax*; and I feel certain, from what I have noticed myself, that this fatality is primarily caused by overcrowding in a water which has too high a temperature. It is generally easier to prevent the appearance of a disease than to stop its ravages when it has once begun. Now it is an ascertained fact that fungi of all kinds require for their development a certain warmth of temperature, and that cold will prevent the spores of a fungus from germinating. This holds good with regard to the larger kinds of fungi, as well as to those almost infinitesimal atoms, such as *Bacteria*, *Bacillaria*, &c., which are doubtless at the root of many zymotic diseases affecting men and other highly organized animals.

On the subject of the fungoid growth known as *Saprolegnia ferax* affecting Salmon, I cannot do better than quote the remarks of my friend, Mr. W. G. Smith, a very competent authority on all questions relating to mycology. He writes:—

"For several weeks past the newspapers have contained accounts of the diseased condition of various fish in several of our northern rivers—principally the Esk and Eden. The disease of the fish is caused by the attack of a fungus. No doubt every one with a slight acquaintance with fungi suspected from the first that the disease was similar to the familiar disease of Goldfish in aquaria, and no other than the common *Saprolegnia ferax*. From material kindly forwarded to the writer for examination from Carlisle by Mr. George Brookter, of Huddersfield, there seems to be no reason to doubt the identity of the parasite with the common pest of Carp—*Saprolegnia ferax*.

According to the newspaper reports we find that the owners of the Salmon fisheries on the Tweed, and the Commissioners to whom the protection of the fisheries is entrusted, have for years been disturbed, distressed, and annoyed by a great mortality which comes over the fish towards the end of the spawning season. Any time during February, and anywhere between Stobo and Berwick, dead Salmon may be seen by the half dozen in every pool. The epidemic is thus described :—Large numbers of Salmon—not only kelts, but clean fish lately arrived from the sea—appear to be affected with an epidemic which destroys hundreds of them. The head and tail first, and gradually the whole body is attacked by a disease which appears to eat away the flesh, turning it white, and giving the fish the appearance of being affected with leprosy. Such fish are entirely unfit for food. Correspondents describe them as leaping out of the water, as if in pain and in frantic efforts to escape; some return to the sea, but many perish in their attempts to reach the salt water. The Salmon caught in the estuary are not diseased in this way, and, as the epidemic is said to be spreading to the Trout, it would appear that some peculiar condition in the fresh water is the cause of the remarkable phenomena. Some of these characteristics of the disease are not confirmed by a more correct observation and less hasty deduction, but what is said enables one to recognise the malady which for several years past has slain its thousands of Salmon on the Tweed. In both rivers the afflicted animals suffer violent pain, and rush blindly about as if brain disease existed through generally inflammatory action, and in both rivers the dead bodies present a similar appearance.

The various theories which have been published in the daily papers as to the cause of the disease and the 'cause of the fungus' have no foundation in fact. The most common theory seems to be that the Salmon die from disease induced from inflammatory action arising from retention of the milt. The theory of the fishery owners and the Commissioners does not afford even the small consolation that the fish die a natural death, for they hold, and are ready to affirm on oath, that the vile pollutions of the woollen mills and towns on Tweedside cause all the evil. The controversy has continued for years, but now some facts have turned up in Cumberland and Westmoreland which must carry a verdict of acquittal for the millowners. A short time ago large numbers of dead Salmon were found in the Kent, a river which is as pure as Thirlemere itself. No pollution, wilful or accidental, could be traced, and the authorities had to confess their ignorance of the cause of death, coming to the illogical conclusion that it arose from exhaustion after spawning, oblivious apparently that this has happened every year since Kent was a river, and the deaths have been heard of only now. From a statement in the *Times* it appears that things piscatorial are much worse in the Eden, which flows through a beautiful country guiltless of the offences of factories.

The *Carlisle Journal* says, 'Large numbers of kelts—that is, fish that have spawned—are found in pools and floating down the stream dead and dying. The appearance of the disease is that of a white fungus. This affects the head of the fish, then it attacks the tail, and subsequently the fins. In some instances the fungus grows so plentifully that the fish appears to be swimming about with a white nightcap over its head. Salmon smolts and Trout are also affected by the disease. An unusual number of kelts have remained in the Eden this year, and many of them have died; so many, in fact, that the water bailiffs have been employed in picking them out of the water and burying them.'

This disease is by no means confined to Salmon and young Salmon (smolts), but Trout, Eels, Lampreys, Flounders, Minnows, and other fish, are equally affected. A watcher on the Esk informed Mr. Brookter that the disease nearly always starts at the nose, and gradually spreads over the head: the fish, he affirmed, would come to a still part of the river with only a small patch on the nose, and in two or three days the patch would have extended over the head, and at the same time have appeared on the base of the fins and tail. The disease is said to be generally confined to the parts mentioned, unless the fish has had a bruise or scar anywhere so as to remove the scales. From an examination of actual specimens, however, it seems proved that the disease by no means always commences at the head. With a very lower power of the microscope the fungus will be seen to consist of a dense mass of matted threads without joints, and a thick forest of minute transparent clubs.

If asked for a reason for the uncommon abundance of the fungus this year, I should be inclined to refer it to the extraordinary mildness of the late winter. Severe weather, or a sudden change of temperature, will generally collapse fungi of the nature of *Saprolegnia ferax*, as will several dilute chemical infusions, and that without damaging the fish; but an experiment, though successful in an aquarium, might possibly fail in a large river.

The fungus has been described as infesting the dead, as well as the living, fish; but with me the fungus has invariably vanished with the death of the fish. Dead fish are certainly covered with a white cottony coating, but on an examination of this flocculent mass, under the microscope, it is found to consist wholly of white granular matter, consisting of bacteria, monads, etc., and no fungus threads or fruit belonging to *Saprolegnia ferax* can be seen.

The disease has been so virulent on the Esk, during the present spring, that the watchers have in some instances buried as many as three hundred and fifty fish in three days between Langholme and Longtown."—*Gardeners' Chronicle, pp.* 560-561, 1878.

Pisciculturists, interested in the artificial rearing of the *Salmonidæ*, should bear in mind the following, as I think, important essentials for success :—*

1. The water in which the ova or young fry are placed should be cold, at a temperature of 37° to 47°.

2. The fry should be always supplied with gravel, stones, or projecting pieces of rockwork, under which they can shelter.

3. The pond, tank, or reservoir should always be covered over with boards or other material, to exclude the hot rays of the sun.

4. Overcrowding must be avoided, or the fish will be attacked with *Saprolegnia ferax*, an epidemic which when once begun, it will be found almost, if not quite, impossible to stop.

5. A stream of pure cold water should incessantly be running, day and night, *briskly* through the preserve.

* The best food for young Trout and Salmon is a hard-boiled egg, passed by pressure and friction through the gratings of a fine strainer.

# BRITISH FRESH-WATER FISHES.

ON THE THAMES, NEAR ROEBUCK INN.

*Order I.*
*ACANTHOPTERYGII.*

*Family*
*PERCIDÆ.*

## PERCH.

### (*Perca fluviatilis.*)

PERKE,      ARISTOTLE, H. A., ii. 9 § 4; 12 § 13, vi. 13 § 2.
*Perca,*     PLINY, xxxii. 9; AUSON., Id. x. 115.
*Perca fluviatilis,*   RONDEL., ii. 196; WILLUGHBY, iv. c. 14, p. 291; LIN., i. p. 481; YARRELL, Brit.
                 Fish., i. p. 1; GÜNTHER'S Cat. i. p. 58; COUCH'S Fish. Brit. Isles, i. 185.

*Characters of the Genus* PERCA.—"Seven branchiostegals. All the teeth villiform, without canines; teeth on the palatine bones, tongue smooth. Two dorsals; the first with thirteen or fourteen spines; anal fin with two spines; operculum spiniferous; præoperculum and præorbital serrated. Scales small; head naked above."—GÜNTHER.

OF the family *Percidæ* there are only two British fresh-water species, the Common Perch (*Perca fluviatilis*) of our ponds, lakes, and rivers, and the Ruffe or Pope. The Perch was known to the ancient Greeks and Romans. Aristotle speaks of it under the name of

Πέρκη; he says that the Perch produces its eggs in a continuous series like frogs, and that the fishermen unwind the broad entangled mass from among the reeds in ponds; this description at once enables us to identify the fish with certainty; but Aristotle under the same name seems to have also included some marine species, as the Bass or Sea Perch. Pliny recommends the burnt ashes of salted perch-heads as a remedy to dispel pustules (xxxii. 9). Ausonius was certainly acquainted with the fresh-water Perch, and appreciated its excellent qualities as food when he says—

> "Nec te delicias mensarum, perca, silebo,
> Amnigenas inter pisces dignande marinis,
> Solus puniceis facilis contendere mullis." (x. 115.)

"Nor will I pass thee over in silence, O perch, the delicacy of the tables, worthy among river-fish to be compared with sea-fish; thou alone art able to contend with the red mullets."

The Perch occurs in many of the fresh waters of Europe, and in Asiatic Russia. In England it is extremely common in rivers, lakes, ponds, and canals; in Wales it is said to be rather a local fish and chiefly confined to stagnant waters; in Scotland it is not found north of the Forth, except where it has been introduced; in all the almost countless waters of the northern counties of Scotland, Yarrell states that the Perch is said to be wanting; farther north, as in Orkney and Shetland, the Perch does not occur, while still farther north, as in various parts of Scandinavia, it is again found. In the rivers and lakes of Ireland the Perch has been long known to occur. According to Couch the Perch is not a native of Cornwall, though it has been introduced within the present century, and where found it thrives well.

Perch deposit their spawn during the month of April and at the beginning of May, and a most curious and beautiful object is the spawn which they produce; it consists of a broad band of network of pearl-like eggs, a foot or considerably more in length; it is unfortunately very readily discerned, as it adheres to bushes or weeds in the water; consequently vast quantities of the spawn are devoured by ducks, swans, and other enemies. The number of eggs contained in one of these pearly festoons has been estimated at the enormous quantity of 155,000 and 280,000; the band is a hollow tube, and can be placed on the wrist as a bracelet.

The Perch attains to about the size of two inches and a quarter in a year, and a two year old will measure about five inches. I believe that when two years old they are able to mature spawn. The growth of Perch, as of other fish, depends in a great measure upon the localities where they are found. In large pools, and in rivers where the fish are not too numerous, and where food is abundant, Perch grow to a large size, but in small ponds they never attain to any size, though they will breed abundantly. Being voracious feeders, food is a very important consideration, and where ponds abound with these fish a sufficiency of food is not easily obtained. Some pisciculturists recommend that the sexes should be separated, the females being placed in one piece of water and the males in another; where this is done the Perch are said to grow well and rapidly. There is no fish, perhaps, that gives better sport to the youthful angler than the Perch; bold, and always ready for a worm, minnow, or other food, they fall easy victims to the baited hook. The following instance of the voracity of the Perch is given by Mr. Cholmondeley Pennell in the *Angler Naturalist*, (p. 61):—

"A very singular, if not unparalleled instance of the voracity of the Perch occurred to me when fishing in Windermere. In removing the hook from the jaws of a fish, one eye was accidentally displaced, and remained adhering to it. Knowing the reparative capabilities of piscine organization, I returned the maimed Perch, which was too small for the basket, to the lake, and being somewhat scant of minnows, threw the line in again with the eye

PERCH

attached as a bait—there being no other of any description on the hook. The float disappeared almost instantly; and on landing the new comer, it turned out to be the fish I had the moment before thrown in, and which had thus been actually caught by his own eye."

Perch are for the most part gregarious, and swim in shoals, so that when the angler has come across a shoal he generally manages to catch several. I have, on some occasions, been very successful in taking large numbers of good-sized Perch by means of eel-lines, the hooks being baited with a lob-worm, and the line thrown into the water with the bait on the ground, the other end of the line being fastened to the bank by a peg. Minnows are very attractive bait to the Perch, and fishing with one of these natural baits is a successful method of taking good fish; but so voracious are they that they will take almost any bait, and I have frequently caught them with an artificial fly when fishing for trout. According to Mr. Jesse, Perch may be attracted to a certain locality by placing a number of live minnows in a glass bottle, the mouth being closed with a piece of perforated zinc to admit ingress and egress of water. A minnow as a bait is then dropped quietly among the assembled Perch, which is immediately taken. A Perch of a pound to two pounds weight may be considered a good-sized fish; instances of their reaching the weight of four, five, six, and even nine pounds are on record.

Mr. F. Buckland mentions a curious epidemic disease as occasionally occurring among Perch. In 1867 a Perch-plague is said to have destroyed hundreds of thousands of these fish in the Lake of Geneva; according to the investigations of Dr. Forel and Dr. Du Plesis this disease was caused by the presence in the blood of the fish of certain minute fungi. This epidemic is said to occur not unfrequently in England (*Famil. Hist. Brit. Fish.* p. 5.)

The flesh of the Perch is excellent, being in my opinion unsurpassed by any non-migratory fresh-water species with the exception of the eel; it more nearly resembles the sole than any other fresh-water fish in the quality and flavour of its flesh.

Some writers speak of a deformed variety of Perch, with an elevated back and distorted tail, as occurring in Sweden, and lakes in the north of Europe, and in Llyn Raithlyn, Merionethshire. A figure of this variety of Perch may be seen in Daniel's *Rural Sports*, p. 247. Perch almost entirely white have been occasionally found, and Yarrell mentions his having received specimens from Yorkshire, which were of a uniform slate-grey colour with a silvery tint, and adds that the fish retained the peculiarity of colour when transferred into other waters. Mr. C. Pennell states that he has taken deformed Perch in some ponds near New Brighton, Cheshire, and that they are not uncommon in other neighbourhoods.

The following is the formula of the number of fin rays in the Perch:—

> Dorsal 14—15, all spinous; 1—2 spinous + 13—14 soft.
> Pectoral 14, all soft.
> Ventral 1 spinous + 5 soft.
> Anal 2 spinous + 8—9 soft.
> Caudal or tail fin 17 rays soft.
> The stomachal appendages or pyloric cœca 3.

The Perch, which is one of the most beautiful of our fresh-water fishes, has the upper part of the body a rich greenish brown, passing into golden yellowish white below; belly white; the sides are marked with about seven broad black transverse bands; the first dorsal fin is large and prickly, having a black patch on the posterior part; the second dorsal and pectoral fin pale brown; ventral, anal, and caudal bright vermilion; the eye large and full, with golden irides; præoperculum notched below and serrated on the posterior edge; operculum smooth, ending in a flattened point directed backwards; branchiostegals seven; lateral line distinct, at first ascending, then gradually descending, ending at about the middle of the tail.

Our English word Perch, which is seen also in the Italian Pergesa and the French Perche, is derived from the Latin *perca*, and that from the Greek Πέρκη, from πέρκος=περκνός, "dark coloured," perhaps from the broad black transverse bands on the sides of the fish.

The figure on the plate is drawn from a fine specimen caught in the month of June.

ON THE AVON STRENSHAM REACH.

# RUFFE OR POPE.

### (*Acerina cernua.*)

| | |
|---|---|
| *Cernua fluviatilis,* | GESNER, De Aquatil. p. 191; WILLUGHBY, p. 334. |
| *Perca fluviat. genus minus,* | GESNER, p. 701. |
| *Perca cernua,* | LINNÆUS; BLOCH, pl. 53, f. 2. |
| *Acerina vulgaris,* | CUV. ET VALENC., iii. p. 4, pl. 41; YARRELL, Brit. Fish., i. p. 17; GÜNTHER's Cat. i. 72. |
| *Aspro,* | COUCH, Fish. Brit. Isles, i. p. 193, pl. 41. |

*Characters of the Genus* ACERINA.—"Seven branchiostegals. All the teeth villiform, without canines; no teeth on the palatine bones or on the tongue. One dorsal, with thirteen to nineteen spines; the anal fin with two; operculum and præoperculum spiniferous. Muciferous channels of the bones of the skull very developed. Scales rather small."—GÜNTHER.

THE Ruffe, Jack Ruffe, Daddy Ruffe, or Pope, as this fish is called, does not appear to be noticed anywhere in the writings of the ancient Greeks and Romans. According to Cuvier, the learned Dr. John Caius (born 1510) first discovered this fish, and sent a figure of it to Gesner, who published it. Gesner, however, knew of the existence of the Ruffe from

what Belon had written before Caius sent the figure to him, and had already given a good description of it.    He says that in England it was known by the name of the Ruffe, "ab asperitate dictus," and that Caius had given it, for the same reason, the name of *aspredo.*

The Ruffe is a much smaller fish than the Perch, and is common in most of the rivers and canals of the midland and some other counties of England.    Couch says it is not found in Cornwall or Devonshire, in Scotland, or the Isle of Wight; nor is it enumerated by Mr. Thompson among the fishes of Ireland.    In Gesner's time it was rarely found in the Thames, but at present it occurs there in greater or less numbers, as is also the case in the Cam. According to Dr. Günther the Ruffe is found in the rivers of France, Switzerland, Germany, Sweden, Norway, Russia, and Siberia.    It is tolerably common in some of the canals and ponds of Shropshire, and I have had no difficulty in obtaining specimens for examination.    In habits it resembles the Perch.    Its food consists of small worms, larvæ of insects, small molluscous animals, etc.    It is a bold biter, and affords good sport to the young angler, being readily taken with a small worm; the Ruffe being, like the Gudgeon, chiefly a bottom swimmer, the baited hook should be near the ground.    No doubt the Ruffe thrives best in rivers or in ponds through which water is constantly running, and in such localities it grows well, sometimes attaining to a length of seven inches and a weight of about two ounces and a half.    The finest Ruffe I ever saw were caught in a pond through which fresh river-water kept flowing, belonging to R. Masefield, Esq., of Ellerton Hall, Shropshire: a fish six inches in length was by no means an uncommon specimen.

The Ruffe, resembling in outward characters and markings both the Perch and the Gudgeon, has sometimes, but erroneously, been considered a hybrid between the two; although there is actual proof that closely allied species do occasionally, and perhaps not unfrequently, cross, this is not true of fishes so very distantly related as the Perch and the Gudgeon.

The spawning season is in April; Mr. Couch says that the roe, which is shed in large quantity, is deposited in deep water on sandy ground.    Mr. Cholmondeley Pennell, on the other hand, asserts that the ova are placed among the rushes and flags at the margin of the water; with this statement also Yarrell agrees.    I am not able to decide between authorities in this case, and as April is now over, I must wait for another spawning season.

The Ruffe is excellent food for the table, resembling that of the Perch, but of a shorter texture; as Dame Juliana Berners says, "it is a right holsom fysshe."    Its general small size, however, prevents its being of much use in this respect; it is better adapted for a bait in Pike trolling.    The spinous character of the dorsal fin of this fish does not in the slightest degree interfere with its being a good bait; the same is the case with the Perch; and it is quite untrue to assert that the Pike, dreading these dorsal spikes, will refuse to attack a Perch.    For myself I prefer a small Perch to any other bait for Pike; I find it quite as attractive as Roach or Dace, and being of firmer flesh, it will last the longer on the spinning tackle.

The Ruffe (rough) derives its name from the character of the scales and the spinous portion of the dorsal fin; with this we may compare the Ruff among birds from its frill-like collar of rough feathers.    The meaning of the word Pope as given to this fish is not at all clear.    From the expression of "Daddy Ruff," applied to it in Shropshire, one would naturally infer that allusion in some way is made to the Pope, Papa, or Father of Rome.    According to Halliwell, Pope is sometimes a term of contempt.    "What a Pope of a thing" is Dorset dialect.    May the reference be to the small size of the fish when compared with the Perch, "the genus minus," indeed, of old Gesner?    I know not.    The scientific generic name of *acerina* must come from the Latin *acer,* in allusion to the "sharp" portion of the dorsal fin. The specific name *cernua,* "with head downwards," requires explanation.

The general colour of the Ruffe is greenish olive, spotted with brown; belly white; dorsal fin continuous, not distinct as in the Perch; first part spinous, the others flexible, spotted with brown, as is also the tail, which assumes a barred appearance; gill cover tinged with greenish pearl; head without scales. The fin rays are

Dorsal 13—15 spinous + 12 flexible.
Pectoral 13.
Ventral 1 spinous + 5 flexible.
Anal 2 spinous + 5—6.
Caudal 17.
Cœca pyloric 3, as in the Perch. Lateral line distinct.

The specimen from which the illustration was made was supplied by Mr. Masefield, of Ellerton Hall, and was taken from a canal in November, 1877.

---

*Order I.*
*ACANTHOPTERYGII.*

*Family*
*TRIGLIDÆ.*

# MILLER'S THUMB.

BULLHEAD.   TOMMY LOGGE.

*(Cottus gobio.)*

| | |
|---|---|
| KOTTOS, | ARISTOT., H. A. iv. 8 § 9; BOÏROS in GESNER De Aquat. p. 401. |
| *Cottus,* | RONDEL., ii. p. 202. |
| *Cottus gobio,* | LINN.; CUV. AND VALENC.; BLOCH; YARRELL, i. p. 71; COUCH, Fish. Brit. Isl. ii. p. 6; GÜNTHER, Cat. ii. p. 156. |

*Characters of the Genus* COTTUS.—"Head broad, depressed, rounded in front; body subcylindrical, compressed posteriorly; head and body covered with a soft and scaleless skin; lateral line present. Two dorsals of moderate height. Pectoral rounded, with some or all the rays simple. Ventral thoracic. Jaws and vomer with villiform teeth (vomerine teeth sometimes absent;) none on the palate. Air-bladder none; pyloric appendages in moderate number." —GÜNTHER.

THIS curiously-shaped little fish, I think there is no doubt, is mentioned by Aristotle when he is speaking on the question whether fishes are able to hear; he says "there occur in rivers certain little fish, found under stones, which some people call *Cotti;* from their lying under stones people catch them by striking the rocks with stones, when the fish being stunned fall out, whence it is evident that fish have the sense of hearing." The Greek word *cottus* means a head, and the little river fish with a large head which is common under stones, can be no other than our Bullhead. Gesner has given a good description and a recognisable figure of *Cottus gobio.* This fish is found in the fresh waters of Europe, and, as Günther says, probably of Northern Asia; it occurs in almost all the fresh-water streams of Europe from Italy to Scandinavia. It is said to be common in Scotland, but according to Thompson it is not found in Ireland. Yarrell, however, mentions its occurrence about

Belfast and Londonderry. Thompson suspects there is some error in the record of this fish being found in Ireland; for it appears that other species of *Cottus*, as the Sea-Scorpion and the Father-lasher, are occasionally called Miller's Thumbs in the North of Ireland. One would suppose that if this fish was once introduced into Ireland, it would grow, thrive, and multiply in the many suitable rivers of that country. From the well-known habits of the fish to lurk frequently underneath stones, and to hide its dusky body among the gravel or sand, it would be pretty secure from the attacks of enemies. However I should not advise its introduction by any means into any waters where Trout or Salmon are found; because it is as I know a most voracious feeder, being especially fond of eggs and the newly-hatched young fry of other species of fish as well as of its own.

I dissected two females the other day, about the 15th. of April; the ovaries were full of eggs almost ready for deposition; the stomachs of the same two fish also contained a great number of their own ova as well as of several of their young newly-hatched fry. Whether the males are guilty of such infanticide I do not know; but I am positive about the females. The spawn consists of a mass of pink eggs, rather large considering the size of the fish; and this mass, which generally covers an area of about one inch and a half to two inches, and is about half an inch thick, is always deposited under stones, to which it adheres by a mucous secretion which accompanies the eggs. The depressed form of the fish's head is admirably adapted for insertion under stones, and when this has been accomplished, the female with her broad and muscular pectoral fins hollows out the sand or mud under the stone, and then, probably, turns her abdomen round and deposits her eggs. The spawning takes place in April and the beginning of May, according to my observation. Johnston and Willughby say that the female collects the spawn into little lumps on her breast, where it is covered with a black membrane until it is hatched. But I feel sure there is some mistake here; the black membrane appears to be the membranous ovisac, which is black in the Miller's Thumb. Linnæus and Fleming say the fish forms a nest on the ground and broods over it, and Blumenbach says the same. I have never found the eggs except in a mass adhering to the under side of stones; I think it probable, however, that the male fish acts as a protector to the eggs, as is the case with the Stickleback. Izaak Walton and some others assert that the Miller's Thumb continues to spawn for several months. I have never found the eggs but in the spring of the year.

I am told by one or two persons who have eaten this fish that it is very good indeed; when the head is excluded, however, there is but little left to eat. It is occasionally eaten in Italy, and according to Pallas it is used as a charm against fever by some persons in Russia; others "suspend it horizontally, carefully balanced by a single thread, and thus poised, but allowed at the same time freedom of motion, they believe this fish possesses the property of indicating, by the direction of the head, the point of the compass from which the wind blows."—(Yarrell, i. 76.) The colour of the flesh after boiling is said to be pink like Salmon; but this is not true; some of the fins occasionally turn slightly pink, but the flesh remains as white as it was before boiling.

The Miller's Thumb is supposed to resemble that organ in the miller, which is said to assume a flattened form from frequently testing the flour. The head is very large, broad, and depressed; a small curved spine on the præoperculum; the body smooth and very slimy; vent nearly midway between the snout and the tip of the tail; body mottled with light and dark brown; belly white; sides below lateral line spotted with black; the lateral line very straight; first dorsal often fringed with orange red; teeth small, villiform in both jaws and on the vomer; irides yellow; pupils bluish black.

The usual length of this fish is about four inches; one of five inches would be above the average. The Miller's Thumb having the first dorsal fin with spines projecting above the membrane is placed in the Acanthopterygian order; but the spines are quite blunt, and there are none which are able to pierce the skin, like some of the fins in the Perch and Ruffe.

The fin-ray formula in specimens I have examined is as follows:—

Dorsal 6 spinous + 16.
Pectoral 11—13.
Ventral 4.
Anal 13.
Caudal 11—12.

The rays in all the fins are very thick and elastic; those of the first dorsal scarcely project above the membrane.

The Bullhead is most tenacious of life; hard blows on the head and complete evisceration I have known to be unable to cause speedy extinction of life. It resembles an Eel in this respect.

EASDALE, GRASMERE.

# THREE-SPINED STICKLEBACK.

BARNSTICKLE.   SHARPLIN.   PRICKLEFISH.

*(Gasterosteus aculeatus.)*

| | |
|---|---|
| *Gasterosteus aculeis in dorso tribus,* | ARTEDI, Spec., p. 96. |
| *Gasterosteus aculeatus,* | LIN., Sys., p. 489; BLOCH, pl. 53, fig. 3; DONOVAN, Brit. Fish. i. pl. 11; GÜNTHER, Cat. i. p. 2; COUCH'S Fish. Brit. Isles, i. p. 167. |
| *Gasterosteus trachurus,* | YARRELL, i. p. 90. |

*Characters of the Genus* GASTEROSTEUS.—"Form of body elongated; eyes lateral; cleft of mouth extending on the sides of the muzzle, oblique; villiform teeth in both the jaws and on the pharyngo-branchials, none on the palate or the tongue. Three branchiostegals. Opercular bones not armed; infraorbital arch articulated with præoperculum; parts of the skeleton forming external mails. Scales none, or in the form of scaly plates along the side. Isolated spines before the dorsal fin; ventral fins abdominal, but pubic bones attached to the humeral arch; ventral with one strong spine, and generally with another single short ray. Swim bladder simple, oblong; cæca pylorica in small number."—GÜNTHER.

THE generic name of *Gastreosteus*, from *gaster*, "the belly," and *osteon*, "a bone," has reference to the strong spiny ventral fin with which the fishes of this family are armed.   Though generally of a small size, the Sticklebacks yield to none in point of interest. There are four well-marked British species, namely, the *G. aculeatus* (three-spined), *G. spinulosus* (four-spined), *G. pungitius* (ten-spined), and the *G. brachycentrus* (short-spined); the other so-called species, as the *G. gymnurus* (smooth-tailed), *G. semiarmatus* (half-armed), and *G. trachurus* (rough-tailed), are probably merely varieties of the *G. aculeatus.*

Our commonest species, the Three-spined Stickleback, is generally an inhabitant of fresh water, and is to be found in ditches, shallow streams, ponds, and canals, but it also occurs in salt and brackish water. If a specimen be suddenly transferred from a fresh-water aquarium to a salt one, this little fish does not seem the least affected by the change, except that it does not quite accommodate itself all at once to the greater buoyancy of the salt water. According to Nilsson these fish are caught in incredible numbers in the Baltic about the middle of November, when they assemble on the coasts of that sea, and are taken by fishermen in boat loads. They are boiled, and the oil they contain is skimmed off the water: a bushel of fish is said to yield two gallons of oil. The refuse is spread over the ground for manure.

The food of the Stickleback consists of small worms, larvæ, and the small crustacea, as the *cyclops*, *cypris*, and *daphnia* among the Entomostraca, and the young of the fresh-water shrimps *(Gammarus pulex)*, and water wood-lice *(Asellus aquaticus)*; but so voracious and bold is this little fish that it will attack almost any living thing. Thompson mentions that a small party of *G. spinulosus*, the Four-spined Stickleback, was observed near Belfast in the act of killing a horseleech, whose head they immediately devoured. I remember some years ago keeping a small Pike in the same vessel with a number of Sticklebacks, and I shall never forget the persistence with which first one and then another of these fish attacked the Pike's tail. Occasionally the larger fish would retaliate and try to swallow one of its tormentors, but the sauce piquant of those formidable spines always proved too potent. After a few violent shakings of the head, the Stickleback was forcibly ejected from the cavernous jaws of its would-be devourer. The result of these repeated attacks on the Pike's tail was a gradual diminution of that organ, and I, feeling sorry for the victim of these cowardly attacks on the rear, took him out of the aquarium and turned him into a pool of water. Sticklebacks are very injurious to the eggs and fry of other fish, and must therefore be carefully excluded from Trout preserves; it is, however, no easy matter to get rid of these little pests when they have once established themselves in a fish-pond. Perhaps the most curious and interesting point in the natural history of these fish is their habit of making a nest and watching over the eggs and young fry. The season for observing this habit is in the month of May. The nest is composed of decayed fibres of aquatic plants, and matted together into a mass more or less round, and placed at the bottom of the water partly covered by the mud or sand; three or four circular holes are to be seen at the top of the nest; the eggs are an aggregated mass of a brown colour, and of the size of small shot. Until pointed out, a Stickleback's nest is a difficult prize to discover, but when once the form has been well impressed on the eye, detection of any number of nests is an easy task. The male fish alone protects the nest; if it were not for his fatherly care, I suspect that the race of Sticklebacks would in time become extinct, the ova and young fry falling easy prey to the other members of the family.

Some years ago I had an opportunity of observing how necessary for the protection of a young Stickleback family is the presence of the male parent. I noticed a brilliant fish hovering over his nest, and fanning the water incessantly with his fins. Having captured him, I placed him with one or two others into my collecting bottle. Here I kept him for about half an hour, whilst I amused myself by watching the manners and customs of the fish in their natural haunts. My eye was soon arrested by the spectacle of a large crowd of hungry marauders in the shape of other Sticklebacks of all ages and both sexes that had gathered around the nest of the very parent whom I had a prisoner in my bottle. They rushed at the nest like terriers at a badger, and began to pull it in pieces, knowing there was something good inside.　Conscience-stricken that I was the author of this terrible catastrophe—for as long as the father-fish was present to protect his property the alien cannibals dared not approach—I restored my prisoner to the water, and gently put him in over the spot where about thirty remorseless strangers were devastating the nest and devouring the contents.　For the space of about half a minute my liberated captive hardly seemed to know where he was, or what he had been doing.　Soon, however, he collects his scattered senses, and discovering the appalling nature of the fact, rushes to the rescue; first one and then another invader is attacked, and compelled to beat a hasty retreat, and wonderful to relate, in the space of about ten minutes not a foe was to be seen, and the brave defender was left in undisturbed possession of the field.　What was to happen next?　The conqueror surveys the ruined state of affairs,

"Haec loca vi quondam et vastâ convulsa ruinâ."

and hastens to repair the fearful breaches which the besiegers had made.　This he does by bringing mouthfuls of weed and bits of rotten twigs and other things, which he places upon the nest, using his nose to hammer the materials together.

The observation of these fish when confined in an aquarium is attended with as much delight as in their native ponds.　The development of the ova may be watched under the microscope—not however so readily as in a Perch's eggs—and the little occupants be seen to jerk about their tails some time before they leave the vitelline membrane.　Strange, undeveloped things in their rudimentary mouth and vitelline sac adhering to the abdomen, they cannot help attracting attention and exciting curiosity.　For the first few days the little fry are seen close to the nest, lying for the most part on their sides inactively; but as they grow they become more vigorous, and anxious to see something of the world.　But the father-fish is slow to encourage such juvenile desires, for is he not well aware that danger lurks on every side? And so, as I myself have seen, should some little occupant of the nursery, moved by piscine curiosity, stray away a little too far from the paternal abode, "does his father know he is out?"　Yes, indeed, very soon, and after him he hies, seizes the young truant in his mouth, as a cat would her kitten, and shoots him out right upon the nest.

I have no personal knowledge of the several varieties of *G. aculeatus;* they are thus described by Günther :—

*G. gymnurus.*—"Four or five scaly plates above the pectoral fin, the remainder of the body naked.　Middle and southern parts of Europe, England, France, South Germany, Baltic." This appears to be *G. leiurus* of Yarrell (i. p. 95), and the Quarter-armed Stickleback of Parnell (*Fishes of the Frith of Forth*, p. 190, pl. 25).

*G. semiarmatus.*—"The front part of the side with a series of ten to fifteen scaly plates. France, Belgium, England."

*G. semiloricatus.*—"The series of scales reaching to the front end of the caudal keel. France, Ireland." (See Thompson's *Nat. Hist. Ireland.*)

*G. trachurus.*—"The sides of body and tail entirely covered with a series of scaly plates. North parts of Europe, North Germany, England, France."　This is the general type of *aculeatus.*

The fin rays in *G. aculeatus* are

> Dorsal 3 spines + 10—12.
> Pectoral 10.
> Anal 1 spine + 8—9.
> Ventral 1 spine + 1.

THE TEN-SPINED STICKLEBACK, (*G. pungitius,*) a well-marked species, is one of the smallest of British fishes.　Though generally distributed, it is not nearly so common as the Three-spined.　I occasionally obtain specimens from the ditches on Preston-Weald Moors,

STICKLEBACKS

1. ROUGH-TAILED   2. HALF-ARMED   3. SMOOTH-TAILED

4. SHORT-SPINED   5. FOUR-SPINED   6. TEN-SPINED

Shropshire; but I have not had much opportunity of studying the habits of this little fish. It is nidificatory like the Three-spined, and probably the rest of the family. It is found in many of the creeks near the coast, and is said to ascend the rivers in the spring to spawn; but like the foregoing species, it is often a permanent resident in our fresh-water ditches and ponds. Sticklebacks are frequently caught with whitebait or young herrings in the lower portion of the Thames, and I have occasionally found some of these little fish on my plate cooked with whitebait. The Ten-spined is distinguished from the rest by having its sides quite naked, or free from lateral plates. It is usually about one inch to nearly two inches in length; the general colour is olive green on the back; belly and sides silvery white, with little black specks; the fins are pale yellowish white. It is sometimes called the Tinker, but wherefore I know not. The fin ray formula is

> Dorsal 10 spinous + 9.
> Pectoral 11.
> Anal 1 spinous + 9—10.
> Ventral 1 spinous + 1.

The Four-spined Stickleback (*G. spinulosus*) appears to be very rare. It was first discovered by Dr. J. Stark in a pond near Edinburgh in 1830. It is the smallest of all the species, being not more than one inch and a quarter in length. Dr. Stark kept some of these diminutive fish in tumblers, and fed them with small leeches and aquatic larvæ. He found them quite as voracious and even more pugnacious than the three-spined species. The specimens in the British Museum are from the Isle of Arran and Berwick. The fin rays are as follows:—

> Dorsal 4 spinous + 8.
> Pectoral 9.
> Ventral 1 spinous + 1.
> Anal 1 spinous + 8.

According to Dr. Stark the Four-spined Stickleback has all the varied colours of the other species of the genus, except the bright red found in the males during the breeding season.

The Short-spined Stickleback (*G. brachycentrus*) is the largest of the family, attaining the length of three inches. It was first procured for Mr. Thompson from pools along the margin of Lough Neagh, Dublin, etc. He gives one English habitat, namely, Stowpool, near Lichfield, whence in July, 1836, he obtained the largest example which had come under his observation (*Nat. Hist. of Ireland*, iv. p. 86). The number of lateral plates above the pectoral fin in this species agrees nearly with *G. aculeatus* var. *gymnurus*, but the spines, as the specific name indicates, are very short. The fin rays are

> Dorsal 3 spinous + 13.
> Anal 1 spinous + 9.
> Pectoral 10.
> Ventral 1 spinous + 1.

All the figures of the species and varieties on the Plate represent the fishes of the natural adult size, with the exception of fig. 5, which is larger than the real fish. On the right hand side may be seen a male in his bright red garb of the month of May, and a female in the act of depositing her eggs in a half-formed nest; after the eggs are impregnated the female retires, and the completion of the nest, as described above, as well as the guardianship of it and its contents, devolves entirely upon the male.

ON THE BRATHAY.

Order IV.
*PHYSOSTOMI.*

*Family*
*CYPRINIDÆ.*

# ARP.

### *(Cyprinus carpio.)*

| | |
|---|---|
| *Kuprinos,* | ARISTOT., H. A., iv. 8 § 4; vi. 13 § 2; viii. 20 § 12. |
| *Cyprinus,* | PLINY, Nat. Hist. ix. 51; GESNER, De Aquatil., p. 309. |
| *Carp,* | WILLUGHBY, H. Pisc. p. 245; COUCH'S Fish. Brit. Isles, vol. iv. p. 4. |
| *Cyprinus cirris quatuor,* | ARTEDI, Syn. p. 25. |
| *Cyprinus carpio,* | LIN., Syst. Nat. i. p. 525; DONOVAN, Brit. Fish. v. pl. 110; YARRELL, i. p. 349; GÜNTHER'S Cat. vol. vii. p. 25. |

*Characters of the Genus* CYPRINUS.—"Scales large; dorsal fin long, with a more or less strong, serrated, osseous ray; anal short. Snout rounded, obtuse; mouth anterior, rather narrow. Pharyngeal teeth 3. 1. 1—1. 1. 3, molar-like. Barbels four."—GÜNTHER.

THE Carp was known to Aristotle under the Greek name Κυπρινος. He speaks of it as a river fish without a tongue, but having a fleshy roof to its mouth; as producing eggs five or six times a year, especially under the influence of the stars; as having eggs about the size of millet seed; and as being occasionally struck by the dog-star when swimming near the surface. Aristotle nowhere tells us whether the flesh of the Carp was used as food; Athenæus, however, speaks of it as excellent in the quality of its flesh, and quotes Dorion as enumerating the Carp among lake and river fish.—"A scaly fish (*lepidotus*) which some people call the Cyprinus." (*Deipnosoph*, vii. 82.) From the Cyprinus being mentioned by Aristotle as having a soft fleshy palate (popularly but erroneously called "Carp's tongue,") and by Dorion in Athenæus as being especially scaly, there is I think no reason to doubt that this fish was known to the ancient Greeks, and as Athenæus says, was eaten by them.

The Common Carp is an inhabitant of the temperate parts of Europe and Asia. It has been long domesticated, and as Günther observes, it has degenerated into many varieties. It was probably introduced into this country, but neither the period when nor the locality whence it was first brought is definitely known. Cassiodorus, a writer of the sixth century, is the first to make use of the term *carpa;* he speaks of it as being delicate and costly, and supplied to princes' tables, and as being produced in the Danube. Writers of the thirteenth century designated this fish by the Latin terms *carpera* and *carpo.* "The Carpo of Cæsarius," says Beckmann, (*Hist. of Invent.*, ii. p. 51, Bohn's Ed.), "appears to have been our Carp, because its scales had a very great resemblance to those of the latter; for we are told......that the devil, once indulging in a frolic, appeared in a coat of mail, and had scales like the fish *carpo.*" The *carpera* of another mediæval writer, Vincent de Beauvais, certainly denotes the Carp, as he speaks of this fish's craft in avoiding nets and rakes, and of its springing out of the water and leaping over the nets. According to Linnæus, Carp were first brought to England about the year 1600; but he is certainly wrong here, because Dame Juliana Berners, in her book on angling, published in 1486, mentions the Carpe. It is "a daynteous fysshe, but there ben but few in Englonde, and thereforre I wryte the lesse of hym. He is an evyll fysshe to take, for he is so stronge enarmyd in the mouthe, that there maye noo weke harneys hold hym." Now since the name of Carp is not to be found in the Anglo-Saxon Dictionary of Ælfric, Archbishop of York, who died in 1051, and since it is spoken of by Dame Berners in 1486 as being a rare fish, it is probable its introduction. into England would be at some date between the years 1051 and 1486. The Carp is once mentioned by Shakspere, namely, in *As You Like It*, Act v, sc. 2.

But from what country Carp were originally introduced into England it is impossible to say. Webster, in his Dictionary, says they first came from Persia, but I know not what may be his authority. When once established they would multiply fast, for they are most prolific, and being entirely hardy and tenacious of life, they could readily be transported from place to place. "Towards the middle of the sixteenth century," says Dr. Badham, "there was scarce a country unacquainted with Carp; in many, stews on a vast scale were stocked exclusively with *Cyprini*, and thus an unfailing supply of orthodox diet for Lent and meagre days was never wanting in larder or pond."

Carp thrive best in temperate and southern climates; when transported to northern parts they are said to decline in size. Carp spawn as a rule at the beginning of June, but the time is in some measure dependent upon the state of the weather. They prefer a warm sunny day, when a female, followed by two or three males, may be readily seen among the various aquatic weeds upon which the little scattered eggs, like poppy seeds, are deposited. They are said to be capable of spawning when three years old. It is not an unusual circumstance for Carp to retain the spawn within the ovary for years; they thus become enormously large and uncomfortably distended. It is thought that they do not always or generally get rid of the spawn at one time, but that they continue occasionally to spawn for four or five months.

The food of the Carp consists in a great measure of the soft parts of aquatic plants, and the growth of algæ, such as *desmideæ* and *diatomaceæ*, with which the plants are often overspread, though it will also eat worms, insect-larvæ, etc.: even small fish are said to be sometimes eaten. From the form of the throat-teeth, which have worn-down crowns, resembling the crowns of the molar-teeth of a quadruped, it would appear that the food of the Carp

CARP

consists mainly of vegetables, and that portions of vegetable food are returned to the throat and remasticated by these pharyngeal grinders. In cold wintry weather the Carp is more or less dormant in the mud, like many other leather-mouthed vegetable fish-feeders. I have on several occasions examined the stomachs and intestinal tract of Carp in the winter season, but never found a vestige of any kind of food in them. Carp are perhaps the most wary and shy of all fish, difficult to take by angling, and clever in avoiding the leads of the net by burrowing under them in the mud, and in leaping over the corks. At the same time they may be readily tamed, and taught to take their food from the hand.

The Carp is believed to be a very long-lived fish; Gesner mentions an instance of one living to be a hundred years old; and Buffon speaks of one living in his time of the age of one hundred and fifty years; but though there is nothing improbable in this supposition, further confirmatory evidence of this extreme longevity would be desirable. The size of Carp varies according as the locality is favourable for their growth. Yarrell says that Carp have attained three pounds weight by their sixth year, and six pounds before their tenth year; they are therefore not so rapid in their growth as some other fish, and on this account are long lived. The largest English Carp I have read of is that mentioned by Mr. Manley, in his pleasant little manual, *Fish and Fishing*. This fish was taken by a net out of Harting Great Pond, near Petersfield, in 1858; its length without the tail was thirty-four inches, the weight twenty-four pounds and a half; some of the scales were said to be of the size of half-crowns. The Carp of the White Sitch Lake, Weston Hall, the seat of the Earl of Bradford, are famous for attaining great size and weight. In a letter, dated April 14th., 1878, his lordship writes to me, "There is a portrait of a Carp at Weston caught in the last century, and mentioned in Daniell's *Rural Sports*, of nineteen pounds and a half, and we caught one the other day which I think was more." It is said that in some of the German lakes they grow to the weight of forty to fifty pounds, and that in Holland fish of twenty pounds are not uncommon. The Carp of the Larian Lake (Como), said by Paul Giovio (Jovius)— born 1483—to attain the enormous weight of two hundred pounds, and to be shot by arrows from a cross-bow, I think we may put down as a fiction.

It is well known that Carp are exceedingly tenacious of life, and will live for a long time out of water. There is no mechanical arrangement for retaining water in contact with the gills, as exists in the Apodal, the Lophioid, and Labyrinthi-branch fishes. Professor Owen associates with the branchial respiration and the apparatus of gristly arches and muscles the peculiar development of the medulla oblongata as the centre of the vagal or respiratory nerves. He writes, "the peculiarly developed vagal lobes may relate to the maintenance of the power of the respiratory organs during a suspension of their natural actions."—(*Comp. Anat. of Vert.*, i. 287.)

In quality of flesh, as an article of food, generally speaking, Carp are little estimated; in ordinary ponds, and indeed even in rivers, the flesh has always more or less a muddy flavour; but after a Carp has been kept for some time in small ponds or stews, whose water is supplied by perennial springs of bubbling fountains, the flesh has not the slightest muddy flavour about it; the vegetable growth in such stews affords ample food, and Carp become exceedingly good and very fat. Such Carp are not often to be met with; but let any connoisseur taste specimens of such fish as Mr. Masefield can supply, and he will acknowledge that the culinary art as practised and recommended by Izaak Walton is not requisite. The Carp should be merely boiled; a little melted butter and walnut pickle is a better condiment for a fountain-feed Carp than old Izaak's sweet marjoram, thyme, parsley, savory, rosemary, onions, pickled oysters, anchovies, cloves, mace, orange and lemon-rinds, and claret wine, etc., etc.

The Greek name *Kuprinos* is probably derived from *Kupris*, "Cypris," a name of Aphrodite or Venus, from the island where she was first worshipped; and applied to the Carp on account of its extraordinary fecundity. The German Karpfen, the English Carp, are probably mere modifications of the Greek Κυπρινος.

The fin rays are

Dorsal 22.
Pectoral 17.
Ventral 9.
Anal 8.

The scales are large; general colour golden olive brown; head and top of the back darker; irides golden; belly yellowish white; tail forked; fins for the most part dark brown.

BEDDGELERT, N. WALES.

*Order IV.*
*PHYSOSTOMI.*

*Family*
*CYPRINIDÆ.*

# CRUCIAN CARP.

*(Carassius vulgaris.)*

| | |
|---|---|
| *Carassius,* | WILLUGH., Hist. P. p. 249. |
| *Cyprinus pinna dorsi ossiculorum viginti,* | ARTEDI, Spec. Pisc. p. 5, No. 5. |
| *Cyprinus carassius,* | LINN. Sys. Nat. p. 526; YARRELL, i. p. 355. |
| *Crucian,* | PENN. Brit. Zool. iii. p. 319, pl. 72; COUCH, Fish. Brit. Isles, iv. p. 28. |
| *Carassius vulgaris,* | SIEBOLD, Süsserwasserfische, p. 98; GÜNTHER'S Cat. vii. 29. |

*Characters of the Genus* CARASSIUS.—"This genus differs from *Cyprinus* in being without barbels; its pharyngeal teeth are compressed in a single series, 4—4. Temperate Asia and Europe. Domesticated and degenerated into numerous varieties."—GÜNTHER.

THE Crucian Carp derives its name from the German word for this fish, namely, *die Karausche*, from whence also the Latin Carassius has been formed. Lacépède calls it the Hamburgh Carp, and some of our Thames fishermen know it by the name of the German Carp. Probably this fish was originally introduced into our own country from Hamburgh, for it is referred to by Linnæus as being called, in the Transactions of the University of Upsal, by the elder Gronovius *Cyprinus Hamburgher*, as the locality where perhaps it was best known.

PRUSSIAN CARP

CRUCIAN CARP

The Crucian Carp was occasionally obtained by Yarrell from the Thames, between Hammersmith and Windsor, where it sometimes attains a considerable size, and weighs a pound and a half. It has been introduced into fishponds by various gentlemen interested in pisciculture, and where the water is constantly supplied by running streams, this fish thrives well; and although its flesh cannot be considered dainty food, yet good well-nourished specimens are by no means to be despised. According to Ekström the Crucian Carp is common in all parts of Scandinavia, inhabiting muddy and grassy lakes. Its spawning time is said to be in May and June, and the eggs to be deposited on weeds. Like many of the species of this family, the Crucian is eminently retentive of life, and will live for a long time either without water or in water whose impurities would poison other fish; it also manages to exist entirely without food for months, though, as may be supposed in such a condition, it grows very thin. It is sometimes called the Bream Carp, because the general form of the fish is flat and bream-like.

The whole length of the specimen before me, from the snout to the origin of the tail, is six inches and a half; the greatest depth at the origin of the dorsal fin, which is in a line with the origin of the ventral, is three inches; the tail is slightly forked, but many specimens have the tail nearly square. The lateral line, proceeding from near the top of the gill-opening to the middle of the tail, is straight, and has thirty-four punctured scales. The back is of a bronze colour, with a slight reddish tinge; below the lateral line the sides are light golden yellow, each scale being minutely dotted with black; the pectoral, ventral, and anal fins reddish brown; the tail is slightly red; the back is very much arched; the irides golden yellow, with a tinge of red; the pupils blue; the first ray of the dorsal and anal fins is serrated on the posterior edge; the scales are large.

The fin-ray formula in this specimen is

Dorsal 20.
Pectoral 14.
Ventral 9.
Anal 8.

The specimen figured was supplied by Mr. Masefield, of Ellerton Hall.

# PRUSSIAN CARP.

## *(Carassius vulgaris, var. Gibelio.)*

THE Prussian Carp, or Gibel Carp, which by Yarrell and some other ichthyologists has been considered a distinct species, is by other authorities, as by Günther, considered merely as a variety of the Crucian. Whether this fish be entitled to rank as a distinct species, I will not pretend to say; at any rate if not specifically distinct, the Prussian Carp is a well marked variety. The Prussian Carp is the *Cyprinus gibelio* of Bloch, Lacépède, Yarrell, Couch, and other writers; the specific name of *gibelio*, from the German Giebel, "a gable" or "ridge of a house," would seem to imply that the term was originally given to the Crucian variety, whose back rises abruptly from the head, and forms a prominent ridge; by modern ichthyologists, however, it is now employed to designate the Prussian Carp.

This variety is far better known than the Crucian, being not uncommon in some parts of the Thames, and abundant in the ponds and rivers of several of our English counties. I believe that the Prussian Carp is common in the Norfolk Broads, where it grows to a good size: it is said to have reached the weight of two pounds. The spawning time is about the end of April or early in May. It is said to be rather a shy biter, and to afford but little sport to the angler. Like the Crucian it is very tenacious of life, and has been known to live out of water for the space of thirty hours. The flesh is said to be white and agreeable, but I have no personal acquaintance with it in this respect. The head is obtuse, body rather short and thick, the tail forked. In a typical specimen of the *C. carassius* var. *gibelio*, a difference from the Crucian will be seen in the less depth of the body, which is more Carp-like than Bream-like, a blunter head, less elevated back, and the caudal fin more decidedly forked; but even in the Prussian Carp varieties seem to exist.

Hybrids are said to be common between the ordinary Carp (*Cyprinus carpio,*) and the Crucian wherever these two fish are kept in a domesticated or semi-domesticated state. Specimens may be seen in the British Museum. One of these hybrids is thus described by Günther —"It resembles the Carp in having four barbels, which, however, are much less developed and smaller. The pharyngeal teeth generally in two series (4. 1—1. 4), sometimes the inner tooth is absent, or another tooth indicates the third series of the Carp. The serrated ray of the dorsal and anal fins varies in strength, being sometimes very feeble."

ON THE AVON.

# GOLDEN CARP.

*(Carassius auratus.)*

| | |
|---|---|
| *Cyprinus auratus,* | LINN. Syst. Nat., i. p. 527; YARRELL, i. 358; GÜNTHER'S Cat. vii. p. 32. |
| *Goldfish,* | PENNANT, Brit. Zool., iii. p. 327. |
| *Cyprinus telescopus,* <br> " *quadrilobus,* | LACÉPÈDE, v. pl. 18, figs. 2 & 3. |

THE Golden Carp, or Goldfish, with the silver and bronze coloured specimens, has its original home in China and Japan. It is subject to as much variation as its western representative, the Crucian Carp, or *Carassius vulgaris*, of which, according to Günther and other ichthyologists, it is merely a domestic variety; "although numerous examples of the Crucian and Goldfish are exactly alike in the shape of the body, the western species appears to have the body more elevated than the eastern, which also has less longitudinal series of scales above the lateral line."—(Günther.) The Goldfish has been domesticated in China for ages, where, as Couch observes, it has contributed to the amusement of the higher classes by its lively actions in luxurious captivity; perhaps no other fish is more subject to variation both in shape and colour, and none more brilliantly beautiful than the vivid golden varieties. The Chinese

GOLDEN AND BRONZE CARP

collect the spawn from the rivers and sell it to merchants, who send it to different parts of the country to be propagated in small ponds, or kept in glass or porcelain vessels in the houses of the rich.

The date of the introduction of these "sportive" fish into England is uncertain; 1611, 1691, and 1728 are each recorded as the year in which they were brought over; it was not, perhaps, till the year 1728 that Goldfish became generally known, when they were brought over in large numbers and presented to Sir Matthew Decker, Lord Mayor of London, who distributed them to various friends over the country. The Goldfish appears to have been introduced into Portugal at an early period; it is now completely naturalised in many of the waters of that country, and a great number of these fish, so commonly exposed for sale in the well-known glass globes of the London and other dealers, have been and are now, I believe, brought into England by trading vessels from Lisbon and other Portuguese towns. In France the Goldfish is said to have been unknown till the days of Louis XV., whose mistress, the Marchioness de Pompadour, had received some as a present.

The temperature of the water has a marked effect in influencing the colour of the Gold-fish; in ordinary ponds of this country the usual prevailing colour is bronze; the golden colour is induced by a warm temperature of the water. "It is a well-known fact that in manufacturing districts where there is an inadequate supply of cold water for the condensation of the steam employed in the engines, recourse is had to what are called engine-dams or ponds, into which the water from the steam-engine is thrown for the purpose of being cooled; in these dams, the average temperature of which is about eighty degrees, it is common to keep Goldfish; and it is a notorious fact that they multiply in these situations much more rapidly than in ponds of lower temperature, exposed to the variations of the climate. Three pairs of this species were put into one of these dams, where they increased so rapidly, that at the end of three years their progeny, which were accidentally poisoned by verdigris mixed with the refuse tallow from the engine, were taken out by wheelbarrows-full. Goldfish are by no means useless inhabitants of these dams: they consume the refuse grease which would otherwise impede the cooling of the water by accumulating on its surface."—(Dr. Edward's *Influence of Physical Agents on Life*, Note, p. 467.)

The question as to the influence of temperature in producing changes of colour, or modifying form, or producing death, is an interesting one. The late Dr. John Davy has published some observations on the vitality of fishes, and on the degree of temperature fatal to them, well worth studying. His experiments on the Goldfish are expressed in a short paragraph, which I will quote.—"One of average size, taken from an aquarium and put into water at ninety-six degrees (Fahr.), immediately became restless, swimming about hurriedly, and making violent leaps, as if attempting to escape. Gradually it became languid, swimming on its side, the caudal fin seldom acting. After a few minutes, when the water had fallen to ninety degrees, it appeared to be motionless: the pectoral fins and the opercula were the last that ceased to act. Now transferred to water of seventy degrees, it rapidly revived, the gills first acting. After an interval of about an hour, it was put into water at ninety-three degrees. This temperature it bore pretty well at first, gradually it became languid, swimming on its side. As the water cooled, its languor abated; and when the temperature had fallen to eighty-eight degrees it had resumed its natural position."—(*Physiological Researches*, p. 301.) From this experiment it would appear that a temperature of about eighty or eighty-eight degrees is well suited to the Goldfish, and that at such a temperature it assumes a brilliant golden, silver, orange, or silver mixed with gold, but that at a temperature of ninety-six degrees the Goldfish will die; such a high temperature would probably be fatal to all other kinds of fish. The statements made by travellers that fish are able to live in water so hot that a man could not bear his hand therein for a single minute must, one would suppose, be incorrect. A temperature of one hundred and fifteen degrees was found by Dr.

Davy to be hardly bearable to his hand, and that of one hundred and twenty degrees not endurable. It is incredible, therefore, to think that a fish could live in a temperature of one hundred and eighty-seven degrees, as recorded by Sonnerat; for, as Dr. Davy remarks, such endurance would imply a different organization from that of fishes generally, when we keep in mind the simple fact that the serum of their blood is coagulated by a temperature of about one hundred and sixty degrees. I must refer any reader interested in these points to Davy's *Physiological Researches* and to Dr. Edward's work on the *Influence of the Physical Agents on Life*, p. 56, 57, Hodgkin's and Fisher's Translation.

The Goldfish presents us with many varieties of form; sometimes the dorsal fin, which in a normal specimen occupies a considerable portion of the back, consists of only four or five rays, or the dorsal may be absent altogether, or the anal fin may be double; the caudal fin or tail may be three or four-lobed; and strangest perhaps of all, in some cases the eyes may be very large and protruding. These, I need hardly remind the reader, are the varieties of Goldfish now frequently to be seen in an aquarium under the name of Japanese fan-tails, telescope fish, etc.

Goldfish seldom exceed a length of nine or ten inches.

The specimens figured were supplied by Mr. Masefield, of Ellerton Hall.

ON THE THAMES

# BARBEL.

## *(Barbus vulgaris.)*

| | |
|---|---|
| *Barbus,* | AUSON., Id. x. 94.  GESNER, Aquat. iv. p. 194.  WILLUGH., Hist. Pisc. p. 259. |
| *Cyprinus oblongus,* | ARTEDI, Spec. Pisc. p. 4, No. 14. |
| *Cyprinus barbus,* | LIN., Sys. N. 527.  DONOVAN, Brit. F. ii. pl. 29. |
| *Barbel,* | PENNANT, Brit. Zool. iii. 312.  COUCH, Brit. Fish. iv. p. 16. |
| *Barbus vulgaris,* | FLEMING, Brit. An. p. 185.  GÜNTHER, Cat. vii. p. 88. |
| *Barbus fluviatilis,* | AGASS. CUV.  SIEBOLD, Die Süsserwasserfische p. 109. |

*Characters of the Genus* BARBUS.—"Scales of small, moderate, or large size.  Dorsal fin generally with the (third) longest simple ray ossified, enlarged and frequently serrated; never, or only exceptionally, with more than nine branched rays, commencing opposite, or nearly opposite the root of the ventral.  Eyes without adipose eyelid. Anal fin very short, but frequently very high.  Mouth arched, without inner folds, inferior or anterior; lips without horny covering.  Barbels short, four, two, or none.  Lateral line running in, or nearly in the middle of the side of the tail.  Anal fins not enlarged.  Pharyngeal teeth 5.4 or 3.3 or 2—2 or 3.3 or 4.5.  Snout but rarely with tubercles or pore-like grooves.  Temperate or tropical parts of the Old World."—GÜNTHER.

THE Barbel is mentioned once only, I believe, in classical authors; in the writings of the ancient Greeks there is no mention of this fish, and Ausonius of the Latins is the only author who notices the Barbel, under the appropriate name of *Barbus*, in allusion to the four

BARBEL

GUDGEON

barbules or beards with which the mouth is furnished. Ausonius speaks of the Barbel as occurring in the river Saravus, the modern Sarre, which joins the Moselle a few miles above Trien.

> "Tuque per obliqui fauces vexate Saravi,
> Qua bis terna fremunt scopulosis ostia pilis,
> Cum defluxisti famæ majoris in amnem
> Liberior laxos exerces, Barbe, natatus;
> Tu melior pejore ævo."        (Id. x. 90—95.)

"And thou, O Barbel, harassed by the narrow passes of the winding Saravus......after thou hast descended a river of greater fame (Mosella) more freely dost exercise spacious swimmings."

According to the above authority the Barbel is a more acceptable article of diet when old—*melior pejore ævo;* its flesh, however, is not generally held in high esteem, though it has been for long, and is now, protected by statute law. Amongst the piscatory restrictions of Queen Elizabeth's reign it is enacted that any one taking Barbel less than twelve inches shall "pay twenty shillings, and give up the fish so wrongfully taken, and the net or engine so wrongfully used." In France the Barbel is more esteemed as food than amongst ourselves; at Tours and other inland places, situated on rivers, as Dr. Badham remarks, '*Les trois Barbeaux*' is a well-known sign, and an abundant supply is always ready for *noces et festins* in water-cages under the bridge.

The Barbel is common in the Danube, the Rhine, and in other rivers in the warm latitudes of Europe, where it grows to a large size, and occasionally attains a weight, it is said, of forty or even fifty pounds; in this country a Barbel of fifteen pounds would be considered a very large fish. The food of the Barbel is partly of an animal and partly of a vegetable nature; its principal food, during those months when it is active, consists of the larvæ of various insects, worms and small fish. It generally keeps near the bottom of the river, and probably uses its four mouth-feelers or barbules as instruments of touch, to enable the fish to detect the nature of its food; these feelers are abundantly supplied with nerves, as indeed is the case in other fish similarly provided.

Anglers generally use ground bait to attract the Barbel to the spots where they intend to fish some hours previously. I have no experience of Barbel-fishing, but those who have been so fortunate speak of this sport, as pursued in a punt on the Thames, as most amusing. Mr. F. Buckland recommends it especially to ladies. Mr. Manley, in his *Notes on Fish and Fishing*, is free to confess that he enjoys a good day's *leger* fishing for Barbel to any other day's fishing "within reach of ordinary, or even extraordinary mortals." The Barbel I believe is exclusively, in this country at least, a river fish, but it is not found in all rivers. The Thames supplies the most abundant and largest fish; in the neighbourhood of Walton and Weybridge, two hundred and eighty pounds' weight of Barbel are said to have been taken by a single rod in one day. The Trent also affords excellent fish. It does not, I believe, occur in the Severn.

The Barbel is a strong and cunning fish, "so lusty and cunning"—to quote from the *Complete Angler*—"as to endanger the breaking of the angler's line, by running his head forcibly towards any covert, or hole, or bank, and then striking at the line to break it off with his tail." I do not know whether this has been verified by modern anglers, but Mr. F. Buckland writes, "When a Barbel is hooked, he always endeavours to strike at the line with his tail to break it." Dame Juliana Berners says of the Barbel, in her own quaint language, "It is an evil fysshe to take, for he is so strongly enarmyd in the mouth, that there may no weake harnesse holde him."

The Barbel spawns in May and June. Yarrell states that the ova, amounting to seven or eight thousand in a full-sized female, are deposited on the gravel and covered by the parent fishes, and that they are vivified in a warm season between the ninth and fifteenth days. Couch says the spawn is discharged in a string, and entwined round some fixed object, as a stone or weed. Gesner says that the Barbel opposite his house, situated near the Danube, spawn at the beginning of August. Siebold mentions May and June as the months. The roe is supposed to be poisonous. Gesner quotes several old writers who affirm that from experiments made on themselves the roe has proved injurious as food; this appears to be alluded to in the *Book of St. Albans*, where it is said, "The Barbyll is a swete fysshe, but it is a quasi meete and a perilous for mannys body. For comynly he yevyth an intro-duxion to ye Febres. And yf he be eten rawe, he may be cause of mannys death; whyche hath oft been seen." Sir John Hawkins, in a note of his edition of the *Complete Angler*, says that even the flesh of the Barbel is deleterious, for a servant of his, who had eaten part of the fish, but not the roe, "was seized with such a violent purging and vomiting as had like to have cost him his life." On the other hand, Bloch asserts that both himself and some members of his family ate of a considerable portion of Barbel roe without any disagreeable results. It is probable that in some cases the effect may be due to idiosyncrasy, or a peculiar disposition of the individual who partook of the roe, but at the same time it is not unlikely that Barbel roe may be, in itself, injurious when eaten. In the time of Sir John Hawkins, Barbel roe used to be taken by country people medicinally, as an emetic and a cathartic. Siebold (*Die Süsserwasserfische* p. 110) on this point writes: "It is strange that although people have of old been warned against eating the spawn of the Barbel, and that frequent experiences still often occur, resulting in vomiting and diarrhœa, (it is strange) that no one has set himself the task of investigating scientifically the spawn of this common fish with a view to test its poisonous effects." Siebold's work, quoted here, bears date 1863. I know not whether since this time any attempts have been made to investigate this matter.

The Barbel, says Yarrell, in the Coat of Bar, forms one of the quarterings of the arms of Margaret of Anjou, queen of Henry the Sixth. These arms are beautifully painted in glass in the windows of a curious old manor-house at Ockwell, in Berkshire, on the banks of the Thames; thus a sort of historic interest, as Badham observes, attaches to this fish.

The flesh of the Barbel is generally pronounced to be poor and insipid; the only way to make these fish eatable, according to Mr. Manley, is to salt and dry them, "and even then," he says, "they are not much better than the bark of a tree would be subjected to a similar process." But Dr. Badham begs to assure citizen anglers, and others who may be incredulous, that these fish, simply boiled in salt and water, and eaten cold, with a squeeze of lemon-juice, will be found by no means despicable fare; he particularly commends "the head and its appurtenances."

The form of the Barbel is rather long, and narrow at the back; the length of the head, which is decidedly pig-like in form, is one-fourth of the whole, not including the tail; snout much produced, lips thick; there are no mouth-teeth, but there are the usual throat-teeth of this family; eyes small; a pair of barbs above the upper lip, and one at each corner of the mouth; colour of the back greenish brown or bluish, sides yellowish, white below; tail deeply forked.

The fin-ray formula is as follows:—

> Dorsal 11.
> Pectoral 16.
> Ventral 9—10.
> Anal 8.

The specimen figured was procured from the Thames near Oxford; I am indebted to Mr. William Hine, of the Anatomical Department, Museum, Oxford, for a fine specimen for examination.

# GUDGEON.

## *(Gobio fluviatilis.)*

| | |
|---|---|
| *Gobio,* | AUSON., Id. x. 134; CUV., R. An. |
| *Gobius fluviatilis,* | GESNER, de Aquatil, p. 399. |
| *Cyprinus gobio,* | LINN., Syst. Nat. i. p. 526; DONOVAN, iii. pl 71. |
| *Gudgeon,* | PENNANT, Brit. Zool. iii. 310; COUCH, Brit. Fish., iv. 20, pl. 182. |
| *Gobio fluviatilis,* | WILLUGHBY, p. 264; YARRELL, Brit. Fish. i. p. 371; SIEBOLD, Süsserwasserf. p. 112; GÜNTHER'S Cat. vii. p. 172. |

*Characters of the Genus* GOBIO.—"Scales of moderate size; lateral line present. Dorsal fin short, without spine, opposite to the ventrals. Anal fin short. Mouth inferior; mandible not projecting beyond the upper jaw when the mouth is open; both jaws with simple lips; a small but very distinct barbel at the angle of the mouth, quite at the extremity of the maxillary. Gill-rakers very short; pseudo-branchiæ. Pharygeal teeth 5.3 or 2—2 or 5.5, hooked at the end. Europe."—GÜNTHER.

IT is not certain whether the Gudgeon is distinctly mentioned by the ancient Greeks, though it was doubtless known to them. It is probable that under the name of Κωβιος (whence the Latin *gobios* is derived,) Aristotle occasionally alludes to the Gudgeon. Ausonius is sufficiently descriptive, and clearly speaks of that most excellent little fish in the following lines:—

> "Tu quoque flumineas inter memorande cohortes
> Gobio, non major geminis sine pollice palmis
> Præpinguis, teres, ovipari congestior alvo
> Propexique jubas imitatus Gobio Barbi."     (Id. x. 131—134.)

"Thou too, O Gudgeon, worthy of being mentioned among the shoals of the river, not greater than the two palms of the hands without the thumb; very fat, round and plumper still when thy belly is full of eggs; Gudgeon imitating the hairs of the pendent-bearded Barbel."

I suspect also that the author of the *Halieuticon* is referring to the Gudgeon in the line—

> "Lubricus et spina nocuus non Gobius ulla."

> "The slippery Gobio harmful with no spine."

The Gudgeon is found in such rivers and streams of this country as flow with moderate velocity, and have a sandy or gravelly bottom. These fish will also thrive in ponds through which fresh water runs; they are gregarious in their nature, and readily taken with a worm, affording capital sport in their small way, to those anglers who care more for numbers than size, and who can appreciate a most excellent food. Their spawning time is in May and June; the ova are very small, and are deposited among stones in shallow water. Yarrell states that the fry are about an inch long by the beginning of August. According to Thompson the Gudgeon is found in many of the waters of Ireland. It is not mentioned as occurring in Scotland. Is this merely negative evidence? Is not the Gudgeon an inhabitant of any of the waters of Scotland? Couch says it is known only of late in Cornwall and the western portion of Devonshire.

In point of flavour the Gudgeon approaches that of the Smelt or Sparling, and in my opinion is one of the best of fresh-water fish we possess. It is a pity, from a gastronomic point of view, that the Gudgeon does not exceed the length of six or seven inches, which is the size denoted by the "two palms of the hand without the thumb" of Ausonius.

The following is Günther's description of the Gudgeon:—"The height of the body is one fifth or nearly one fifth of the total length (without caudal); tail compressed; snout obtuse, with the upper profile convex; eye a little behind the middle of the length of the head (in adult specimens). Barbels not extending beyond the centre of the eye (in adult examples), frequently shorter. A series of round blackish spots along the lateral line, sometimes confluent posteriorly. Dorsal and caudal fins with transverse series of black dots."

The fin rays are

> Dorsal 9—10.
> Pectoral 15.
> Ventral 8.
> Anal 8.

The English word Gudgeon comes directly from the French *goujon*, that from the Latin *gobio*, which must be referred to the Greek Κωβιος. The expression "to gudgeon a man," *i. e.* to deceive him, may have originated from the ease with which a Gudgeon is taken by a bait, as Gay sings—

> "What gudgeons are we men,
> Every woman's easy prey!
> Though we've felt the hook, again
> We bite and they betray!"

Or it may have reference to the ease with which so delicate a morsel as a Gudgeon is swallowed. According to the French expression given by Rouchi (*Patois of the Hainault*, Wedgwood's *Etymolog. Dict.*), *Cha passe come un gouvion*, meaning "that which is easily swallowed;" so also *Faire avaler des gouvions*, "to make one believe a lie," literally "to make Gudgeons be swallowed." On this point Latham, in his *Large Dictionary* (s.v. *gudgeon*) observes: "Of Gudgeons having been swallowed with particular ease there is no very good evidence; though there is a good deal in favour of the Loach having been so treated. The Loach is said, in most notices, to have been not unfrequently tossed off in toasts, or swallowed in a glass of wine, by the gallants of the Elizabethan period. It is suggested, then, that the *Gudgeon* when suggestive of credulity is the Loach. How much the two fishes have in common is well known. Both keep on the ground; both are marked or mottled; both have a beard or wattles."

# ROACH.

## (Leuciscus rutilus.)

| | |
|---|---|
| *Rutilus sive Rubellus fluviatilis,* | GESNER, de Aquat., p. 820. |
| *Cyprinus iride pinnis ventralibus ac ani plerumque rubentibus,* | ARTEDI, Spec. Pisc. p. 10, No. 18. |
| *Cyprinus rutilus,* | LINN., Sys. N. i. p. 529. |
| *The Roach,* | PENNANT, Brit. Zool. iii. p. 319; COUCH, Brit. Fish. iv. 47, pl. 191; YARRELL, i. p. 399. |
| *Leuciscus rutilus,* | FLEMING, Brit. An. p. 188; SIEBOLD, Süsserwasserf. p. 183; GÜNTHER, Cat. vii. p. 212. |

*Characters of the Genus* LEUCISCUS.—"Body covered with imbricate scales; lateral line generally complete, running in, or only a little below, the median line of the tail. Dorsal fin short, without stiff ray, commencing opposite, rarely behind the ventrals. Anal fin rather short or moderately developed, generally with from nine to eleven rays, rarely with eight (in small species only), and still more rarely with fourteen rays. Mouth with structural peculiarities; lower jaw not trenchant; barbels none. Pseudo-branchiæ. Pharyngeal teeth conical or compressed in a single or double series. Intestinal tract short, with only a few convolutions. Palæ- and Nearctic regions."—GÜNTHER.

THE Roach is generally distributed throughout England, Wales, and Scotland. In Ireland, however, it is said not to occur, the Rudd (*Leuciscus erythrophthalmus*), or Red-Eye, which is exceedingly common in the north of Ireland, being mistaken for the true Roach. According to Couch, the Roach is not known in Cornwall, and in Devonshire only in the lake called Slapton-Ley. Its European geographical distribution is north of the Alps.

Roach are gregarious, and swim generally in shoals; they spawn at the end of May and the beginning of June, and at this season the scales are peculiarly rough to the touch; the spawn is deposited among weeds or upon submerged bodies in immense quantities. In the Aqualate Mere belonging to Sir Thomas Boughey, Bart., Staffordshire, this spawning process is utilized in the capture of eels; certain wattle-work constructions are set up in different parts of the mere, to which the Roach resort, and upon which they fix their spawn; here large quantities of eels congregate to feed on the Roach or spawn, and are taken in wicker traps. The Roach is not in much request as an article of diet, the flesh being generally soft and woolly; nevertheless large specimens in September and October are not to be despised when nicely fried.

"The art of Roach fishing," says Mr. Manley, "rightly holds a high place in the angler's estimation. Anyone can catch the half-bred and half-starved Roach of a muddy and weedy pond, and I dare say Dame Berners spoke rightly of the uneducated fish of her day when she said 'the Roche is an easy fysshe to take.' Probably, too, Walton was justified in speaking of the Roach of his day as being 'accounted the *water-sheep* for his simplicity or foolishness.' But a river Roach, say of the Thames, or Colne, or Trent, of our era is a very different fish, and he is not to be had by any tyro. He has, too, his times and seasons, his offs and ons, and the general capriciousness of the scaly tribes, being subject to all kinds of atmospheric and terrestrial influences, which affect both the time and manner of his taking a bait. Moreover, Roach of a much-fished river, like the Thames, are highly educated, and are pretty wide awake to the fisherman's proceedings—the fixing of the punt, the plumbing the depth, and the scattering of the ground-bait. Of course the latter attracts them, and they come to see 'what's up,' and if inclined to feed they will constantly take the baited hook for an innocent morsel of favourite food. But to make a good basket of Roach, even when they are 'on,' requires very careful attention to a number of details."— (*Notes on Fish and Fishing*, p. 300.)

The usual length of a Roach is about eight or ten inches, but it is said sometimes to attain fourteen inches; a Roach of one pound in weight would be considered a good fish; but instances are on record of fish having been taken two, three, and even five pounds weight. This last fish is mentioned by Pennant, and its weight may fairly be questioned.

The food of the Roach, like other members of the family, is partly of a vegetable and partly of an animal nature. The throat-teeth are large and well developed, arranged generally in a single series; they form an important character in distinguishing this fish from its relative the Rudd; in this latter fish the teeth are minutely but distinctly serrated, which is not the case in the Roach.

The Azurine or Blue-Roach, the *Leuciscus cœruleus* of Yarrell, is probably only a variety of the Rudd. Hybrids between the Roach and the Rudd are supposed to occur, and I think there is no doubt from an examination of several specimens, that the so called Pomeranian Bream is merely a cross between the Roach and the Common Bream, as first stated by Professor von Siebold.

The following is Dr. Günther's description of the Roach:—"Body generally somewhat elevated, its depth being about one third of the total length (without caudal). Mouth terminal, the upper jaw but slightly projecting beyond the lower. There are three longitudinal series of scales between the lateral line and ventral fin. Origin of the dorsal fin above, but not in advance of the root of the ventral. Body silvery, the lower fins generally with a red tinge in adult examples. Pharyngeal teeth 6, or 5—5, (or 6)." The position of the dorsal fin with regard to that of the ventral will at once distinguish the Roach from the Rudd; in the former the origin of the dorsal is only slightly behind that of the ventral; in the latter it is conspicuously so.

The definition of our English word Roach is far from clear. The Anglo-Saxon is *reohche*, which also signifies "a thornback" or "skate-fish;" this seems to bring one to the root *reoh*, "rough." Possibly reference may be implied to the roughness of the fish during the season of spawning. The expression "as sound as a Roach," is supposed by some to have been originally "sound as a rock." Ray has the proverb "as sound as a Trout;" "but sometimes people will express it *as sound as a Roach;* which is by no means a firm fish, but rather otherwise; and on that account Mr. Thomas surmises it should rather be *as sound as a roche,* or rock; and it is certain, the Abbey of de Rufe, in Yorkshire was called Roche Abbey, implying that *roche* was formerly the pronunciation of *rock* here, in some places at least." (Latham's *Dict.* s.v.) That the proverb however originally referred to a fish, and not to a rock, seems probable from Ray's expression "sound as a Trout," as well as from the French saying "*être frais comme un gardon,*" "to be fresh as a *gardon,*" (Roach or Ide); which Littré (s.v., *gardon*) thus explains, "to have an air of freshness and health, an expression derived from the brilliancy of the scales of this fish." Littré gives another proverb, "*Fraîche comme un gardon, droite comme une perche,*" "fresh as a Roach, right as a Perch."

The scientific name of *leuciscus* is from the Greek *leucos,* "white," a term which we generally employ to denote the bright and silvery Roach, Dace, &c.

The fin formula of the Roach is

> Dorsal 12.
> Pectoral 17.
> Ventral 9.
> Anal 12.

The specimen figured was supplied by E. H. Reynard, Esq., of Sunderlandwick.

ROACH

ON THE LEA

<table>
<tr><td>*Order IV.*<br>*PHYSOSTOMI.*</td><td>*Family*<br>*CYPRINIDÆ.*</td></tr>
</table>

# HUB.

## *(Leuciscus cephalus.)*

| | |
|---|---|
| *Capito,* | AUSON, Id. x. 85. |
| *Capito seu Cephalus fluviatilis,* | GESNER, de Aquatil, p. 182. |
| *Mugil fluviatilis,* | WILLUGHBY, p. 261. |
| *Chub or Chevin,* | WILLUGHBY, p. 255; PENNANT, Brit. Zool., iii. p. 322; YARRELL, i. p. 419; COUCH, Fish. Brit. Isles, iv. p. 44. |
| *Cyprinus oblongus macrolepidotus,* | ARTEDI, Sp. p. 7, No. 10. |
| *Cyprinus cephalus,* | LINN., Syst. i. p. 527. |
| *C. jeses,* | DONOVAN, Brit. Fish. v. pl. 115. |
| *Leuciscus cephalus,* | FLEMING, Brit. An. p. 187; GÜNTHER, Cat. vii. p. 220. |
| *Squalius cephalus,* | SIEBOLD, Süsserwasserfische, p. 200. |

IN three short lines Ausonius, in his Idyl on the Moselle, appears to speak of the fish now under our consideration, namely, the Chub—

> "Squameus herbosas Capito interlucet arenas,
> Viscere prætenero fartim congestus aristis,
> Nec duraturus post bina trihoria mensis."   (Id. x. 85-87.)

"Among the weedy sands the scaly Chub glitters, completely stuffed in its very soft flesh with awn-like bones, a fish which will not keep for the table beyond six hours."

The large broad head of this fish implied in the Latin word *Capito*, the large scales denoted by the term *squameus*, the woolly and exceedingly bony nature of the flesh as mentioned in the second line, and the liability to spoil by being kept, all truthfully point to the Chub as the fish of which Ausonius speaks.

The Chub is common in the deep rivers of this country, as in the Thames, the Wye, and many other streams. It prefers, as Couch remarks, "those streams in which the water flows with some considerable rapidity, along a clean bottom of sand or gravel; and so needful to its well-being is a supply of what is afforded by a current, that it is not easy to keep it alive in a tank, or within the narrow limits of a pond." This is quite true as a general rule, though I have known Chub to do fairly well in a strip of water through which there was no constant fresh-water current flowing; indeed the specimen figured was taken from such a piece of water described. It is found also in some of our canals, where the water is pretty clear and wholesome. The Chub is found in various parts of Europe, and in Asia Minor. According to Siebold it is pretty common in almost all the lakes, rivers, and streams of Middle Europe, attaining to a good size and weight of eight pounds or more, but on account of the flesh abounding in little bones it is nowhere in much repute. In the north of Scotland it is said not to occur, nor in the west of England. However, it is probable that the Chub may be artificially increased by its introduction into rivers where it is not at present found, but its poor reputation as an article of diet is not likely to induce pisci-culturists to take much interest in it.

The spawning time is at the end of April and the beginning of May; according to Siebold, in the months of May and June, during which time the males are covered with fine granules breaking out over the body.

I have but little experience in angling for Chub, though I have occasionally caught them with a worm or an artificial fly. From an angler's point of view, according to Mr. Manley, "the Chub, as a fish for sport, is by no means to be despised, though he is not so strong, plucky, and determined as some others when hooked." The same writer says there is this peculiarity about the Chub, that no other fish can be captured in such a variety of methods and with such a variety of baits; he also recommends that the fisherman, whatever fly he uses, should attach to the bend of the hook a narrow strip of white kid, about half or three quarters of an inch long, as adding some attraction to the fly. The Chub is a wary and shy fish, choosing deep quiet holes under bushes, where it is screened from view. Its natural food is the larvæ of various insects, worms, etc., though from the presence of strong and decided throat-teeth there can be no doubt that the Chub is partly also a vegetable feeder, like the *Cyprinidæ* generally.

As to the quality of the flesh as food, the Chub is almost universally esteemed poor; I have tried it in various ways, and I must say that, in my opinion, it is not worth cooking. On one occasion I tried Izaak Walton's receipt, which is as follows:—"First scale him and then wash him clean, and then take out his guts, and to that end make the hole as little, and near to his gills as you may conveniently, and especially make clean his throat from the grass and weeds that are usually in it; for if that be not very clean, it will make him to taste very sour. Having so done, put some sweet herbs into his belly; and then tie him with two or three splinters to a spit, and roast him, basted often with vinegar, or rather verjuice and butter, with good store of salt mixed with it." I must say that I did not find the Chub—and he was a fine specimen—thus dressed "a much better dish of meat" than anglers imagine; and I never again cared to repeat the process. The French, it is said, call the Chub *un vilain*, and condemn him altogether. Mr. Francis, speaking of the Dace and Roach, recommends them to be pickled or potted, or plainly broiled, salted and peppered, a slice of butter being laid on them while hot, and says that even Chub can be eaten in this way. Mr. Manley endorses the statement of Ausonius to some extent when he says, that

Chub are to be cleaned as soon as possible after being taken, split open, and rubbed with salt or lemon, and that if anglers will insist on eating of their spoil, they must, above all, remember "that a Chub *kept for a single night uncleaned is absolutely unedible.*"

A Chub of three or four pounds weight would be considered a good-sized fish; Yarrell states that one of five pounds is the most that he can find recorded; Mr. Cholmondeley Pennell, who has given a table of comparative weights and lengths of Chub, records, as three of the biggest fish, the following lengths and weights :—

A Chub weighing 5lbs. 5¼oz. measured 21 inches.
"          "          6      2½          "      22      "
"          "          7      0½          "      23      "

Our English word *Chub* has clearly been given to the fish to express the broad size of the head; it is the Anglo-Saxon *copp*, German *kopf*, the Latin *caput*, the Greek κεφαλη, the Sanskrit *kapâla ;* but Mr. Manley is quite right in objecting to the term as implying the idea of a clumsy logger-headed fish, because the Chub's head does not justify such an appellation in the least; the head is certainly broad, but not at all out of proportion; and the Chub, as Mr. Francis says, "is a well-shaped, handsome-looking member of the Carp tribe," and I hope my readers, on referring to the plate, will acknowledge this fish to be so. The Latin name of *Capito* is given by Ausonius as the name of the Chub, and other writers have merely followed his nomenclature as having the claim of priority. In some parts of the north of England, as about the Eden, the Esk, the Lowther, Eamont, and other rivers, the Chub is called the *Skelly,* a term no doubt having reference to the large scales of the Chub. A very similar word, *Schelly,* is in the neighbourhood of Ullswater applied to a very different fish, namely, to the *Coregonus clupeoides,* one of the Salmonidæ, known at Bala as the Gwyniad, and at Loch Lomond as the Powan. The term Schelly, as applied to this latter named fish, may refer to its bright shining scales, or to the ease with which the scales fall off from the body when handled; with this we may compare the expression to scale a fish, or the term *shale* in geology.

The specific distinctions of the Chub are as follows :—"Body oblong, its depth being one fourth or rather more than one fourth of the total length (without caudal). Head very broad, the width of the interorbital space being about two fifths of the length of the head. Mouth wide, its cleft extending to below the front margin of the orbit; upper jaw slightly over-lapping the lower. The hindmost suborbital bone is rather larger than the first, *the width of the third much less* than that of the last. Origin of the dorsal fin opposite to the root of the inner ventral rays. Length of the ventral fin more than one half that of the head. There are three longitudinal series of scales between the lateral line and ventral fin. Coloration uniform; margins of the scales greyish. Pharyngeal teeth hooked, slightly denticulated, 5.2—2.5."—(Günther).—

The fin formula is

Dorsal 11.
Pectoral 16.
Ventral 9—10.
Anal 11.

The specimen figured was supplied by Mr. Masefield, of Ellerton Hall.

CHUB

PONT ABERGLASLYN, NORTH WALES.

*Order IV.*
*PHYSOSTOMI.*

*Family*
*CYPRINIDÆ.*

# ACE.

*(Leuciscus vulgaris.)*

| | |
|---|---|
| *Leucisci secunda species,* | GESNER, De Aquatil. p. 26. |
| *Dace,* or *Dare,* | WILLUGHBY, Hist. Pisc. p. 260; PENNANT, Brit. Zool. iii. p. 320; COUCH, Fish. Brit. Isl. iv. p. 54, pl. 194. |
| *Cyprinus novem digitorum, &c.,* | ARTEDI, Spec. Pisc. p. 9 No. 16. |
| *Cyprinus leuciscus,* | LACÉP., v. p. 572; DONOVAN, Brit. Fish. iv. p. 77. |
| *Vandoise,* | BELLON, p. 314; BLOCH. |
| *Leuciscus vulgaris,* | FLEMING, Brit. An. p. 187; YARRELL, i. p. 404; GÜNTHER'S Cat. vii. p. 226. |
| *Leuciscus lancastriensis (Graining),* | YARRELL, i. p. 406. |
| *Dobule Roach,* | YARRELL, i. p. 397. |
| *Squalius leuciscus (Hasel, Häsling),* | SIEBOLD, Süsserwasserfische p. 203. |

THE Dace is one of the most elegant-shaped fish which we have; it is of a beautiful silvery whiteness, and exceedingly quick in its movements, darting like an arrow away from any person or object that may alarm it. It is common in most of the rivers and streams of Central Europe. In England the Dace is found in many of our clear waters, but it is said not to occur in Ireland or Scotland. The Dace is gregarious, like the Roach, swimming generally in shoals; it feeds on the larvæ of various kinds of insects, as well as on the insects themselves, and on worms; its food is also partly of a vegetable nature. The spawning time is in the month of June, at which season these fish may often be seen to congregate on the weedy shallows of rivers, upon which they deposit their ova.

Dace rise freely at the artificial fly, and, as Mr. Pennell says, "make a gallant fight when hooked." They are in good condition in September and October, and though not held in great repute in a gastronomic point of view, being rather soft in flesh and full of small bones, fine specimens out of our clear rivers are not to be despised when nicely fried. The Thames fishermen catch considerable number of Dace, using a light red worm as a bait; bottom-fishing is said to be at its best in October, November, and even in December and January. The Jews have a great liking for Dace, and indeed for white fish generally, and, as Mr. Manley says, they consume them in large numbers (at least when they can get them) during their fasts. Very fine Dace are said to be produced in the New River, near Hornsey, specimens of three-quarters of a pound being by no means uncommon; according to Mr. Pennell, the people residing in the neighbourhood are said to prefer them to Trout for the table. The Dace, from its brilliant appearance, is an excellent bait in trolling for Pike, especially when the water is discoloured. The usual size to which the Dace attains is about eight or nine inches, though larger specimens are found.

The length of the specimen before me from point of nose to the bifurcation of the tail is seven inches and a half; the greatest depth is two inches; the length of the head is one inch and a half; mouth narrow, the cleft not extending as far as the front margin of the orbit, upper jaw overlapping the lower; the origin of the dorsal fin is just opposite the hind part of the root of the ventral; three or four longitudinal series of scales between the lateral line and the ventral fin; upper part of back brownish blue, or blue by angularly reflected light; below lateral line silvery white; irides white or light straw-colour; pectoral and ventral fins slightly tinged with red; anal white; caudal brown, deeply forked.

The fin rays are

> Dorsal 9.
> Pectoral 15.
> Ventral 9.
> Anal 10.

The word *Dace* appears to have been formed by what philologists term "phonetic decay" from the fuller form of *dart*, a name which, with another synonym of *dare*, is applied to the fish under our consideration. As early as the time of Gesner we learn that this species of *Leuciscus* was called the *Dard* by the Santones and Pictones (the old names for the inhabitants of the provinces of Saintonge and Poitou), because the fish moves rapidly, like an arrow or "dart." "Alia Leucisci species est ea quæ hodie à Gallis Vandoise vocatur, a Santonibus et Pictonibus Dard, quod sagittæ modo sese vibret."—(*De Aquatil.* p. 26.) Mr. Manley aptly quotes Drayton as having in his mind the "darting" Dace when he says—

> "Oft swiftly as he swims, his silver belly shows;
> But with such nimble flight, that ere ye can disclose
> His shape, out of your sight like lightning he is shot."

Slightly altering a line in Keble's *Christian Year*, we may apply it especially to Dace as

> "Living shafts that pierce" the stream.

Vandoise or Vaudoise is at this day one of the French names of the Dace; it reminds one of the Vendace, or *Coregonus vandesius*, of Loch Maben in Dumfriesshire, one of the Salmonoids, but what the derivation of the word may be I know not, and M. Littré in his French Dictionary gives no explanation.

# GRAINING

DACE, like most other kinds of fish, are subject to variety, and ichthyologists now regard the Graining, first mentioned by Pennant, and described as a different species by Yarrell in the Linnæan Society's Transactions (vol. xvii., pl. i., p. 5), under the name of *Leuciscus lancastriensis*, as merely a variety of the Dace. Pennant says, "in the Mersey, near Warrington, and in the river Alt, which runs by Sephton, Lancashire, into the Mersey near Formby, a fish called the Graining is taken, which in some respects resembles the Dace, yet it is a distinct and perhaps new species."—(*Tour in Scotland and Voyage to the Hebrides*, pp. 11, 12.) The Earl of Derby, grandfather of the present Earl, supplied Yarrell with numbers of this fish, which that naturalist considered was entitled to rank as a distinct species. Mr. Thompson also obtained specimens of the Graining from the river Leam, near Leamington, and at Guy's Cliff, Warwickshire. The nose of the Graining is said to be more rounded than in the Dace, the scales rather larger, the radiating lines on the scales of the lateral line less numerous than those of the Dace; in colour the upper part of the head and body is pale drab, tinged with red, and separated from the lighter parts of the body below by a well-defined line. In the Dace the number of scales forming the lateral line is about fifty-two, as near as I can count from specimens before me; in the Graining Yarrell gives the number as forty-eight. There seems to be no recorded difference in the form of the throat teeth in the Dace and Graining. I have been unable to see any specimens of this fish, which is probably a mere variety of the Dace; the same perhaps may be said of the Dobule Roach *(Leuciscus dobula)* of Yarrell, which seems to be a young Dace.

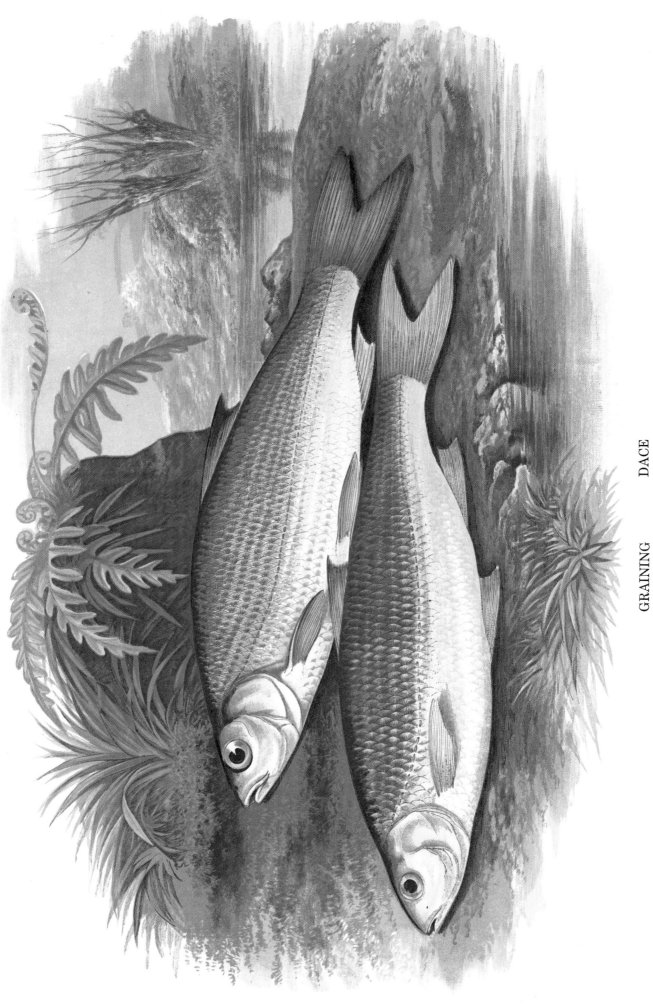

GRAINING    DACE

ON THE PART.

<table>
<tr><td>*Order IV.*</td><td></td><td>*Family*</td></tr>
<tr><td>*PHYSOSTOMI.*</td><td></td><td>*CYPRINIDÆ.*</td></tr>
</table>

# RUDD, OR RED-EYE.

### *(Leuciscus erythrophthalmus.)*

| | |
|---|---|
| *Rootaug (das Rothauge), Red-eye,* | |
| *i.e. Erythrophthalmus Germanicus dictus,* | WILLUGHBY, p. 249. |
| *Cyprinus iride, pinnis omnibus caudaque rubris,* | ARTEDI, Gen. Pisc. p. 3 No. 2. |
| *Cyprinus erythrophthalmus,* | LIN., Syst. Nat. i. p. 530; DONOVAN, Brit. Fish. ii. pl. 40. |
| *Rud,* | PENNANT, Brit. Zool. iii. p. 318; COUCH, Fish. Brit. Isl. iv. p. 49. |
| *Roud (Norfolk), Finscale, Shallow,* | |
| *Red-eye, Rudd,* | YARRELL, i. p. 412. |
| *Leuciscus erythrophthalmus,* | FLEMING, Brit. An. p. 188; CUVIER; THOMPSON, Nat. Hist. Irel. iv. 138; GÜNTHER's Cat. vii. p. 231. |
| *Azurine,* | YARRELL, i. p. 416. |
| *Scardinius erythrophthalmus,* | SIEBOLD, Süsserwasserfische p. 180. |

T HE Rudd is not uncommon in some of the rivers and ponds of this country; it is very like a Roach in general appearance, and often mistaken for one. There is one character, however, which at once reveals the difference between the Rudd and the Roach; in the

Roach, the origin of the dorsal fin is only slightly behind that of the ventral fin, while in the Rudd it is conspicuously behind it. The Rudd is generally distributed throughout the level counties of England; it occurs in the Thames and other waters near London, in Oxfordshire, Warwickshire, Shropshire, and other counties. In the Cam it is called the Shallow; but perhaps the Norfolk Broads are the waters where the handsomest and largest Rudd are produced. According to Thompson it is found from north to south of Ireland, chiefly in lakes and slow rivers; it is generally called a Roach throughout the island, where the true Roach does not occur.

The Rudd spawns in April and May, among the weeds of pools; its food consists of larvæ of insects, worms, small molluscs, and vegetable matter. In quality of flesh it is said to be preferable to the Roach. Where ponds are crowded these fish never attain to any size, but in suitable waters, as in the Norfolk Broads, they not unfrequently attain to a weight of two pounds. Mr. Manley recommends fishermen who want to make the special acquaintance of Rudd, to betake themselves to Slapton Ley and fly-fish for them on the sandy shallows in the summer months. "I am almost afraid," he adds, "to say how many score I have taken there in a few hours with a single-handed fly-rod and common red-palmer fly, but, remember, with a small piece of white kid glove the size of a gentle flying on the head of the hook. *Erythrophthalmus* at Slapton runs up to two pounds, is fairly sportive, but is such an easy prey to the seductive kid, that fishing for him loses part of its interest." A Rudd of one or two pounds is a very beautiful fish, with its bright red eyes and fins, and reddish gold body.

It is often thought that the Rudd is not a distinct species, but a hybrid between the Bream and the Roach. This seems to have been the common opinion in the time of Izaak Walton. "There is a kind of bastard small Roach," he says, "that breeds in ponds, with a very forked tail, and a very small size, which some say is bred by the Bream and right Roach, and some ponds are stored with these beyond belief; and knowing men that know their difference call them Ruds; they differ from the true Roach as much as a Herring from a Pilchard. And these bastard breed of Roach are now scattered in many rivers." The Rudd, however, fairly claims specific distinction, though hybrids between the Rudd and the Roach, as well as between the Rudd and the White Bream, have been observed in Germany and Holland.

The specific characters of the Rudd are thus given by Günther:—"Body elevated, its depth being generally more than one third of the total length (without caudal). Mouth terminal, narrow, very oblique; jaws even in front. There are three longitudinal series of scales between the lateral line and ventral fin. Origin of the dorsal conspicuously behind the root of the ventral. Belly behind the ventrals compressed into an edge, covered by the scales extending across it. Fins generally red, especially the lower. Pharyngeal teeth distinctly serrated."

The fin rays are

Dorsal 10—11
Pectoral 15.
Ventral 9—10.
Anal 13—15.

# AZURINE.

THE Rudd, like fish generally, is subject to variety, and it would appear that the Azurine, or Blue Roach, first described by Yarrell under the name of *Leuciscus cæruleus* (Lin. Soc. Trans. vol. xvii. p. i. p. 8), is merely a variety of the Rudd. At the time Yarrell obtained specimens of the Graining from some of the Knowsley waters through the kindness of the Earl of Derby, he received also specimens of fish which he called the Azurine or Blue Roach. Through the kindness of Mr. T. J. Moore, of the Liverpool Museum, I have been able to examine a great number of these Azurines which came from the Knowsley pools; of course, having been for many years in spirits, they have lost their original blueness of colour. The position of the dorsal fin relative to the ventral, the narrow oblique mouth, and above all the serrated throat-teeth, which in no respect differ from those of the Rudd, all point to the conclusion that the Azurine is a variety of the Rudd or Red-eye. As to colour it is never safe to depend much on any peculiarity; we would do well to remember the admonition of the Roman Poet—"nimium ne crede colori." I am informed that these Azurine fish are not now found in the Knowsley ponds. The specimens in the Liverpool Museum are all of a small size, few being more than six or seven inches in length.

---

# DOBULE.

THE Dobule Roach, a single specimen of which Yarrell took with the mouth of a White-bait net in the Thames below Woolwich, and which is regarded by Günther as a small Dace, is thus in its principal characteristics described by Yarrell:—"Body slender in proportion to its length; nose rather rounded, upper jaw longest; ventral fins arise just in advance of the line of the origin of the first ray of the dorsal fin; tail considerably forked; scales of moderate size, fifty forming the lateral line; the colour of the top of the head, nape, and back dusky blue, becoming brighter on the sides, and passing into silvery white on the belly; dorsal and caudal fins dusky brown; pectoral, ventral, and anal fins pale orange red; irides orange; cheeks and operculum silvery white."

The *Leuciscus dobula* of Agassiz, Cuvier and Valenciennes, is given by Günther as a synonym of the *Leuciscus cephalus*, or Chub.

AZURINE    DOBULE    RUDD

ON THE THAMES.

*Order IV.*
*PHYSOSTOMI.*

*Family*
*CYPRINIDÆ.*

# TENCH.

## *(Tinca vulgaris.)*

| | |
|---|---|
| *Tinca,* | AUSON., Id. x. 125; GESNER, De Aquatil. p. 984; WILLUGHBY, Hist. Pisc. p. 251. |
| *Cyprinus mucosus totus nigrescens,* | ARTEDI, Spec. Pisc., p. 5 No. 7. |
| *Cyprinus tinca,* | LIN., Syst. Nat. i. p. 526; DONOVAN, Brit. Fish., v. pl. 113. |
| *Tench,* | PENNANT, Brit. Zool. iii. p. 314; COUCH, Fish. Brit. Isl. iv. p. 22. |
| *Tinca vulgaris,* | CUV., Régne Anim.; YARRELL, i. p. 375; SIEBOLD'S Süsserwasserf. p. 106; GÜNTHER'S Cat. vii. p. 264. |

*Characters of the Genus* TINCA.—"Scales small, deeply imbedded in the thick skin; lateral line complete. Dorsal fin short, without spine, its origin being opposite the ventral fin; anal short; caudal sub-truncated. Mouth anterior; jaws with the lips moderately developed; a barbel at the angle of the mouth. Gill-rakers short, lanceolate; pseudo-branchiæ rudimentary. Pharyngeal teeth 4 or 5—5, cuneiform, slightly hooked at the end. Europe."—GÜNTHER.

THIS handsome and valuable fish is mentioned once only in classical authors, namely, by Ausonius in his Idyl on the Moselle. Ausonius appears to have shared what was probably the popular opinion of his day, which held the Tench in poor estimation as an article of diet; he mentions this fish in company with White-fish and Shad in the lines—

> "Quis non et virides vulgi solatia Tincas
> Norit, et alburnos prædam puerilibus hamis,
> Stridentesque focis obsonia plebis Alausas?"     (Id. x. 125—127.)

"Who is not acquainted with the green Tench, the solace of the common people, and the Bleak, the spoil captured by boys' fish-hooks, and the Shad which hiss in the fire-pans, plebeian fish-fare?"

Tench thrive best in good-sized ponds, where there is plenty of water weeds of various kinds, as pond-weed, *Potamogeton, Myriophyllum,* &c.; the ponds must not be overstocked, otherwise the fish will not grow to any size, but keep small and thin. Tench are also found in some of our rivers; the Thames, in certain localities where the water is sluggish, being fairly well supplied with them. Deep clay-pits and broad shallow waters on muddy bottoms are productive. Yarrell states that some very extensive tracts of water a few miles north of Yarmouth, not far inland from a point called Winterton Ness, abound with Tench, which, when removed to stews, feed and thrive on a mixture of greaves and meal till fit for the table, and that the flesh is nutritious and of good flavour. As to the quality of the food opinions vary; some people regard the Tench as excellent, others will not touch it; for my own part, I think a well fed Tench of about two pounds in weight one of the best fresh-water fish that we possess, and that it does not in the least require rich and savoury sauces to make it palatable.

The Tench spawns in June; the saying that this happens when "wheat is in flower" is as old as the time of Willughby, who writes "parit vere et æstate cum triticum floret." The female fish when about to deposit her spawn is attended by two or three males, who follow her about; at this time of the year they are very easily taken in a net. The eggs are small, and are, like those of the Carp, deposited on the weeds. The young fish grows rapidly. Couch states that in twelve months it may weigh from half a pound to a pound, and that an instance is known where a Tench, placed in a pond, in six years and a half attained to the weight of four pounds and a half, which would be considered in this country a fish of large size, though they have been taken of five or six pounds weight. The food of the Tench consists of worms and insect larvæ, but it also feeds extensively on vegetable matter. During the winter months it lies buried more or less deeply in the mud, and is dormant, like the Carp. From an examination of the stomachs of several Tench and Carp taken out of the mud in mid-winter, which, together with the whole intestinal tract, were quite empty, it appears that during this time these fish do not take food. It is well known that Tench are eminently tenacious of life, and are able to breathe with a very small supply of oxygen.

Izaak Walton calls the Tench the *physician of fishes,* especially for the Pike, which "being either sick or hurt is cured by the touch of the Tench;" he says that "the tyrant Pike will not be a wolf to his physician, but forbears to devour him though he be never so hungry." This is an old conceit, and is mentioned by Willughby and other authors; some modern writers appear to think there is some truth in the belief. I think we may safely dismiss the whole story as a myth; the Pike will certainly take a Tench just a well as he will another fish, when he is in the humour, and I have caught Pike occasionally when trolling with a small Tench as a bait; Mr. Masefield, of Ellerton, who has perhaps as much experience as any man living, tells me that Pike will eat a Tench as soon as any other fish, and that he has frequently taken Pike with this bait.

The male of the Tench is readily recognised from the female by the large cup-shaped ventral fins.

The fin-formula is

Dorsal 10—11.
Pectoral 17.
Ventral 10.
Anal 9.

The scales of the Tench are very small, and the whole body is abundantly supplied with mucus.

---

# GOLDEN TENCH.

THE Golden Tench is an extremely handsome fish; it is merely a variety of the *Tinca vulgaris*. It is said by Mr. F. Buckland to have been introduced in 1867, by Sir Stephen Lakeman, into this country; but we are not informed where from. In a letter I received last May (1878) from Mr. Higford Burr, of Aldermaston Park, Reading, that gentleman informs me that Mr. Buckland gave him two Gold Tench in September, 1862, and that these fortunately proved to be male and female. These two fish were placed in a pond by themselves and have bred. "I have now," says Mr. Burr, (May 8th., 1878), "a great number; what we catch with rod and line in the summer I place in a small pond until cool weather sets in, when I am happy to distribute them to any gentleman who may apply for them." I do not know in what part of Germany or Austria this golden variety is found. Siebold, writing in 1863, says,—"This magnificent, black-spotted, orange-yellow or red variety of the Tench, which is known by the name of Gold Tench (*Gold-schleihe*), and which I have met with as a cultivated and an ornamental fish in Upper Silesia, has never yet been seen by me in the fish market here (Munich), nor was it noticed by Günther in the Neckar district; according to Heckel it occurs in the still waters of the Salzach, which, however, I must doubt."—(*Die Süsserwasserfische von Mitteleuropa*, p. 107.)

The specimen figured, which weighed one pound, was given to me by Mr. Masefield, who has set apart one of the ponds at Ellerton Hall for the breeding of these fish.

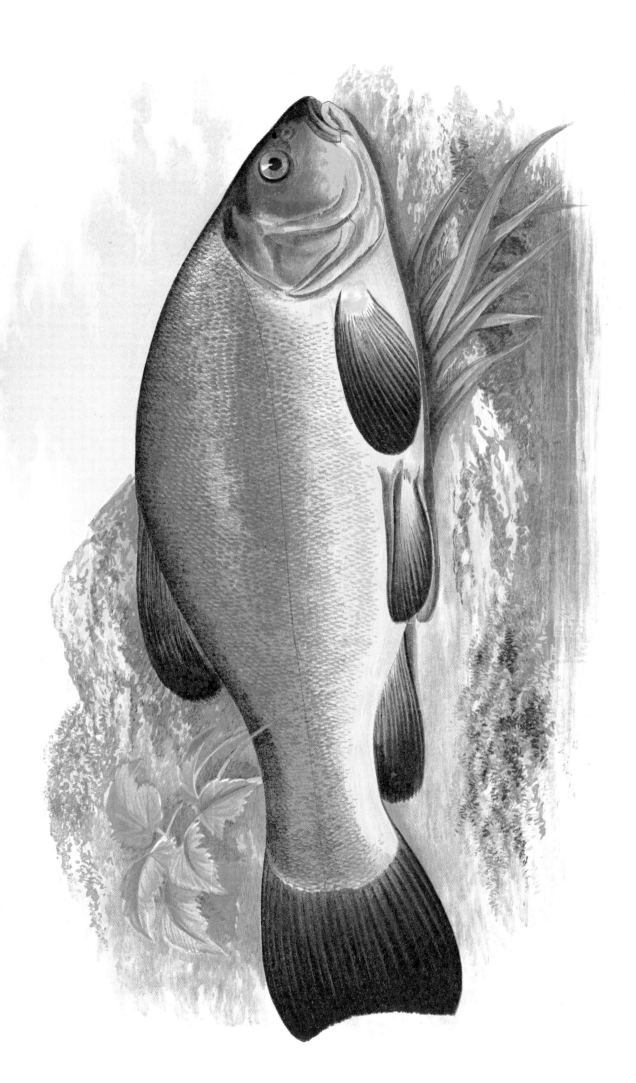

TENCH

RYDAL WATER.

<table>
<tr><td>*Order IV.*</td><td></td><td>*Family*</td></tr>
<tr><td>*PHYSOSTOMI.*</td><td></td><td>*CYPRINIDÆ.*</td></tr>
</table>

# COMMON BREAM.

## (*Abramis brama.*)

| | |
|---|---|
| *Cyprinus latus sive Brama,* | GESNER, De Aquatil. p. 316. |
| *Cyprinus pinnis omnibus nigrescentibus,* | ARTEDI, Spec. Pisc. p. 4 No. 2. |
| *Bream,* | WILLUGHBY, Hist. Pisc. p. 248; PENNANT. Brit. Zool. iii. p. 317; |
| | COUCH, Fish. Brit. Isl. iv. p. 36. |
| *Bream, or Carp-Bream,* | YARRELL, i. p. 382. |
| *Cyprinus brama,* | LIN., Syst. Nat. i. p. 531; DONOVAN, Brit. Fish. iv. pl. 93. |
| *Abramis brama,* | FLEMING, Brit. An. p. 187; GÜNTHER'S Cat. vii. p. 300. |
| *Abramis Brama, Brachsen, Blev,* | SIEBOLD'S Süsserwasserf. p. 121. |

*Characters of the Genus* ABRAMIS.—"Body much compressed, elevated or oblong; scales of moderate size; dorsal fin short, without spine, opposite to the space between ventrals and anals; anal fin long, many-rayed. Lower jaw generally shorter, and rarely longer than the upper; both jaws with simple lips, the lower labial fold being interrupted at the symphysis of the mandible; upper jaw protractile. Gill-rakers rather short; pseudobranchiæ. Pharyngeal teeth in one or two series, with a notch near the extremity. Belly behind the ventrals compressed into an edge, the scales not extending across it. Europe, north of the Alps, and adjoining parts of Asia; North America."—GÜNTHER.

ABRAMIS is the name of a fish mentioned by Oppian and Athenæus; the former speaks of these fish swimming in shoals, and frequenting the rocks and shores of the sea, together with other marine species; and therefore the Bream, which is exclusively a fresh-water fish, cannot be intended (*Halieut.* i. 244). Athenæus enumerates the *Abramis* among several other fishes found in the Nile. The *Abramis* of the Greeks has been referred to some species of Bream, therefore, without sufficient reason.

There are two undoubted British species of Bream, namely, the Common or Carp-Bream (*Abramis brama*), and the White Bream, or Breamflat, (*Abramis blicca*); the so-called Pomeranian Bream, the *Cyprinus Buggenhagii* of Bloch, being almost certainly a hybrid between the Common Bream and the Roach. The two first-named species, when young, are difficult to distinguish, for both are nearly white in colour; but older specimens of the Common or larger Bream become yellowish or yellowish brown, and are then readily to be distinguished from the silvery white Breamflat. An examination of the throat-teeth, however, will clear up any doubts as to the species, because those of the Common Bream are arranged in a single series of five on each bone, while the other species has a double row or series of five teeth in one and two in the other.

Bream are common in many of the lakes, ponds, rivers, and canals of this country. They thrive best in large pieces of water, and have been known to attain the weight of twelve or even fourteen pounds. Many parts of the Thames produce fine Bream, as at Walton, Hampton, Kingston, &c. In the Midland Counties, as in the Trent and the Ouse, Bream are abundant; Mr. Manley says that the Ouse is decidedly the best Bream river in England. The Norfolk Broads are also mentioned as producing Bream of a large size. In Shropshire I have seen great quantities of large Bream taken out of the Aqualate Mere, belonging to Sir Thos. F. Boughey, Bart.

Bream swim in shoals, and feed on worms and the larvæ of water insects, together with vegetable matter. Like some other of the *Cyprinidæ*, the males during the spawning season, which is in May, have white tubercles on the scales, and are rough to the touch. These disappear when the season of reproduction is over. The Thames fishermen bait their hooks with small red worms and brandlings; when hooked in deep water, according to Mr. Francis, the Bream "has a disagreeable nack of boring head down, and rubbing and chafing the line with its side and tail, so that the line often comes up for a foot above the hook covered with slime."

The flesh of the Bream is generally soft, insipid, and full of fine bones, and in little estimation for the table; but Mr. Francis assures us that when taken off a clean gravelly or sandy bottom in the winter time, "when the weed is out of them," they are by no means bad eating. This is quite probable, as the quality of the flesh of various fish depends to a considerable extent on the character of the water inhabited by them, and on the season of the year. In more ancient days the feeding and eating of Bream were more in fashion than at present. Chaucer says of his Frankeleyn—

> "Ful many a fat partrich had he in mewe,
> And many a brem, and many a luce in stew."
>
> (*Prologue Cant. T.* 349.)

Juliana Berners says that "the Breme is a noble fysshe and a deynteous." Dr. Badham quotes a French proverb, "*Qui a brême peut bramer ses amis;*" "he who has Bream is able to ask friends to his table." Sir William Dugdale mentions that about the year 1419 a single Bream was valued at twenty pence, when the day's labour of a mason or master carpenter was less than sixpence, for which three-halfpence was deducted if his food was supplied to him. He also tells us that a pie containing four Bream was sent from Sutton, in Warwickshire, to the Earl of Warwick at Mydlam in the north country, at the cost of sixteen shillings; which amount included the wages of two men employed for three days in catching the fish, together with the spices and flour for making the pie.—(*Hist. Warw.*, p. 668.)

Bream are caught in enormous quantities in some places on the Continent. Nilsson tells us that when the fishing is being carried on in Sweden, in some of the parishes near the lakes it is forbidden to ring the church bells, that the noise may not alarm the fish. Ten to forty thousand pounds weight of Bream have been taken at a single haul of the net. Siebold (*Süsserwasserf.*, p. 124), states that Bream, being eminently gregarious in their habits both at spawning and other times, are caught in immense number in the Spirdingsee and Bodensee below Constanz. "Even now," he says, "from time to time many hundred tuns (*mehrere hundert Tonnen Brachsen*) of Bream are taken from the Spirdingsee at a single draught of the large winter nets."

Bream, like Carp and Tench, are tenacious of life, and will live for some time out of water. Though poor fare for the table, Bream are most useful fish in large ponds and lakes where there are many Pike, to which they contribute a constant supply of food.

The derivation of the word *Bream* is obscure; clearly it is only another form of the German *Brachsen*, French *Brème*, Old High German *Brahsema*, Dutch *Brassem*. The Low Latin form of the word is *Bresmia;* I suspect this is merely an altered form of the Greek Αβραμις, the derivation of which I have been unable to discover.

The head of the Bream is small; body very deep and compressed behind the ventral fin; tail much forked. The colour of large or moderate-sized specimens is yellow and brown on the back, pale below.

The fin rays are

> Dorsal 12.
> Anal 26—30.
> Ventral 10.

The throat-teeth are 5—5.

The specimen figured was caught by a net in the Aqualate Mere last May (1878), and obligingly given to me with any other fish that I required by Sir Thomas F. Boughey, Bart.

COMMON BREAM

ON THE THAMES, NEAR ETON.

Order IV.<br>PHYSOSTOMI.
Family<br>CYPRINIDÆ.

# WHITE BREAM, OR BREAMFLAT.

### (Abramis blicca.)

| | |
|---|---|
| *Blicca, Ballerus, Plestya,* | GESNER, De Aquatil. p. 24. |
| *Cyprinus admodum latus et tenuis,* | ARTEDI, Spec. Pisc. p. 12 No. 24. |
| *Cyprinus björka,* | LIN., Sys. Nat. p. 532. |
| *Cyprinus blicca,* | BLOCH, i. p. 65 pl. 10. |
| *Abramis blicca,* | CUV., R. A. ii. p. 274; GÜNTHER, Cat. vii. p. 306. |
| *White Bream,* | YARRELL, i. p. 387; COUCH, Fish. Brit. Isl. iv. pl. 188. |
| *Blicca björkna,* | SIEBOLD'S Süsserwasserf. p. 138. |

THE White Bream is a much smaller species than the Common Bream, and is far less widely distributed over the country; it seldom exceeds one pound in weight, and is worthless as an article of diet; it is of bright silvery hue, and quite destitute of the yellow or golden lustre of its near relation. It is hardly possible to distinguish this species from the young individual of the Common Bream, because though the White Bream has never any yellowish tint, generally observable in large or middle-sized specimens of the other species, yet young Common Bream are very frequently white, and so similar in appearance and form to the Breamflat, that discrimination is difficult until the throat-teeth are examined. The difference has already been pointed out in my notice of the Common Yellow Bream.

This species was first observed in this country in 1824, by the Rev. Revett Sheppard, who obtained specimens from the river Trent, near Newark; it was subsequently found by the Rev. L. Jenyns in the Cam, where it is called the Breamflat. It is much more common on the Continent, breeding in lakes and slow-running rivers; it is valued simply as affording food for Pike and other voracious fishes. The specific name, *blicca*, is from the Anglo-Saxon verb *blican*, "to shine," to which also the name Bleak *(Alburnus lucidus)*, another Cyprinoid, must be referred. The geographical distribution of the White Bream, according to Günther, is Europe, north of the Alps.

The fin rays are

Dorsal 10—11.
Pectoral 14.
Ventral 9—10.
Anal 22—27.

Hybrids between the White Bream and the Roach have been observed in Holland, Belgium, and Germany.

# POMERANIAN BREAM.

THE fish to which Mr. Yarrell has given the name of the Pomeranian Bream, from the country in which it was first discovered by Bloch, viz. Swedish Pomerania, and which has been generally regarded as a species of *Abramis* distinct from the Common Yellow and White Breams, is in all probability a hybrid between the Common Yellow Bream *(Abramis brama)*, and the Roach *(Leuciscus rutilus)*. Bloch, who has figured and described this fish in his work, *Naturgeschichte der Fische Deutschlands*, p. 95, gave to it the name of *Cyprinus Buggenhagii*, from the name of the gentleman, M. Buggenhagen, from whom he had received specimens. The late Mr. Yarrell received specimens of this fish from the waters at Dagenham Breach, Essex, in the year 1836. Mr. William Thompson, the Natural Historian of Ireland, noticed a specimen of this fish taken from the sluggish river Lagan near Belfast *(Nat. Hist. Ireland*, iv. p. 137). It has also been found in Cambridgeshire, in a tributary of the Colne near Hanworth, Middlesex, and in the Avon. I have had an opportunity of seeing a great number of these so-called Pomeranians which were caught in a net in different parts of the Aqualate Mere, Staffordshire, on the 7th. of May, 1878. Through the kindness of the proprietor, Sir Thomas F. Boughey, Bart., I was invited to be present when parts of this great sheet of water were netted, and allowed to take home with me such specimens as I desired. Siebold *(Süsserwasserfische*, p. 134), identifies this fish as the *Abramis Leuckartii* of Heckel, and states that it has been found in the Somme and Moselle by Selys-Longchamps, and in the Dniester by Nordmann; he certifies that it belongs not only to the basin of the Lower Rhine, but that it is also found in its middle course and its tributaries. Professor von Siebold is strongly of opinion that this fish is a hybrid between the Common Bream and some *Leuciscus*, although he has promoted it to the rank of a genus by giving it the name *Abramidopsis Leuckartii*. He says at the conclusion of his observations, "I will only remark now that, although I have taken Heckel's *A. Leuckartii* to be a particular species, and have raised it to a genus, I have doubts whether this fish really deserves this special classification. The more specimens I have had to pass through my hands of *A. Leuckartii*, from different countries of Middle Europe, the more it appears to me that this Cyprinoid is nothing but a hybrid *(Bastard)* between an *Abramis* and a *Leucisus*."—(P. 137.)

The Pomeranian Bream has been admirably described by Dr. Günther as "a Roach-like modification of the Bream, or a Bream-like modification of the Roach." It differs from an *Abramis* in having a low back, less compressed body, a much less extended anal fin with rays not more than eighteen or nineteen, whereas in the Bream that fin has twenty-eight to thirty; it has not the long, scaleless, compressed ridge at the fore part of the back so characteristic of a true *Abramis;* the shape of the dorsal fin is different, it does not diminish sharply from the anterior extremity to the posterior basal portion; the belly behind the ventral fins is covered with angularly bent scales, in *Abramis* the scales do not extend across it; on the other hand this part of the belly is strongly Bream-like, being compressed into an edge; the throat-teeth in all the specimens I examined were in a single row of five; Siebold found six teeth on the left throat-bone twenty-four times in forty-five specimens, while in one specimen he found on the left throat-bone a double series, namely 1.6, and on the right a single series of 5; in another he found 1.5 teeth on the left and 5 on the right. Although the form and number of the throat-teeth in the *Cyprinidæ* afford a good guide in seeking to determine species, and although the number of teeth, whether in a single or double series, is generally more or less characteristic of a species, I have found that here, too, there is no rule without exceptions. On the whole the throat-teeth of this hybrid presents us with such a combination as one would expect in a fish intermediate between a Bream and a Roach. I have specimens of the pharyngeal teeth and throat bones of the Roach, Bream, and of the fish under consideration, and can confidently affirm that in this case also Günther's description of this fish, quoted just now, is most appropriate and correct. I may notice that when netting the large mere of Aqualate, only portions of which, on account of its great size, are available for this purpose, sometimes the net would bring to shore an immense quantity of Bream without any Roach; in such cases there were no Pomeranians; sometimes Roach and no Bream were caught, here again there was an absence of the Pomeranians; but in every case where the net secured both Bream and Roach, there was always found a certain number of these fish. The evidence, therefore, taken on the whole, satisfies me with the correctness of Professor von Siebold's opinion that the so-called Pomeranian Bream is merely a hybrid—but an exceedingly interesting one—between *Abramis* and *Leuciscus*, and that in the specimens I have been fortunate enough to examine that *Leuciscus* is the *L. rutilus*, or the Roach.

One of the names which the German fishermen give to this fish is *Leiter*, which means "a guide." Bloch states that the fishermen are greatly delighted when they take this fish in their nets, because they say they may then expect a successful haul. They have an idea that other Bream follow this fish. Siebold mentions this name when he says, "Very large specimens grown in the Frische Haff have been given to me at Tolkemit by the fishermen as so-called *Leiter* (guides)."

In a specimen from Aqualate Mere, measuring eleven inches from the snout to the bifurcation of the tail, the greatest breadth was four inches, the length of head two and a half; the origin of the ventral fin was about an inch in advance of that of the dorsal; the lateral line descending at first, then straight, then gradually and slightly ascending to a point nearer to the lower portion; irides pale straw; colour of pectoral, ventral, and caudal fins brownish, slightly tinged with red; scales large; whole body much more full and round than in the Bream, not compressed in the upper part of the back; belly compressed towards the anal fin and tail. Back at the upper part bluish black; sides and belly silvery white.

The fin-ray formula was

> Dorsal 12.
> Pectoral 16.
> Ventral 9.
> Anal 18.

The specimen from which the illustration was made was captured in the Aqualate Mere.

ON THE DERWENT

# BLEAK.

### (*Alburnus lucidus.*)

| | |
|---|---|
| *Alburnus,* | AUSON., Id. x. 126. |
| *Alburnus Ausonii,* | GESNER, De Aquatil. p. 23; WILLUGHBY, p. 263. |
| *Cyprinus quincuncialis, &c.,* | ARTEDI, Spec. Pisc. p. 10 No. 19. |
| *Cyprinus alburnus,* | LIN., Sys. Nat. i. p. 531; DONOVAN, Brit. Fish. i. pl. 18. |
| *Bleak,* | PENNANT, Brit. Zool. iii. p. 324; COUCH, Fish. Brit. Isl. iv. pl. 195. |
| | YARRELL, i. p. 419. |
| *Alburnus lucidus,* | GÜNTHER'S Cat. vii. p. 312; SIEBOLD, Süsserwasserf. p. 154. |

*Characters of the Genus* ALBURNUS.—"Body more or less elongate; scales of moderate size; lateral line running below the median line of the tail; dorsal fin short, without spine, opposite to the space between ventrals and anal; anal fin elongate, with more than thirteen rays. Lower jaw more or less conspicuously projecting beyond the upper. Lips thin, simple....Upper jaw protractile. Gill-rakers slender, lanceolate, closely set; pseudobranchiæ....Pharyngeal teeth in two series, hooked; belly behind the ventrals compressed into an edge....Europe; Western Asia."—GÜNTHER.

IZAAK WALTON has admirably described the little Bleak, which he aptly calls the Fresh-water Sprat, as "a fish that is ever in motion;" "and therefore," he adds, "called by some the river swallow; for just as you shall observe the swallow to be ever in motion, making short and quick turns when he flies to catch flies in the air, by which he lives, so does the Bleak at the top of the water." How often have I in Oxford days, while waiting to take the accustomed oar in the University or College Boat, sat watching these silvery little fish, so abundant in the Thames and Cherwell, and admired their swallow-like movements! The Bleak is supposed to be referred to by Ausonius in his Idyll on the Moselle, in the line—

"Norit et Alburnos prædam peurilibus hamis."

"Who does not know the Bleak, the prey of boys' fish-hooks?"

The Bleak, which is found in many of our English rivers, as in the Thames, the Lea, the Trent, is said by Couch not to be a native of Ireland, that doubt exists as regards Scotland also, and that it is unknown in Cornwall and Devonshire. It is gregarious in its habits, is readily taken by a small artificial fly, or with a small bit of red worm, at a depth of ten to twenty inches. The spawning time takes place in May, at which time, as is the case with several other Cyprinoids, the head and gill-covers are rough to the touch. The little Bleak, says Siebold, as it swims near the surface of the water, often perceives when some rapacious Perch make a rush at it from underneath, when it jerks itself for a considerable space out of the water, and thus eludes the pursuit of its enemy.

From its surface swimming habits, as Siebold also remarks, it becomes very often the prey of birds, as the Sea Swallow (Tern), and as these fish generally are infested more or less with parasitic entozoa, the birds that swallow them become infested also.

We must never despise anything because it is small; everyone is familiar with those little, shining, brittle globules known as artificial pearls; the apparently insignificant, yet withal beautiful Bleak used to be the chief element in their production. A French bead-maker, by name Jaquin, found out how to make these artificial pearls, which, as Beckmann observes, "approach as near to nature as possible, without being too expensive." Jaquin noticed that when these fish, called *ables* or *ablettes* (a word evidently formed from *alburnus*), were washed, the water was filled with fine silver-coloured particles. This he allowed to settle, and then collected the sediment, which had the lustre of most beautiful pearls; this soft shining powder he called essence of pearl, or *essence d' orient*. At first he coated with it beads of gypsum or hardened paste, and, as Beckmann observes, "since everything new, particularly in France, is eagerly sought after, this invention was greatly admired and commended." It was found, however, that when exposed to the heat the pearly coat came off and adhered to the skin, which gave it a brightness far from desirable, so the ladies, for whose use it was chiefly intended, proposed to M. Jaquin that small hollow glass beads should be coated over in the inside with this essence of pearl. This he succeeded in doing; small glass tubes were dipped in, and the pearly pigment injected into hollow glass globules of various sizes and slightly different forms. The Bleak were caught in enormous numbers in the Seine, the Loire, the Saone, and the Rhine; four thousand fish producing about a pound weight of pearl essence, worth to the fisherman about twenty-five francs. The scale-deprived fish were sold at a cheap rate as food for the common people. Jaquin's date is uncertain, Reaumur mentions the year 1656. From France the invention found its way to this and other countries. I do not know whether the art of making these Bleak-scale pearls is practised at the present day or not. I may mention that Dr. Badham states that the manufacture of pearls from Bleak scales was at length superseded by that of Roman pearls, of soft unrivalled lustre; the Roman pearl-powder was obtained from the swim-bladder of some species of *Atherina* caught in immense numbers in the Tiber.

According to Izaak Walton, Bleak are "excellent meat;" Mr. Cholmondeley Pennell says that "a few dozen Bleak marinated form an excellent breakfast dish;" Mr. Francis considers them "very delicate eating when cooked in the way in which Sprats are commonly cooked;"

BLEAK

LOACH

MINNOW

SPINED LOACH

Mr. Manley holds that they "are neither worth the cooking nor eating, having a muddy flavour, or at the best being tasteless, while they are too large to eat like Whitebait, and too small to get a solid mouthful from."

From the Bleak's preference to feed in places where drains pour in their foul water, some have supposed arises the presence of a kind of tapeworm which infests the intestines of this fish, and that the agitated manner in which it often swims on the surface of the water is to be accounted for by the presence of its parasitic guest; hence the term "Mad Bleak," as applied to this fish when performing these uneasy gyrations. This may be so, but why are not other fish equally affected in a similar way? I have opened a great number of fish belonging to various families, and my experience is that they always contain parasitic entozoa, and very frequently *tæniæ* or tapeworm. A glance at Diesing's *Systema Helminthum*, vol. ii. p. 383 to 423, will show how extremely liable are all fish to various parasitic entozoa in different parts of their bodies. In the Roach Diesing enumerates as many as fourteen species as occurring; in the Bleak he mentions six, the species of tapeworm in the latter fish being the *Tænia torulosa* of Batsch.

The Bleak seldom attains to a length beyond seven inches; the colour when fresh is light greenish, or light brown with a slight tinge of blue; sides, cheeks, and belly brilliant silver; eye very large; the dorsal fin is situated far back; cleft of the mouth directed upwards.

The fin-ray formula is

Dorsal 10.
Pectoral 17.
Ventral 9—10.
Anal 18.

The specimen figured was taken from the Thames at Oxford.

Hybrids between the Bleak and Chub, and the Bleak and Rudd have been described.

*Order IV.*　　　　　　　　　　　　　　　　　　　　　　　　　　　　　　*Family*
*PHYSOSTOMI.*　　　　　　　　　　　　　　　　　　　　　　　　　　　　*CYPRINIDÆ.*

# MINNOW.

### (*Leuciscus phoxinus.*)

| | |
|---|---|
| *Phoxinus,* | BELON, De Aquatil. p. 322. |
| *Pisciculus varius ex Phoxinorum genere,* | GESNER, p. 715. |
| *A Pink* or *Minim* or *Minnow,* | WILLUGHBY, Hist. Pisc. p. 268. |
| *Cyprinus tridactylus varius oblongus teretiusculus,* | ARTEDI, Spec. Pisc. p. 12 No. 23. |
| *Cyprinus phoxinus,* | LIN., Syst. Nat. p. 528; DONOVAN, Brit. Fish. iii. pl. 60. |
| *Leuciscus phoxinus,* | FLEMING, Brit. An. p. 188; YARRELL, i. p. 423; THOMPSON, Nat. Hist. Ireland iv. p. 138; GÜNTHER'S Cat. vii. p. 237. |
| *Phoxinus laevis,* | SIEBOLD'S Süsserwasserf. p. 222. |
| *Minnow, Minim* or *Pink,* | YARRELL, i. p. 423; COUCH, Fish. Brit. Isl. iv. 64. |

IT is not at all certain that the fish of which Aristotle speaks under the name of Φοξινος is the Minnow of our rivers and streams, although this term has been applied to this little fish ever since the time of Belon (born about A.D. 1518). The Greek word signifies "tapering to a point," which may have reference to the hinder part of the body of a Minnow, which is somewhat elongated and slender. Aristotle speaks of the *phoxinus* as having ova inside it as soon as it is born, and as depositing its ova in a stream, and adds that the males devour great numbers of them, while other ova perish in the water.

The Minnow, as its name declares, from *minimus*, "very little," is the smallest of the British *Cyprinidæ*, seldom exceeding three inches and a half; it is found in many rivers and streams of this country. It is believed not to have been originally a native of the Irish rivers, and to be still a very local fish in that country. In Scotland it is said to be common.

The Minnow is a very prolific breeder; the abdomen of the females in June being greatly distended with ova; the spawning season lasts only a short time, generally not more than two or three days, and the eggs soon become young fish. Yarrell says he has taken them three-quarters of an inch long by the first week in August. The young fellows are quite transparent with the exception of the large black eyes; it is said that in this state the larvæ of the May-fly (*Ephemera vulgata*) are among their greatest enemies; the diminutive fry seem to be aware that they owe their safety to concealment, for when exposed they immediately bury themselves in the gravel. In an aquarium, or in a small clear pond they become tame. It is quite amusing to observe a whole host of hungry Minnows chasing a bit of bread about. These little fish are free biters and are readily caught with a small hook and a piece of a worm; as spinning-bait for Trout, Perch, and small Pike, the Minnow cannot be surpassed; he is moreover a very handsome little fish. "Lay one when in full season," Mr. Manley enthusiastically says, "on the palm of your hand, examine and admire him. Mark his shape —a miniature Salmon in symmetrical configuration. Mark his beautiful colouring—every shade of olive, white, pale brown, silver, pink, and rosy harmoniously blended, and producing that beautiful mottled appearance which reminds one of the Mackerel and of the *Salmo fontinalis*, the lovely American Brook-trout, which I hope before long will be naturalized in many of our waters." According to Mr. Manley, small Minnows are an excellent substitute for real Whitebait.

The Minnow is said occasionally to eat its own dead, a feature which can hardly recommend itself to our admiration. A writer in the fifth volume of Mr. Loudon's *Magazine of Natural History* relates that, crossing a brook, he saw from the foot-bridge something at the bottom of the water which had the appearance of a flower. "Observing it attentively," he adds, "I found that it consisted of a circular assemblage of Minnows; their heads all met in a centre, and their tails diverging at equal distances, and being elevated above their heads, gave them the appearance of a flower half-blown. One was longer than the rest, and as often as a straggler came in sight he quitted his place to pursue him; and having driven him away, he returned to it again, no other Minnow offering to take it in his absence. This I saw him do several times. The object that had attracted them all was a dead Minnow, which they seemed to be devouring." This ring or flower-like arrangement of their bodies round some attractive morsel as a nucleus I have repeatedly witnessed myself.

The characters of this species are thus given by Dr. Günther:—"Dorsal fin opposite to the space between ventrals and anal. Mouth anterior; upper jaw slightly overlapping the lower; body cylindrical. A blackish spot at the base of the caudal (which is forked); a more or less distinct series of blackish spots along the side of the body, the spots sometimes confluent into a band. Pharyngeal teeth uncinate, 5 or 4.2, 2.4 or 5. Gill-rakers very short and few in number; pseudobranchiæ. Europe."

The fin rays are

Dorsal 9.
Pectoral 16.
Ventral 8—9.
Anal 9—10.

# OACH.

### (*Nemachilus barbatulus.*)

| | |
|---|---|
| *Cobitis fluviatilis barbatula,* | GESNER, De Aquatil, p. 404. |
| *The Loche;* Germanis, *Grundel,* | WILLUGHBY, Hist. Pisc. p. 265. |
| *Cobitis tota glabra maculosa, corpore subtereti,* | ARTEDI, Spec. Pisc. p. 2 No. 1. |
| *Cobitis barbatula,* | LIN., Sys. Nat. i. p. 499; YARRELL, i. p. 427; DONOVAN, Brit. Fish. i. pl. 22; SIEBOLD, Süsserwasserf. p. 337. |
| *The Loach, Loche* or *Beardie,* | YARRELL, i. p. 427: COUCH'S Fish. Brit. Isl. iv. pl. 199. |
| *Nemachilus barbatulus,* | GÜNTHER'S Cat. vii. p. 354. |

*Characters of the Genus* NEMACHILUS.—"No erectile suborbital spine. Six barbels, none at the mandible. Dorsal fin opposite to the ventrals. Air-bladder enclosed in a bony capsule."—GÜNTHER.

THE Loach, Loche, Stone-Loach, Beardie, or Groundling is a well-known little fish, common in most of our brooks and streams; but on account of its habit of hiding with its body more or less concealed from view under stones or under submerged bodies it is not often seen. It is found in various streams throughout Europe, with the exception of Denmark and Scandinavia.

The Loach delights in clear running rivulets, which it prefers to broad rivers; during the day-time it keeps chiefly to the bottom, and thus affords great pleasure to country lads, who have to exercise a little ingenuity and skill in catching the slimy creatures, which dart rapidly away when disturbed from their places of concealment. From the possession of the six barbules which fringe the upper lip, four in front and one at each angle, it may be inferred that the Loach principally obtains its food from the bottom of the water; these barbules are most beautifully and abundantly supplied with nerves, and no doubt serve as instruments of touch, whereby the little fish is enabled to discover the nature of its food. The small size of the Loach renders it an excellent subject for dissection under a binocular microscope, and an examination of the nerves with which these cirri or barbules are supplied will repay anyone who cares to study the matter.

The Loach spawns in March and April; the number of eggs, which are very small, must be very great, for at this period the females have their abdomens very much distended with the ova. The fecundity of this fish seems to be alluded to by Shakespeare:—"Your chamber lie breeds fleas like a Loach;" that is, I suppose, is as prolific of fleas as a Loach is of spawn.

This fish has been, and still is by some persons, accounted an excellent food. "In some parts of Europe," says Yarrell, "these little fishes are in such high estimation for their exquisite delicacy and flavour, that they are often transported with considerable trouble from the rivers they naturally inhabit to waters contiguous to the estates of the wealthy." Siebold also tells us that owing to the savoury flesh of this fish, it is in universal estimation, and frequently brought to market.

The Loach feeds on the larvæ of aquatic insects, and such small worms as it can meet with; it will not unfrequently bite at a baited hook. Their small size, however, is no inducement for the fisherman, unless he wants them as bait for Trout, small Pike, or Perch, and even for this purpose they are not to be recommended, for the flesh is delicate.

The Loach, and the Spined Loach, the next species to be described, are the only two British fresh-water fishes which have their air-bladder enclosed in a bony capsule, a peculiarity, however, which is common to all the group of the *Cobitidinæ*. This bony capsule, in the Loach, consists of two globular cases connected together by a short transverse channel. It is situated near the second vertebræ. By means of a fine needle these osseous capsules may be broken, and the air-bladder disengaged. This organ is figured in Yarrell, who, however, mistook its nature, he regarding "these circular bones as analogous to the scapulæ."

The Loach seldom exceeds the length of five inches, and generally does not attain to that size; the head is somewhat depressed or flattened; eyes small; snout produced; body round at first, then flattened; origin of the dorsal fin about half way between the end of the snout and the root of the tail. Colour prettily marbled or mottled with dark brown; tail and dorsal fin with brownish-black spots in cross bands; ground colour of head, body, and sides yellowish white.

The fin rays are

Dorsal 9—10.
Pectoral 12.
Ventral 7.
Anal 6.

The generic name of *Nemachilus* (*i.e.* "thread-lipped") contains such species of the group as do not possess an erectile suborbital spine, like the Spined Loach. "The Common Pond-Loach," (*Cobitis fossilis*), to which Dr. Badham and Mr. Manley refer, whose favourite pastime is to roll and wallow in the mire of his pond, the *Schlammpitzger* and *Moorgrundel* of the Germans, found in Central and Eastern Europe, is not known to occur in this country. The origin of our English word Loach, with which the French *Loche* and the Spanish *Loja* are identical, is obscure. The German names of this fish are *Bartgrundel* and *Schmerle*.

*Order IV.*                                                         *Family*
PHYSOSTOMI.                                                   CYPRINIDÆ.

# SPINED LOACH, OR GROUNDLING.

## (*Cobitis tænia.*)

| | |
|---|---|
| *Cobitis aculeata,* | GESNER, De Aquatil. p. 404. |
| *Cobitis barbatula aculeata,* | WILLUGHBY, p. 265. |
| *Cobitis aculeo bifurco infra utrumque oculum,* | ARTEDI, Spec. Pisc. p. 3 No. 2. |
| *Cobitis tænia,* | LIN., Sys. Nat. i. p. 409; BLOCH; LACÉPÈDE; CUV. AND VAL.; SIEBOLD, Süsserwasserf. p. 338; GÜNTHER'S Cat. vii. p. 362. |
| *Botia tænia,* | YARRELL, i. p. 432; COUCH, Fish. Brit. Isl. iv. p. 72. |

*Characters of the Genus* COBITIS.—"Body more or less compressed, elongate; back not arched. A small, erectile, bifid suborbital spine below the eye. Six barbels, only on the upper jaw. Dorsal fin inserted opposite to the ventrals; caudal rounded or truncate. Air-bladder enclosed in a bony capsule. Europe; East-Indian Continent."— GÜNTHER.

THE Spined Loach is a very small fish, seldom exceeding three inches in length, and but little known in this country. It is said to occur in the Trent near Nottingham, in the clear streams of Wiltshire, Warwickshire, and Cambridgeshire. Its habits are probably similar to those of the Stone-Loach. According to Siebold, the Spined Loach—the *Dorngrundel* or *Steinbisser* of the Germans—is the smallest of the species known on the Continent, never exceeding four inches at most. "Its propagation is similar to that of the *Bissgurre* (*Cobitis fossilis*), and it lives in concealment like it, only with this difference, that it does not increase to the same extent, and chooses for its abode brooks and streams as well as ponds."

The spawning time is during the warm months of spring.

The spine is forked and moveable, but what its functions may be I know not; I have been unable to get hold of a specimen of this fish. According to Yarrell, the form of the body is still more elongated, slender, and compressed than that of the Loach; the nose more pointed; the mouth and eyes smaller in proportion; the pectoral fin longer and narrower; all the fins occupy the same relative situation. The colours are similar, both of the body and fins, but a row of dark brown spots ranged along the side is the most conspicuous.

The fin-ray formula is said to be

Dorsal 8 (but 10 according to Günther).
Pectoral 9.
Ventral 6—7.
Anal 7.

ON THE WYE.

# ALLIS SHAD.

## (*Clupea alosa.*)

| | |
|---|---|
| *Alausa,* | Auson., Id. x. l. 127. |
| *Clupea alosa,* | Cuv., R. A. ii. p. 319; Jenyns' Man. p. 438; Günther's Cat. vii. p. 433. |
| *Alosa communis,* | Yarrell, ii. p. 213; Parnell, Mem. Werner. Soc. vii. p. 330. |
| *Alosa vulgaris,* | Siebold, Süsserwasserf. p. 328. |
| *Allis,* | Pennant's Brit. Zool. iii. p. 307. |
| *Allis Shad,* | Couch's Fish. Brit. Isl. iv. p. 117. |

*Characters of the Genus* CLUPEA.—"Body compressed, with the abdominal serrature extending forwards into the thoracic region. Scales of moderate or large, rarely of small size. Upper jaw not projecting beyond the lower. Cleft of the mouth of moderate width; teeth, if present, rudimentary and deciduous. Anal fin of moderate extent, with less than thirty rays; dorsal fin opposite to the ventrals; caudal forked. Inhabitants of the coasts of every part of the globe; many species entering fresh water."—Günther.

TWO British species of Shad are known to occur in the waters of our coasts and in some of our rivers, namely, the Allis Shad and the Twaite Shad, and so similar are they in general form and appearance, that they have, both in ancient and modern times been frequently confounded. There seems to be no doubt that under the name of θρισσα, τριχια, and other similar forms, certain species of the *Clupeidæ* were known to the ancient Greeks, but I do not agree with those authors who refer the θρισσα of Aristotle, Ælian, Oppian, Athenæus, and others, without the slightest hesitation exclusively to either of our Shads, although it is probable these fish were known both to the ancient Greeks and Romans. The Greek word θρισσα is derived from θριξ, τριχος, "a hair," and probably has reference to the hair-like bones which are contained in the flesh of most of the Herring family; and consequently the Shad may be, with others of the *Clupeidæ*, included under the Greek name. Be this as it may, ancient authority has referred the θισσα of the Greeks, and the *alausa* which Ausonius mentions, to a Shad. From this latter word the Germans have formed their *alsen*, *elson;* whence also our English word Allis as applied to the species under our consideration. Dr. Badham says that the Shad "forms one of an elaborately finished group of mosaic fish in a house at Pompeii." Here, then, there is evidence of these fish having been known to the Romans. Ausonius, in the line—

"Stridentesque focis opsonia plebis alausas,"

speaks of the Shad as pauper's fare; whether this was the general opinion amongst his countrymen one cannot say.

The Allis Shad ascends some of our rivers in the months of April and May for the purpose of spawning. It is a local fish, being of rare occurrence in the Thames, but in some seasons abounding in certain parts of the Severn and the Wye. It is said to be frequently taken on the north-eastern coasts of England, as at Berwick; also at the mouth of the Tweed in autumn. According to Parnell, it is of rare occurrence in the Firth of Forth; the same writer says that "it is frequently reported that Herrings of a large size, measuring from twenty to twenty-four inches in length, are occasionally taken off the Dunbar and Berwickshire coasts, and which the fishermen name the Queen of the Herrings, but that it is probable the fish they allude to is the Allis Shad."—(*Fishes of the Firth of Forth*, p. 332 in vol. vii. *Mem. Wern. Nat. Hist. Soc.*) Mr. Buckland tells us that he once received a telegram from a gentleman saying that a monster Herring had been taken in the fresh-water part of the Tay, weighing five pounds and a half. This of course proved to be the Allis Shad. The Shad used at one time to ascend the Severn as far as Shrewsbury, but I am told it is never now found higher up than Worcester. I may mention that the Flounders used to ascend the Severn as far as Shrewsbury several years ago, but that they have long ceased to do so. The Severn navigation weirs prevent the ascent of Shad and Flounders beyond certain parts of the river; excepting in very high tides Shad seldom come up as far as Diglas, which is about one mile below Worcester. The spawning of both species of Shad has often been observed in the gravelly pools near Powick, on the Teme, near Worcester. The Shad spawns in May and early June, and chooses shallow rocky places. The fishermen near Worcester call the Shad the "May-fish," as do the Germans. Couch says that the "proceeding is conducted at night, at which time the fish may be heard to make a rattling noise, as if beating the water with their tails." After spawning the Shad soon return to the sea, where they are occasionally caught with a line by those who are *whiffing* for Pollacks, the bait being either the Mud Lamprey or a slice of Mackerel; they have also been caught with a trammel in deep water.

When in the rivers, where they remain on an average about two months, they are taken in nets of two hundred yards long, the mesh being one of three inches. Couch states that seventy to eighty dozen have been caught in a night, the time chosen for taking this fish, which has the character of being shy and timid.

The flesh, as an article of diet, is fair, and though far inferior, in my opinion, to that of a Herring, it is nevertheless good food. I believe that the London markets and the markets

ALLIS SHAD    TWAITE SHAD

of the large towns are supplied with Shad to a considerable extent from Holland, a country famous for its fisheries.

I have already remarked that the two species of Shad are similar, and that it is not easy to distinguish the one from the other on mere external inspection; there is, however, a character which reveals itself on an examination of the gills, and which is a decisive test as to the species, whether it be the Allis or the Twaite (*alosa* or *finta*). In *alosa* the gill-rakers are fine and long, in number from sixty to eighty, on the horizontal part of the outer branchial arch; in *finta* these gill-rakers are strong and bony, in number varying from twenty to twenty-seven.

The Allis Shad, or "King of the Herrings," as it is sometimes called, grows to the length of two feet or more, with a weight of about three pounds, and this is not uncommon; but fish of five pounds' weight and more have been noticed. The specimen I had for examination measured twenty inches in length, and about six inches in its greatest breadth above the dorsal fin; its weight was three pounds and a half.

The height of the body compared with the length is as one to four and a half; ventral fins behind the origin of the dorsal; tail deeply bifurcated; there is a large blackish blotch just behind the upper portion of the gill-cover, which is sometimes followed by a series of smaller black patches. As a rule, the next species (*Clupea finta*) is more generally marked with these smaller patches.

The fin-ray formula is

Dorsal 19.
Pectoral 15.
Ventral 9.
Anal 20—24.

*Order IV.*
*PHYSOSTOMI.*

*Family*
*CLUPEIDÆ.*

# Twaite Shad.

(*Clupea finta.*)

| | |
|---|---|
| *Twaite Shad,* | YARRELL, ii. p. 208; COUCH, Fish. Brit. Isl. iv. p. 123. |
| *Clupea apice maxillæ superioris bifido, maculis nigris utrinque,* | ARTEDI, Spec. Pisc. p. 15 No. 2. |
| *Clupea fallax,* | LACÉPÈDE, v. p. 452. |
| *Alosa finta,* | YARRELL, ii. p. 208; SIEBOLD, Süsserwasserf. p. 332; CUV., Règne Anim. |
| *Clupea finta,* | JENYNS' Man. p. 437; GÜNTHER, Cat. vii. p. 435. |

THIS species is both in general appearance and habits very similar to the Allis Shad, with which it has often been confounded; the distinction, first pointed out by Troschel, lies, as noticed in what has been said when speaking of the Allis Shad, in the shape and number of the gill-rakers. The Twaite Shad never attains to the size of the other species, nor is it considered as good a fish for the table. It enters some of our rivers about May for the purpose of spawning; on which account this fish, as well as the Allis Shad, is on the Continent sometimes called "May-fish;" it remains in our rivers for two or three months, and then descends to the sea. These fish were formerly very abundant in the Thames. Yarrell says that Twaite Shads appear during the months of May, June, and July, in great numbers in the Thames from the first point of land below Greenwich, opposite to the Isle of Dogs, to the distance of a mile below, and that many are taken, but that they bring a small price to the fishermen, being in little repute as food, "their muscles being dry and full of bones." The present condition of the Thames, I suspect, prevents this periodic migration of the Twaite Shad.

Some writers have supposed that the Twaite can be distinguished from the Allis by its possessing teeth in both jaws, and by having a row of dusky spots along each side of the body, the Allis having one spot only near the head; but Dr. Günther has shown that it is impossible to form "a systematic arrangement of a group of animals based exclusively on differences in an organ which has become rudimentary, or where it is subject to even individual variations." The teeth in the members of the genus *Clupea* are a very unsafe guide whereby to lead to real characteristic distinctions; "they are more or less completely lost in a number of individuals either by accident or by age; those on the tongue, if present, are a more constant part of the dentition; yet there are numerous species in which the lingual teeth are few in number, and as readily lost as those in the jaws. Nearly the same may be said with regard to the teeth on the palate; and innumerable instances may be met with in which it is impossible to say whether a certain bone has been provided with teeth or not." In the two Shads there is no real difference in the dentition; neither species has teeth on the palate, the vomer, the tongue, or on the under jaw, while the teeth on the intermaxillary and the maxillary (upper jaw) are deciduous. Both species are occasionally marked with a series of blackish patches along the sides of the body; in the discrimination, therefore, of these two Shads, recourse must be had to the examination of the gill-rakers as the only safe guide.

What the derivation of the terms Shad, and Thwaite or Twaite may be, I know not; the specific name of *finta* is the Italian *finta*, "simulation." The French name of this Shad is *La Feinte*, and doubtless, as Littrè says, was given to this species because it resembles the Allis Shad; "*Ainsi dit parce que c'est une alose feinte.*" The Germans generally call the Allis Shad *Die Maifisch*, or *Mutterhäring*, and the Twaite Shad *Die Finte*.

There is no real difference in the fin rays of this species from the other Shad.

ON THE DOON.

Order IV.<br>PHYSOSTOMI.
Family<br>ESOCIDÆ.

# PIKE.

## *(Esox lucius.)*

| | |
|---|---|
| *Lucius,* | AUSONIUS, Id. x. 122; GESNER, De Aquat. p. 500; WILLUGHBY, Hist. Pisc. p. 236. |
| *Esox rostra plagioplateo,* | ARTEDI, Spec. Pisc. p. 26 No. 1. |
| *Esox lucius,* | LIN., Sys. Nat. i. p. 516; DONOV., Brit. Fish. v. pl. 109; JENYNS' Man. p. 417; GÜNTHER'S Cat. vi. p. 226; SIEBOLD, Süsserwasserf. p. 325. |
| *Pike* or *Pickerell,* | WILLUGHBY, p. 236; PENNANT, Brit. Zool. iii. p. 424, ed. 1812; YARRELL, i. p. 434; COUCH, Fish. Brit. Isl. iv. p. 150. |

*Characters of the Genus* ESOX.—"Body elongate, covered with small cycloid scales, many with a muciferous channel; lateral line distinct; eye of moderate size. Snout elongate, broad, depressed, with the lower jaw the longer; cleft of the mouth very wide. Teeth of the mandible in a single series, unequal in size; some large; intermaxillary, vomer, palatine, and hyoid bones with bands of cardiform teeth; maxillary toothless. Dorsal fin opposite the anal. Caudal forked."—GÜNTHER.

THE Pike was probably unknown to the ancient Greeks; at any rate there is no mention of this fish in any Greek author; among the Latins, Ausonius is the only writer who clearly alludes to it in the following lines:—

PIKE

Hic etiam Latio risus prænomine, cultor
Stagnorum querulis vis infestissima ranis
Lucius, obscuras ulva cænoque lacunas
Obsidet: hic nullos mensarum lectus ad usus,
Fervet fumosis olido nidore propinis.     (120—124.)

"Here also, under a name ridiculous in Latium,* an inhabitant of the ponds, a most hostile power to the croaking frogs, the Pike (Lucius) haunts the pools dark with weed and mud; this fish, chosen for no uses of the table, steams with a bad smell in the smoking cook shops."

Dr. Badham renders the passage in verse, less literally,—

"The wary luce midst wrack and rushes hid,
The scourge and terror of the scaly brood,
Unknown at friendship's hospitable board,
Smokes 'midst the smoky tavern's coarsest food."

The Pike is supposed by some to be an introduced fish into this country, and although it is now very common in the rivers, ponds, and lakes of England, Wales, Scotland, and Ireland, there is evidence to show that at one time it was considered rare. " In the latter part of the thirteenth century," says Yarrell, "Edward the First, who condescended to regulate the prices of the different sorts of fish then brought to market, that his subjects might not be left to the mercy of the vendors, fixed the value of Pike higher than that of fresh Salmon, and more than ten times greater than that of the best Turbot or Cod." Pikes are mentioned in an act of the sixth year of the reign of Richard the Second, 1382, which relates to the forestalling of fish, (see Pennant, *Brit. Zool.* iii. p. 425, ed. 1812); and they were served at the great feast given by Archbishop Neville in the year 1466. Pike are said to have been so rare in the reign of Henry the Eighth that a large one sold for double the price of a lamb in February, and a Pickerel (or small Pike) for more than a fat capon.

According to Couch the Pike is known in almost every part of England except Cornwall. It is found in the fresh waters of the temperate parts of Europe, Asia, and North America; in American specimens, according to Günther, there are generally seventeen anal rays, and only exceptionally nineteen; whilst the European examples have nineteen, a less number being of very rare occurrence.

The usual haunts of the Pike in the deep pools of slow-flowing rivers, and weedy ponds, did not escape the notice of Ausonius as quoted in the lines above. "In such places, shrouded from observation in his solitary retreat, he follows with his eye the motions of the shoals of fish that wander heedlessly along; he marks the water-rat swimming to his burrow, the duck-lings paddling among the water-weeds, the dabchick and the moorhen leisurely swimming on the surface; he selects his victim, and like the tiger, springing from the jungle, he rushes forth, seldom indeed missing his aim: there is a sudden rush, circle after circle forms on the surface of the water, and all is still again in an instant."—(*British Fish and Fisheries.*)

I need not give many instances of the well-known voracity of the Pike; such as may be seen in the works of some of the old writers, as Gesner, Rondeletius, Walton, and others. But the following quite modern story (for it happened in June 1856) is well authenticated, and is given by Mr. Cholmondeley Pennell in his excellent handbook *The Angler Naturalist;* it is headed "Particulars of an Encounter with a Fish in the month of June, 1856." The account is given by the boy's father, Mr. George Longhurst, of Sunning Hill. "One of my sons, aged fifteen, went with three other boys to bathe in Inglemere Pond, near Ascot Racecourse; he walked

---

* Lucius was a favourite prænomen among the Romans, as is attested by the frequent occurrence of the letter L. at the beginning of inscriptions. King Lucius Tarquinius Priscus appears to have been the first important personage who bore the name, which is evidently derived from *lux*, "light." Ausonius means to say that it is ridiculous for so worthless a fish as the Pike to be called after a name which kings and nobles have borne.

gently into the water to about the depth of four feet, when he spread out his hands to attempt to swim; instantly a large fish came up and took his hand into his mouth as far up as the wrist, but finding he could not swallow it, relinquished his hold, and the boy turning round, prepared for a hasty retreat out of the pond; his companions who saw it, also scrambled out of the pond as fast as possible. My son had scarcely turned himself round when the fish came up behind him and immediately seized his other hand, crosswise, inflicting some very deep wounds on the back of it; the boy raised his first-bitten and still bleeding arm, and struck the monster a hard blow on the head, when the fish disappeared. The other boys assisted him to dress, bound up his hand with their handkerchiefs, and brought him home. We took him down to Mr. Brown, Surgeon, who dressed seven wounds in one hand; and so great was the pain the next day, that the lad fainted twice; the little finger was bitten through the nail, and it was more than six weeks before it was well. The nail came off and the scar remains to this day." And what became of the Pike? Retribution quickly followed this would-be boy-devourer! "A few days after this occurrence, one of the woodmen was walking by the side of the pond, when he saw something white floating. A man, who was passing on horseback, rode in, and found it to be a large Pike in a dying state; he twisted his whip round it and brought it to shore. Myself and my son were immediately sent for to look at it, when the boy at once recognised his antagonist. The fish appeared to have been a long time in the agonies of death; and the body was very lean and curved like a bow. It measured forty-one inches, and died the next day, and was, I believe, taken to the castle at Windsor."

There is an old myth that the Pike will spare the Tench, his piscine "physician." The following story, communicated by Dr. Genzik to Mr. C. Pennell, will show that he does not hesitate to attack a human physician, or at any rate a medical student. "In 1829 I was bathing in the swimming school at Vienna with some fellow-students, when one of them— afterwards Dr. Gouge, who died a celebrated physician some years ago—suddenly screamed out and sank. We all plunged in immediately to his rescue, and succeeded in bringing him to the surface, and finally in getting him up on to the boarding of the bath, when a Pike was found sticking fast to his right heel, which would not loose its hold, but was killed and eaten by us all in company the same evening. It weighed thirty-two pounds. Gouge suffered for months from the bite."

Referring back to the Pike sparing the Tench, because the former fish is grateful for supposed services rendered by the latter in rubbing itself against the Pike's wounds, and thus healing it by the application of mucus, I should hardly have thought it necessary to refute the story, were it not that some modern authors are inclined to think there is some truth at the bottom of it.

> "The Pike, fell tyrant of the liquid plain,
> With ravenous waste devours his fellow train;
> Yet, howsoe'er by raging famine pined,
> The Tench he spares—a medicinal kind;
> For when, by wounds distrest or sore disease,
> He courts the salutary fish for ease,
> Close to his scales the kind physician glides
> And sweats a healing balsam from his sides."

That Pike may prefer one kind of fish to another is not only probable in theory, but known as a fact, and it is likely enough that this "fell tyrant of the liquid plain" would rather dine on a fat Gudgeon or bright-scaled Dace than on a slimy Tench; but it is not true that the Pike refuses to swallow Tench; I have frequently caught Pike when trolling with a small Tench, and others have the same experience. Moreover, the late Rev. W. Bree gives the following evidence, which is pretty conclusive:—"I turned into a pit fifty-seven small Tench, and upwards of three score Crucian Carps; and not a great while afterwards, having discovered the presence of Pikes in this piece of water, a net was employed, with which three of that species were taken, which weighed respectively about three pounds, two, and a pound and a half; but all that remained of the other fishes which had been placed in this pond were one Tench that weighed a pound and a half, and eight Crucians of about a pound each. I cannot have the smallest doubt that the Pike devoured the fish that were missing, and those nine that remained only escaped because they were rather too large for these Pikes to swallow."—(*Zoologist*, 1853, p. 4125.)

When a Pike is hungry, in that frantic state so well described by Charles Kingsley as partly induced by the north-east wind,

> "Hungering into madness
> Every plunging Pike,"

almost any kind of food is acceptable; water-voles, rats, young ducks, little goslings, young moorhens, dabchicks, and fish of all kinds enter into a Pike's food-list; besides garbage occasionally; and even it is on record that the head of a swan, as the bird was feeding under water, has been seized by one of these ravenous fish. Toads seem to be the only creatures the Pike refuses to swallow.

Pike spawn in March and April, and sometimes in February; Siebold gives April and May; there is doubtless difference as to time in this respect. The roe is small, and in canals and ponds is deposited among the weeds; where possible, a pair of Pike will seek the small bays, creeks, and shallows of the waters inhabited by them, and place their spawn there, returning after the season to more open waters. The young are said to be produced in about thirty days, and their growth to be rapid; but of course growth depends in a great measure on the amount and quality of food they can get.

The size to which Pike, under favourable circumstances, will attain, is very considerable. The largest on record is the one mentioned by Gesner, who relates that in the year 1497 a Pike was caught in a pool near Hailprun (Heilbronn) in Suabia (Neckar-Kreis, Würtemberg), with a brass ring fixed in the skin under the gills, a portion of which ring was still bright. Gesner gives a figure of this ring, which is before me as I write; its diameter, measuring from the outer periphery, is just three inches and a half; the breadth of the margin is just a quarter of an inch; at the bottom of the ring is a double series of round metal balls of the size of large peas, three in each series, which is separated by an interval, and the balls are attached to the ring each by a pedicle; engraved round the margin of the ring is a Greek inscription, easily read, the translation of which is as follows:—"I am that fish that was first put into this lake by the hands of the Emperor Frederick the Second, on the fifth day of October, 1230." On the top of this ring a smaller one was fastened, by which it was attached to the fish. The six circular balls are supposed, by Gesner, to signify the Imperial Electors. The diameter of the smaller ring is an inch and five-eighths; its margin is a quarter of an inch in breadth. If this story is correct, the Pike in question would have been two hundred and sixty-seven years old from the time it was placed in the lake; it is said to have weighed three hundred and fifty pounds, but I do not find this on the authority of Gesner. Mr. Cholmondeley Pennell, who has very accurately reproduced old Gesner's figure of the ring, with its inscription, mentions one Leham, who had seen a drawing of both Pike and ring, in a tower on the road between Heilbronn and Spires; this writer says that as late as the year 1612 the water from which the Pike was taken was still named *Kaiserwag* (?) or the Emperor's Lake. "The ring and the skeleton of the Pike," adds Mr. Pennell, "are stated to have been long preserved in the cathedral at Mannheim, the skeleton measuring nineteen feet; but upon subsequent examination by a clever anatomist, it was discovered that the bones had been lengthened to fit the story—in other words, that several vertebræ had been added." Considering that we have authentic records of Pike attaining to the weights of forty, seventy, and even ninety pounds, there seems no reason to disbelieve entirely the old "Ring-story." As Mr. Pennell says, "taking all the circumstances of the case into consideration, as well as the amount of concurrent testimony produced, there appears to be no reason to doubt that a Pike of extraordinary size and age was actually taken at the place and time stated. It is to be observed, in estimating the probabilities of the narrative, that it was certainly the custom in earlier times to put metal rings into the gill-covers of fish; and as late as 1610 a Pike was taken in the Meuse bearing a copper ring, on which was engraved the name of the city of Stavern and the date of 1448."— (*Angler Naturalist*, p. 190.)

One of the largest recorded British Pike was taken in Loch Ken, Kirkcudbrightshire; it is mentioned in Daniell's *Rural Sports* and by other writers. The head is now in the possession of the Hon. Mrs. Bellamy Gordon, of Kenmure Castle, Kirkcudbrightshire, to whom I am indebted for some particulars concerning this monster fish. It is said to have weighed over seventy-two pounds, and to have been about seven feet in length.* The Pike from some of the Continental lakes, however, exceed even this weight. Dr. Genzik, of Lintz, assures Mr. Pennell that in the fish markets there, as well as in those of Vienna and Munich, Pike of eighty and ninety pounds weight and upwards are not unfrequently exposed for sale; the same gentleman saw a Pike taken at Oberneukirchen which after being cleaned weighed ninety-seven pounds and some ounces; and he was informed by an officer of Tyrolese Rifles that he was present when in 1862 a fish was caught at Bregentz of more than one hundred and forty-five pounds weight.

Large Pike are not unfrequently caught in the pools at Weston Park, Shropshire, the seat of the Earl of Bradford. His lordship mentions to me a specimen of Pike in his possession which weighed thirty-seven pounds and a half. "One year," he says, "I remember taking two at the same time which weighed thirty and thirty-three pounds." In Mr. Frank Buckland's Museum, South Kensington, several casts of Pike, admirably executed and well coloured, may be seen; I particularly noted one fish, of thirty-five pounds weight, caught in a net at Rabley Lake, Windsor, in October, 1874. It must have been in splendid condition; the breadth and depth were enormous. There is also a cast of one Pike being partly swallowed by another; the pair weighed nineteen pounds; both were found dead in Loch Tay in 1870. As Mr. Buckland remarks, "they were probably charging at the same bait."

As to the quality of the flesh of this fish there is much difference of opinion; some persons will not eat it on any account, others regard it as most excellent food. In the case of Pike, as in that of fresh-water fish generally, much depends on the waters inhabited, the amount of food, and the time of the year. A Pike of four, six, or ten pounds weight, taken out of a river where White Fish and other kinds abound is almost always, in my opinion, a good fish; the same may be said of Pike taken from lakes and large ponds well supplied with food; but Pike taken from small muddy pools insufficiently stocked with other fish, and caught soon after spawning, are worthless, I confess, and such specimens, I suspect, must have come under the notice of the Roman poet who, as we have seen, considered the Pike unworthy of a gentleman's table, and fit only to "steam away with unpleasant odour in smoky cookshops."

Trolling for Pike is a sport which is deservedly in high favour with anglers generally; the baits employed are Roach, Dace, Perch, Bleak, Gudgeon, and small Tench—a Goldfish is an attractive lure. Pike are sometimes caught with a large artificial fly, as in Salmon fishing.

---

* The Honourable Mrs. Bellamy Gordon tells me that this fish, which was caught about one hundred and twenty years ago by John Murray, keeper at Kenmure, was taken by an artificial fly made of peacocks' feathers; that the head has lost some of its bones, and that in consequence it looks smaller than it used to do, but that it is still large in comparison to the head of a Pike of twenty-seven pounds weight also caught in Loch Ken about forty years ago, and preserved in the same case.

In discoloured water the spoon bait is often very effective. But I must refer my readers, who require information on such points, to Mr. Cholmondeley Pennell's *Book of the Pike* and to Mr. Francis Francis's *Book on Angling*, where the fullest information and instruction will be found.

The body of the Pike is elongated, of uniform depth from the shoulder to the origin of the dorsal fin, then narrowing; the head flat and wide; under jaw the longest; gape excessively wide; eyes large and prominent; distinct mucous pores on the lower jaw, as also on the upper surface of the head. The dorsal fin and the anal are very far back, and are opposite; tail forked and broad. Colour of head and upper part of the back olive brown, becoming lighter on the sides, and broadly specked or mottled with green or yellowish green, with many scattered roundish yellow spots; belly white or silvery white.

The fin-ray formula is

> Dorsal 19.
> Pectoral 15.
> Ventral 10.
> Anal 19.

The name of Pike doubtless alludes to the length and shape of this fish's body. In Halliwell's *Dictionary of Archaic Words* we learn that Luce was generally applied to large full-grown fish, in the last stage of life; "first a Jack, then a Pickerel, thirdly a Pike, and last of all a Luce." "The Pike of the fisherman," says Yarrell, "is the Lucie of heraldry, from the Latin or old French name. Three silver Pikes in a red field were the arms of the ancient baronial families of Lucie of Cockermouth and Egremont." Shakespeare *(Merry Wives of Windsor,* i. 1,) refers to this fish in the arms of Sir Thomas Lucy, of Charlecote, Warwickshire.

A fine specimen was presented for the use of this work by Major Brooksbank, of Middleton Hall.

# SALMONIDÆ.

———

D R. GUNTHER has well remarked that "the *Salmonidæ* and the vast literature on this family offer so many and so great difficulties to the ichthyologist, that as much patience and time are required for the investigation of a single species as in other fishes for that of a whole family. The ordinary method followed by naturalists in distinguishing and determining species is here utterly inadequate; and I do not hesitate to assert that no one, however experienced in the study of other families of fishes, will be able to find his way through this labyrinth of varieties without long preliminary study, and without a good collection for constant comparison. Sometimes forms are met with so peculiarly and constantly characterized, that no ichthyologist who has seen them will deny them specific rank; but in numerous other cases one is much tempted to ask whether we have not to deal with a family, which, being one of the most recent creation,* is composed of forms not yet specifically differentiated."

The difficulties here spoken of by Dr. Günther, in his preface to the sixth volume of his *Catalogue of the Fishes in the British Museum* (London, 1866), have been in a great measure overcome, thanks to the great knowledge and the laborious patience of the eminent ichthyologist himself, and although no doubt a good many questions relating to the life history of some of the members of this family remain at present unanswered, yet it may be safely asserted that Dr. Günther has successfully combated most of the difficulties which beset the study of the *Salmonidæ*, and that in him we have an excellent and most trustworthy guide in threading our way through what was before, what he so well describes, a labyrinth of confusing variations. I was well aware of some of these difficult questions before I undertook to write this present work, and therefore from the very day almost on which I embarked, I kept my eye and mind almost without intermission on questions relating to this family of the *Salmonidæ*; I have visited various parts of England, Wales, and Ireland, in order to make enquiries, and especially to procure specimens, and on the whole I may congratulate myself on my success.

Under the family name of British *Salmonidæ* are included the various species of Salmon proper, whether migratory or non-migratory, the Charrs of the North of England and of Wales, the Pollan, the Gwyniad, and the Vendace of Ireland, Wales, and Scotland respectively,

———

* "No fossil true *Salmo* is known at present; the nearest fossil approaching to it is a *Mallotus*."

the Grayling, and the Sparling, or Smelt. But it is only in the first sub-generic group (*Salmones*) that we meet with such infinite variations as to cause the difficulties alluded to; these variations are dependent on age, sex, and sexual development, and the properties of the water, as Günther has remarked. There is, however, another fact in the history of some of them which serves still further to increase complications, and that is that some of these Salmonoids interbreed.

As to points of variation we find that there is great difference in the *colouration* between the different individuals of the same species. Again, colouration varies in the *same* individual, according to age and sexual development; thus the young of the Salmon, as indeed of all the *Salmonidæ* perhaps, are striped transversely with dark bars; the colour of a male or a female Salmon in the spawning season (November, December,) is often adorned with various tints of red, yellow, and blue, totally unlike the colouration of the same fish earlier in the year with its bright silvery scales. "Nimium ne crede colori" must ever be remembered, because colour rarely assists in distinguishing a species, there being perhaps not one which has the same colour at all periods of its life.

The *size* of some of the *Salmonidæ* is subject to variation; and this depends mainly, if not entirely, on the amount of food to be obtained. I have seen a Trout two years old, taken out of a fair-sized piece of water where food was abundant, which weighed nearly three-quarters of a pound; whereas another individual of the same age, which had lived in a small pond with many other Trout for the same length of time and with little food, would weigh not more than two ounces and a half.

*Structural variation* occurs in the snout in a most marked degree. The long pointed snout of a male ready to spawn is different from that organ before the milt is matured; so in the form of the mandible or lower jaw, which in the breeding season is generally bent upwards, there is great difference. The tail, moreover, is subject to variation; in young specimens, in the parr state, that organ is always more or less deeply incised in all the species of *Salmo*; in the grilse state the tail is still incised, but not so deeply as in the parr state, whilst in a full grown Salmon the tail is almost square; so that here we should follow a very fallacious guide did we fail to remember that variation occurs relating to the age and the sexual development of the fish. But not only is the caudal fin thus liable to structural variation; we are assured by Dr. Günther that the form and length of all the fins may vary. Species inhabiting rapid streams, as well as still waters, show considerable variations; "those individuals which live in rapid streams, being in almost constant motion, and wearing off the delicate extremities of the fins, have the fin rays comparatively shorter and stouter, and the fins of a more rounded form, particularly at the corners, than individuals inhabiting ponds or lakes; moreover, one and the same individual may pass a part of its life in a lake, and enter a river at certain periods, thus changing the form of its fins almost periodically."—(P. 5.)

In the *texture* of the surface of the body variation occurs. In old males the epidermis is always tough during the spawning season, the scales are more or less deeply imbedded in the skin, and therefore not easily deciduous; this is not the case at other seasons of the year.

Thus it will be seen that in all these instances of variation, whether in colouration or in structure, it would be unsafe to depend on them as guides in discriminating species, because such characters are not constant; they are variable according to the age and sexual development of the fish. But it may be asked, have we no reliable guides on which to depend? Are there no constant characters? Dr. Günther draws attention to the following points upon which, he thinks, the chief stress should be made in discriminating species.

1. "The form of the præoperculum of the adult fish." This will be readily seen by the subjoined woodcut. *a* is the præoperculum of the Sewen (*S. cambricus*), which at *a** has

SALMON (MALE.)

a distinct and well-developed lower limb; *b* is that of *S. brachypoma*, which at *b** has scarcely a trace of a lower limb. This character may be said to be constant, and I have always

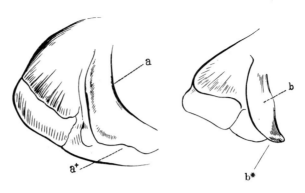

Fig. 1.      (After Günther.)      Fig. 2.

found it a safe guide in discrimination. It should be remembered, however, that in the young of all the Salmonoids the præoperculum has a short lower limb, and that whilst "in some species it lengthens with age, its development in a horizontal direction is arrested in others."

2. "The width and strength of the maxillary of the adult fish." This character is well shown in the accompanying woodcuts. *a* is the maxillary or upper jaw of the Common Trout, *b* that of the Lochleven Trout, each fish being of the same size, namely, twelve

*a*, Common Trout.                    *b*, Lochleven Trout.
(After Günther.)

inches long. I have before me a young specimen of the Common Brown Trout with parr marks distinct, from Ellerton Hall; it is about four inches long. I have also before me a parr Salmonoid from the Dee, near Min-yr-Afon, the residence of Mr. Bigge, caught in August, 1878; it is about five inches in length. The young parr state in all the Salmon family is very similar, and a general examination of the young of the different species would fail to detect any difference. Now in the first of these two specimens (*S. fario*) the maxillary reaches almost to a level with the posterior orbit of the eye; in the Dee Salmonoid the maxillary reaches only to the centre of the eye. Here is a most important character, for I know at once that this young Dee Salmonoid is the parr state of the *Salmo cambricus*. There are other indications as to this being the species, but I pass over them for the present.

3. "The size of the teeth, those of the intermaxillaries excepted."

4. "The arrangement and the permanence or deciduousness of the vomerine teeth." This is a character of some importance; in some species the teeth are arranged on the vomer in a double series, in others in a single one; but as the teeth forming a single series are often arranged alternately, or in a kind of zigzag way, presenting somewhat the appearance of a double series, and other irregularities also occur, a definite arrangement is not always evident. In some fish these vomerine teeth are persistent, in others deciduous.

5. "The form of the caudal fin in specimens of a given size, age, and sexual development."

6. "A great development of the pectoral fins when constant in individuals from the same locality."

7. "The size of the scales, as indicated by the number of transverse rows above the lateral line." Dr. Günther regards this as one of the most constant characters.

8. "The number of vertebræ; the constancy of this character is truly surprising, excess or diminution in the number being of rare occurrence."

9. "The number of pyloric appendages." In some species the number varies from thirty to fifty; in others, as in the Salmon and Charr, it is very constant; in the Lochleven Trout these cæcal appendages are generally very numerous, from seventy to ninety; and where the normal number is diminished, this has been brought about by the confluence of some of the cæca. I may mention a striking instance of the value of this character in the case of the Galway Sea Trout (*Salmo gallivensis*); in a specimen before me, a fish about ten inches long, the pyloric appendages are very short, the longest is not more than half an inch, and about a line in diameter.

Certain points in the life history of the Salmon or other species of the *Salmonidæ* which yet remain obscure will be noticed in the accounts of the different fish as they come before me. I give here a tabular arrangement of the various species of British *Salmonidæ*, which I hope will be found useful.

# SALMONIDÆ.

## FIRST GROUP—SALMONINA.

### First Sub-generic Group—*SALMONES.*

#### MIGRATORY SPECIES.

Salmo salar, LIN., (Salmon.)
S. trutta, FLEM., (Salmon- or Sea-Trout.)
S. cambricus, DONOV., (Sewen.)
S. brachypoma, GTHR., (Short-headed Salmon.)
S. gallivensis, GTHR., (Galway Sea-Trout.)
S. argenteus, CUV. & VALENC., (Silver Salmon.)
S. eriox, YAR., (Bull Trout of the Coquet.)

#### NON-MIGRATORY SPECIES.

Salmo fario, LIN., (Common Brown Trout.)
S. ferox, JARD. & SELBY, (Great Lake or Black Lough Trout.)
S. stomachicus, GTHR., (Gillaroo Trout.)
S. nigripinnis, GTHR., (The Black-Fin.)
S. levenensis, WALK., (Lochleven Trout.)

### Second Sub-generic Group—*SALVELINI.*

#### NON-MIGRATORY SPECIES.

Salmo alpinus, LIN., (Alpine Charr.)
S. willughbyi, GTHR., (Windermere Charr.)
S. perisii, GTHR., (Llanberris Charr.)
S. grayii, GTHR., (Gray's Charr.)
S. colei, GTHR., (Lord Enniskillen's Charr.)
S. killinensis, GTHR., (Loch Killin Charr.)

Coregonus clupeoides, LAC., (Gwyniad of Bala.)
C. pollan, THOMPS., (Pollan, or Fresh-water Herring of Ireland.)
C. vandesius, RICH., (Vendace of Loch Maben, Dumfriesshire.)

Thymallus vulgaris, NILSS., (Grayling.)

#### MIGRATORY OR NON-MIGRATORY.

Osmerus eperlanus, LIN., (Smelt or Sparling.)

## SECOND GROUP—SALANGINA.

No British species; (rivers and seas of China and Japan.)

ON THE TWEED

<table>
<tr><td>Order IV.<br>PHYSOSTOMI</td><td style="text-align:right">Family<br>SALMONIDÆ.<br>Sub-generic group—SALMONES.</td></tr>
</table>

# SALMON.

## (Salmo salar.)

| | |
|---|---|
| *Salmo fluviatilis,* | PLINY, Nat. Hist. ix. 18. |
| *Salmo,* | AUSONIUS, Id. x. l. 97; WILLUGHBY, Hist. Pisc. p. 189. |
| *Salmo rostro ultra inferiorem maxillam* | |
| *sæpe prominente,* | ARTEDI, Spec. Pisc. p. 22 No. 1. |
| *Salmo salar,* | FLEM., Brit. An. p. 169; JENYNS' Man. p. 421; YARRELL, ii. p. 1; PARNELL, Fish. of Firth of Forth, p. 278 (Wern. Nat. Hist. Soc.); GÜNTHER'S Cat. vi. p. 11. |
| *Salmon,* | PENNANT, Brit. Zool. iii. p. 382 ed. 1812; COUCH, Fish. Brit. Isl. iv. p. 163; ALEX. RUSSEL, EDMONSTON AND DOUGLAS, 1864. |
| *Salmulus,* | RAY, Syn. Pisc. p. 63. |
| *Salmo salmulus,* | JENYNS' Man. p. 426; PARNELL, Wern. Nat. Hist. Soc. p. 298. |
| *Salmo gracilis,* | COUCH, Fish. Brit. Isl. iv. p. 216. |
| *Samlet* and *Parr,* | PENNANT, Brit. Fish. iii. p. 404 ed. 1812; YARRELL, ii. p. 83; COUCH, Fish. Brit. Isl. iv. 245 pl. 221. |
| *Trutta salar,* | SIEBOLD, Süsserwasserf. p. 292. |

*Characters of the Genus* SALMO.—"Body covered with small scales; cleft of the mouth wide, the maxillary extending to below or beyond the eye. Dentition well developed; conical teeth in the jaw bones, on the vomer and palatines, and on the tongue, none on the pterygoid bones. Anal short, with less than fourteen rays. Pyloric appendages numerous; ova large."—GÜNTHER.

GRILSE OR YOUNG SALMON

*Characters of the Sub-generic Group* SALMONES.—"Teeth not only on the head of the vomer, but also along its body; in a few species the posterior teeth are lost with age, and only a more or less conspicuous ridge remains along the median line of the bone, which becomes visible after removal of the membrane."—GÜNTHER.

THE Salmon, "the King of Fresh-water Fish," as old Izaak Walton rightly calls him, was unknown to the ancient Greeks; being chiefly a northern fish, and not found in the Mediterranean, it did not come within their knowledge. Pliny and Ausonius amongst Roman writers allude to the Salmon; the former merely states that "in Aquitania the River-Salmon is preferred to all sea fish." Ausonius gives a very good description of a Salmon, and doubtless had both seen its movements in the Moselle and had tasted its delicious flesh, as is evident from his lines—

> "Nec te puniceo rutilantem viscere, Salmo
> Transierim, latæ cujus vaga verbera caudæ
> Gurgite de medio summas referuntur in undas
> Occultus placido cum proditur æquore pulsus.
> Tu loricato squamosus pectore, frontem
> Lubricus, et dubiæ facturus fercula cœnæ,
> Tempora longarum fers incorrupta morarum,
> Præsignis maculis capitis, cui prodiga nutat
> Alvus, opimatoque fluens abdomine venter."        (97—105.)

"Nor will I pass over thee, O Salmon, blushing with thy red flesh, the roving strokes of whose broad tail are borne from the middle of the stream to the top of the water, at such time as the hidden lash betrays itself on the calm surface. Thou, clothed in scaly armour, slippery as to thy fore part, and able to constitute a remove for a most excellent dinner,* dost bear keeping fresh for a long time; thou art conspicuous with thy spotted head; thy full paunch trembles, and thy belly overflows with abdominal fat."

My own translation is literal. Pennant gives the following in blank verse, but with less faithfulness to the original:—

> "Nor I thy scarlet belly will omit,
> O Salmon, whose broad tail with whisking strokes
> Bears thee up from the bottom of the stream
> Quick to the surface: and the secret lash
> Below, betrays thee in the placid deep.
> Arm'd in thy flaky mail, thy glossy snout
> Slippery escapes the fisher's fingers; else
> Thou makest a feast for nicest-judging palates;
> And yet long uncorrupted thou remainest:
> With spotted head remarked, and wavy spread
> Of paunch immense o'erflowing wide with fat."
> *Anonymous* (*Brit. Zool.* iii. p. 383-4, ed. 1812.)

The Salmon is an inhabitant of the fresh waters of the northern and temperate parts of the world, occurring in Scandinavia, Iceland, Russia, Germany, Holland, France, Great Britain, and North America. It is said also to occur in Northern Asia. Its geographical range in temperate Europe reaches to about 43° north latitude; it extends southwards to the Bay of Biscay, and appears to inhabit Northern Asia and America to latitude 41° north. It does not occur in any of the rivers which flow into the Mediterranean. It is migratory in its habits, descending to the sea after it has deposited its spawn on the gravelly beds of the rivers. "The natural history of the Salmon," as Mr. Russel well says, "is not only interesting in itself—interesting for what is known and settled, for what is guessed and controverted, and for what remains as utter mystery and dire perplexity—but is also important as having a bearing upon, or rather forming an essential part of the commercial and legislative questions."

* The *dubia cœna* of the Romans implied so many good things that you did not know what to choose.

It has long been a disputed point as to whether the parr is the young of *Salmo salar* or a distinct species. There are, I believe, some people who still persistently maintain that the parr is not the young of the Salmon, but a distinct species, notwithstanding the evidence derived from the careful experiments of Mr. John Shaw, of Drumlanrig, in the years 1833-6, who proved beyond a shadow of doubt that the parr was a young Salmon. This gentleman, in a valuable memoir, before me as I write, succeeded in tracing the life history of the Salmon from the egg up to its smolt stage of two years' growth.

The diameter of the ovum of a Salmon is one fourth of an inch; according to Mr. F. Buckland every female Salmon carries as a rule, about nine hundred eggs to a pound of her weight; the spawning time is in November and December; "the female throws herself on her side, and while in that position, by the rapid action of her tail, she digs a receptacle in the ground for her ova, a portion of which she deposits, and again turning upon her side, she covers it up by a renewed action of the tail—thus alternately digging, depositing and covering ova, until the process is completed by the laying of the whole mass, an occupation which generally occupies three or four days."—(*Experimental Observations on the Development and Growth of Salmon Fry*, p. 565.) The only part the male fish performs, beyond the mere sexual function, consists in the unwearied vigilance which he exhibits in protecting the spawning-bed from the intrusion of rival males, all of which he assiduously endeavours to expel. The hatching period lasts from ninety to one hundred and thirty days, according as the temperature of the water facilitates or retards the development of the spawn. In a temperature of 40° the fish has been observed to be hatched the one hundred and eighth day after impregnation; when the temperature did not exceed 33°, the hatching did not take place till one hundred and thirty-one days after impregnation, though in this case the temperature of the river during the last forty days of that period had risen to an elevation of 60°. According to Mr. Shaw's experiments the growth of the Salmon is as follows, though no doubt this growth is not the same in all individuals, some growing faster than others. A young Salmon, with its attached umbilical sack of one day old, is about seven eighths of an inch in length; at two months old it has attained the size of about one inch and three quarters, and bears many transverse dark bars; the little fish is at this stage called a parr; at four months of age the young Salmon, or parr, is two inches and three eighths long; at six months about three inches; at twelve months four inches and a quarter; at eighteen months it is nearly five inches and a half, still bearing the parr marks; at two years it attains the size of six inches, the parr marks now disappearing, or being only faintly visible, and the fish assuming the characteristic aspect of the smolt, commonly so called. In this latter's stage the young fish is in colour and form very like the parent Salmon; it is in this stage also that it rises most readily to an artificial fly, and used to be caught by the angler in large quantities before the law interfered with its capture.

The sexual development of the male is subject to variety, for in some cases young smolts of seven or eight inches long have their milt fully developed, and attend the older fish on the spawning beds. Mr. Shaw succeeded in impregnating Salmon-ova with the milt of the male parr in several instances. With the young female smolt the case appears to be different, for the female smolt does not mature her ova. "No parr," says Günther, "has ever been found with mature ova." "Some advocates for the opinion of the specific distinctness of the parr," he adds, "pretend indeed to have found female parrs. Those fish which were pointed out to me as females were invariably specimens which had fed freely on the ova of their congeners, and their stomachs had been regarded as the ovary! Some persons were so anxious to convince me of the correctness of their opinion, that they sent me specimens with ova in the abdominal cavity. On closer examination these fishes turned out to be immature *male* specimens, the ova having been introduced by a cut into the abdomen, said to have been made to admit the spirit."—(*Catalogue*, vi. p. 9, note.) It may, of course, be asked, why may not the females occasionally mature their ova as the males do their milt?   Mr. Shaw says that solitary instances have occurred of large female parrs having been found in Salmon rivers with the roe considerably developed, "and I find," he adds, "by detaining the female smolts in fresh water until the end of the third winter, that individuals are found in this comparatively mature condition."

Without denying the possibility of the female smolt partially maturing the ova, it must be admitted that no case has been brought forward in which a female smolt has been shown to have ova fully developed and ripe for impregnation.   Even if such an instance should ever be proved, it does not follow that the parr is a distinct fish.   The large parr, nine or ten inches in length, occasionally found in rivers, are simply the young of the Salmon, which, not being ready for migration at the usual time, had remained for another year in the fresh water of the river, and feeding, as we know they do, voraciously in this stage, it is possible that a female smolt may occasionally partially develope the ova.

As to the length of time during which Salmon-fry remain in the rivers before they descend to the sea, it would appear from experiments made at Stormontfield, on the Tay, in 1853-4, that there is, in this respect, a great amount of variation even amongst individuals living under the same apparent conditions; it seems that a considerable number of young fish descend to the sea when they are about fifteen months old.*   A parr hatched in February, 1878, say, may be ready to take its journey seawards in May or June, 1879; it has also been shown that a large number remain in the river till they are a little over two years old; a parr hatched in February, 1868, may remain in the fresh water till May or June, 1870, and I suspect that this is usually the case.

The young Salmon after remaining for some time in the sea returns to the river; it is then called a grilse.   How long does it remain in the sea before it returns to the fresh-water?   In experiments made at Stormontfield, a great number of smolts were marked by cutting off the adipose fin, others by cutting the tail, and others by the fixing of silver rings.   Between twelve and thirteen hundred smolts were marked by cutting off the adipose fin and turned out of the pond the first year, of these twenty-two are stated to have been caught as grilse that same season; of those that left the pond the second year eleven hundred and thirty-five were marked by cutting the tail, and of these several are reported to have been caught as grilse in the course of their season.   "Of all the smolts marked by the attachment of rings or other effective means," says Mr. Russel, "whether in the Tay or other rivers, *none have been got,* as either grilse or Salmon, *the first year,* and *several have been got the second year.*   Of the Stormontfield smolts of the second year—descending in spring, 1856—three hundred were marked by silver rings, and of those none were got.   It is quite possible indeed that all of the three hundred that escaped their enemies in the sea, or even, we will suppose, the entire three hundred, 'no wanderer lost,' may have returned to the Tay as grilse that season, and yet none of them have chanced to be caught.   But from other quarters we have what seems positive evidence in favour of the second season.

In various years a great number of Tweed smolts were marked by a silver wire passed through and fastened to the back part of their tails; none of them were got as grilse or Salmon the season they were marked, but the next season several of them were caught as most indubitable grilses.   Still later experiments on the Tweed, apparently on a smaller scale, but conducted with great care, have brought out the same results.   The Duke of Roxburghe has preserved in his possession a fish which was marked as a smolt by the insertion of a peculiarly shaped wire on the 14th. of May, 1855, and which was caught on July 21st. of the *following* year as a grilse weighing six pounds and a half.   The more

---

* I do not believe, as some have maintained, but never proved, that a young fish ever grows so fast as to be able to descend to the sea in the same year as that in which it was hatched.

recent experiments of Mr. Ramsbottom, of Drohulla, have also gone to support the doctrine that the fish does not return until after thirteen to fifteen months in the sea; smolts turned out of the nursery ponds and marked in May, 1862, having been caught as grilse in June, July, and August, 1863, though there is in this case a possibility that the smolts may have been turned out before they were ready to emigrate, and may after their expulsion have spent in the river one of the two years which Mr. Ramsbottom assumes that they spent in the sea. To what conclusion, then, on this point do these experiments conduct us? To nothing absolutely certain; but as a probability, supported by evidence small in amount, but strong in quality, to this—that some at least of the smolts do not ascend as grilse, or as anything else, till *next* year, or fifteen months after their descent; and as another probability, supported by evidence greater in amount, but not so strong in quality, that some of them return the *first* year, or three months after descent. It may then be that both views are correct."—(*Natural Hist. of the Salmon*, p. 54-56.)

Growth in a grilse or young Salmon takes place very rapidly during its sojourn in the sea; this is no doubt owing largely to the abundance of food in the form of Sand-eels, young Herrings, Shrimps, etc., etc. I have taken as many as five large Herrings out of the stomach of a Salmon that had been caught in the sea; indeed I have invariably found sea fish to have their stomachs full of food, whereas I have never been able to detect a particle of food in a river fish. A smolt descending to the sea weighing only a few ounces may return to the river weighing six, eight, or even fourteen pounds after some time feeding in salt water. A remarkable instance of rapidity of growth is given on the authority of the Duke of Athol (*Quarterly Review*, April, 1863). The fish caught was first caught as a grilse forty miles from the sea on the 31st. of March; it then weighed ten pounds. It went down to the sea, and returned again in the short space of thirty-seven days, when it was again caught; it weighed twenty-one pounds and a quarter. This fact of a grilse returning so soon to the river a second time would seem to show that the same individual may change the salt for fresh water several times in the year, as thought probable by Dr. Günther. It is well known, that although the majority of the mature individuals ascend a river during floods at a fixed period, for the especial purpose of spawning, others, either singly or in troups, enter the fresh water early in the year, and indeed continue to come up every month in the year. The cause of these non-periodic ascents to the river is unknown. These early or clean-run fish of the spring months are always found to be in excellent condition; they are very fat, not only in the substance of their flesh, but in the large quantity of adipose matter which is found on the pyloric appendages; this serves as an internal source of sustenance which supports the fish in its sojourn in the fresh water where it scarcely ever feeds. These clean-run spring fish avail themselves of the spring floods and enter some of our rivers; but whether they remain in the fresh water from March to November,—the spawning season,—or whether, in some cases, they go down again to the sea before spawning, one cannot say. It seems a long while for the internal supply of fat to last a fish—from March to November—without food. "These fish," as Mr. F. Buckland says, "if there had been no floods in the spring, would probably have remained in the sea, and would have appeared in the river either in the first floods in July or August, or if there were no floods in these months, they would have come up in November and December as large fish, which, as experience shows, are generally the latest to come into the river, and which for the most part spawn in the lower portions of the river."—(*Famil. Hist. Brit. Fish.*, p. 369.)

The question of early and late rivers is a very important one; according to the present law it is illegal to take Salmon with a net after the end of August, the fishing beginning again in February. This law "applies to all rivers, little or big," as Mr. Buckland says, "those that run long courses and those that are of short length, those that have lakes at or near their origin, those whose tributaries are simply rivulets rising high up in the mountains, and those which have long reaches of spawning-grounds......There are rivers which Salmon never enter till the end of June and during July, August, and September; their numbers then increase during October and November; to the fishermen of these rivers the months of February, March, (and often April,) are of no commercial use whatever; nor do the anglers even profit, because the waters contain not clean-run 'up fish,' but only 'down fish' that have lately spawned, and are not fit either for food or sport. The fishermen on these rivers, therefore, are anxious to be allowed to prolong their netting season into September, and in some cases even further; and at the same time they are willing to give up fishing altogether in February and March, and in many cases even in April."—(P. 370.) The same authority is of opinion that *the presence of a lake at the head of a river* has a great influence in causing an early ascent of Salmon, as its "innate self-preserving faculty prompts the Salmon to leave the security of the sea and make a run for the lake at the head of the river, which it somehow knows exists—a most marvellous faculty, a faculty not possessed by man—and wherein its instinct teaches it that it will be safe till the spawning time arrives, when it can run up the tributaries of the lake." Mr. Buckland instances the Tay as being proverbially an early river, fresh-run fish being found in Loch Tay as early as January; on the other hand he adduces the river Conway as a good example of a late river; in this case there is no lake at the head of the river, but there is a broad expanse of water near Conway Bridge, or *a lake at the bottom of the river.* Here the fish remain for a long time, till such time, in fact, as the spawning instincts prompt the fish to ascend the river at all hazards. "I am certain sure," Mr. Buckland adds, "that this is right, and hope eventually to see the day when angling in Conway and many other late rivers of Wales, Devon, and Cornwall is made legal in November; only no gaff must be used—only a landing-net—and all the hen-fish returned carefully and uninjured to the water." Mr. Buckland's explanation of the cause, or rather of one of the causes, which create early and late rivers is most suggestive, and seems to me to be very probable. I may mention Loch Melvin as an instance of early water; the river Ban-drows has the Lake of Melvin at its head, and the Salmon run from the sea up the river into the lake chiefly in the early spring months.

The question as to the migratory *Salmonidæ* returning to the rivers in which they were bred appears to carry evidence of an affirmatory character; experiments have proved this to be the case as a general rule; though doubtless numerous individuals perish either from exhaustion after spawning, or from the attacks of various enemies, such as Porpoises, Dog-fish, etc. Deaths from the first mentioned cause—exhaustion after spawning and the journey back to the sea—appear to be of frequent occurrence. If the parents succeed in getting down to the sea in tolerable health, they soon recruit their strength by abundance of food; but a large number are found dead every year. Buckland having examined a large number of these dead fish could find no cause of death "except an anæmic condition, and a laxity of fibre in the muscular tissue. I conclude therefore," he says, "that the natural cause of death is (except in cases of violence or wounds from fighting) simply exhaustion; most of these fish found dead are males. It is very possible that the law of nature is that the large males shall die in certain numbers, and thus leave room for the smaller males to keep up the breed. The females are found dead much more rarely than the males; these facts may also have some bearing on the interpretation of the male smolt having its milt fully developed, and capable, as I myself have proved by experiment, of fecundating the ova of adult fish. The female smolt has the ova developed in a very minute degree at the time that the male smolt contains ripe milt."—(P. 322.)

The male Salmon in the breeding season has its snout much produced, and the lower jaw is bent upwards in the form of a hook, which fits into a hollow of the upper jaw; giving the fish an unsightly appearance. As no individuals, thus sexually characterised, are found in spring or summer-run fish, it has been supposed that this hook—sometimes an inch or more in length—has been absorbed, during the fish's sojourn in the sea. But it is more probable that these old males perish, according to the observations of several ichthyologists.

The non-feeding of the Salmon during its abode in fresh water I have already alluded to. That this is a fact I have verified myself in numerous instances; other observers have done the same. If it be asked how can muscular force be maintained for some months without food, the answer is an easy one. The Salmon lives on its own internal fat, stores of which are laid up throughout the whole body of the fish, especially in the abdominal regions, and around the pyloric cæca. Let any one compare the difference in the quality of the flesh between a sea-fed Salmon and one that has been some time in a river. In the first case the abdomen is tremulous with fatty matter, whilst the flesh of the river fish, though firm, is comparatively destitute of fat. And this continued abstinence from food is no doubt, to a considerable extent, the reason of the fish's gradual deterioration, till the exhausting process of spawning renders the Salmon now quite unfit for food. The Salmon's abode, therefore, in fresh water, should be regarded as a quasi-hybernation, during which life is maintained by stores already laid up in the organism. That muscular force may be maintained, and in fact that it is chiefly kept up by the combustion, not of the nitrogenous elements, but of the carbonaceous, has been rendered tolerably certain, and the circumstance that a Salmon may move about for a long time in fresh water without supplies of food beyond its own abundant fat, is not actually much more than a further instance of what takes place in hybernating animals, as the bear, which goes fat into winter quarters, and comes out very thin. The same may be said with regard to experiments that have been made, showing that the Swiss mountains may be ascended solely upon the strength afforded by butter and other non-nitrogenous food.

It may be objected again that the Salmon occasionally taking an artificial fly, must show that it does take natural food in the river. But a fish will sometimes seize a bait more for sport than from a desire to swallow it. What does an artificial Salmon-fly, with its glittering tinsel and gaudy colours, resemble in nature? Certainly no kind of winged insect, not even a brilliant dragon-fly, either in form or motion; no *libellula* or *agrion* ever swims in the water, least of all after the fashion in which the artificial fly is made to locomote by the angler. Sir Humphrey Davy thought "that the rising of Salmon and Sea-trout at these bright flies, as soon as they come from the sea into rivers, depends upon a sort of imperfect memory of their early smolt habits." Perhaps so, but be this as it may, the undoubted fact that the stomach and all intestinal tract are always found empty, it is a convincing proof that the Salmon, as a rule, abstains from food during its sojourn in fresh water.* I have never found anything in the stomach of a river Salmon except some whitish or yellowish mucus, and a lot of tape-worms, whose presence, according to my experience, is almost constant.

It has been shown by Siebold that sterility often occurs in the *Salmonidæ;* that some individuals are not sexually developed, and that such differ from the ordinary fish. According to Siebold this sterile state extends over the whole lifetime of the individual. It appears, however, that this sterility is merely a temporary immaturity, and that a part of the individuals arrive at a full sexual development at a later or much later period than others. Dr. Günther adds, that "many Salmonoids cease to propagate their species after a certain age, and that all so-called overgrown individuals (that is, specimens much exceeding the usual size of the species,) are barren, though they externally retain the normal specific characters."—(P. 8.)

Salmon, like the other migratory species generally, cannot be retained in fresh water for any length of time; they may live for two or three years, but do not thrive, and seem quite unable to accommodate themselves to a permanent abode in fresh water. It would seem,

---

* I am speaking specially of fish before spawning; as kelts they may feed. I have never examined the stomachs of kelts, but I suspect they are in too great a hurry to rush down to the sea—their natural larder—than stop to feed in the river.

however, that certain hybrids, as between the Sewen and Trout, continue to grow in fresh water.

The ova of the Salmon are capable of being impregnated by the milt of a Trout, or of some other Salmonoids, and I believe the young are hatched in due time; but from inquiries I have made, they do not thrive or live any length of time. The colouration in an adult Salmon is not subject to much variety—being different in this respect from the Sewen and Common Trout—excepting in the breeding season, when both male and female are marked with large black and red blotches; at this time the skin has become tough, and the scales are deeply imbedded therein. Mr. F. Buckland says that the skins of such fish after spawning are admirably adapted for tanning, and he advises his piscatorial friends to skin all the old kelts the water-bailiffs find dead; "when prepared these skins will make slippers, gloves, or binding for books."

Salmon grow to a large size; the following is a list of the largest Salmon in Mr. Buckland's Museum at South Kensington:—

|  | Weight * | Length |
|---|---|---|
| 1.—Tay Salmon | 70lbs. | 4ft. 8in. |
| 2.—Rhine Salmon | 69 | 4 8 |
| 3.—Shannon Salmon | 54 | |
| 4.—Tay Salmon, Kinfauns | 53 | 4 0 |
| 5.—Rhine Salmon | $51\frac{1}{2}$ | 4 3 |
| 6.—Tay Salmon | 51 | 4 3 |
| 7.—Wye Salmon | 50 | 4 2 |
| 8.—Shannon Salmon | 46 | 4 3 |
| 9.—Wye Salmon | $44\frac{1}{2}$ | 3 $10\frac{1}{2}$ |
| 10.—Tay Salmon, Kinfauns | 42 | 3 8 |

Mr. Buckland draws attention to the fact that a great number of our cathedral towns stand upon rivers in which Salmon either now exist or from which they have disappeared. "When monasteries were first established, previous to cathedrals themselves being built, the founders selected sheltered spots where, for the most part, they could get a plentiful supply of fresh-water fish, especially Salmon, for the use of the table on fast-days."—(P. 341.)

Formerly Salmon were more or less abundant in the Thames; between the years 1794 and 1821, according to a record published in *Land and Water* (iii. No. 58), seven thousand three hundred and forty-six pounds weight were taken. Even now, says Günther, "almost every year Salmon and Sea-trout in the grilse state make their appearance at the mouth of the Thames (where the migratory Salmonoids have become extinct for many years) ready to ascend and to restock this river as soon as its poisoned water shall be sufficiently purified to allow them a passage."—(P. 10.)

Every one who happens to be in London in the month of November must have viewed with wonder the magnificent Salmon of many pounds weight and of bright silvery hue, exposed for sale on the slabs of the fishmongers' shops. According to our Salmon laws it is illegal to take or expose for sale any Salmon between the 2nd. of November and the 1st of February. Of course, therefore, these must be foreign fish; they come from the Rhine, not a great way from Rotterdam. The following short account of the Rhine fisheries, given by Mr. Buckland, is interesting:—"Mr. D. Van Elst, who lives at Rotterdam, holds a lease from the government of the fisheries on the Maas, the only one of the three mouths of the Rhine through which Salmon migrate. The principal fishing station is at Orange Nassau, about fourteen miles from the sea; the river is here about nine hundred yards in width, and the nets used are about eight hundred yards long, thirty feet in depth, and the meshes two and

---

* Yarrell mentions a Salmon in the possession of Mr. Groves, (now Crump,) of Bond Street, London, that weighed eighty-three pounds,—this was in 1821; "flesh fine in colour, and of excellent quality."

SALMON TROUT

half inches from knot to knot, or nearly ten inches in circumference. This gigantic net is worked by a steamer of twelve horse power and a windlass driven by two horses on shore; the fish are not at once killed, but are kept alive in a well-boat, which is towed to Kralingen, three miles from Rotterdam, and there sold alive to the merchants. There are five private fishing stations above Rotterdam: three are worked by steamers and horses. The nets are only worked during the ebb tide." These Rhine fish are in splendid condition, often weighing forty, fifty, and sometimes sixty pounds. The sandy tracts which compose the coast of Holland abound with Smelts and Sand-eels; even, it is said, the fields are manured with them; on these favourite fish the Salmon feed, and on these they fatten, and thus grow into the "gigantic and plump" fish which in the month of November may be seen in the London fish shops.

The female Salmon is mature when about fifteen inches long; the male, however, as we have seen, may be mature when in the smolt stage, and about six or seven inches long. The præoperculum in the Salmon has a distinct lower limb, and the angle rounded; the maxillary, which in mature specimens is slender and rather feeble, is stout and broad in young ones; it extends to a little below the posterior margin of the orbit, but in the parr state only to the middle of the eye; the head of the vomer is toothless, the single series of small teeth on the body of the vomer is at an early age lost from behind towards the front, so that half-grown and old examples have only a few (from one to four) left. The caudal fin is deeply cleft in young specimens of twenty-eight inches in length, being truncate only in very large examples during or after spawning. (See plate of male Salmon.) The hind part of the body is elongate and covered with relatively large scales, *there being constantly eleven or sometimes twelve in a transverse series* obliquely forwards to the lateral line. (See Günther, p. 13.)

A good-sized female Salmon, caught in Bala Lake on September 28th., 1878, which I had the opportunity of examining, had on its spawning-dress. Above the lateral line there were numerous large black round spots, many of which were confluent, and a number of reddish blotches or thick wavy lines; below the lateral line the colour of the sides was yellowish pink; the gill-covers were yellow below, spotted and lined with brown and red blotches; the tail square, with pale oblong pinkish brown spots; the upper part of the head was bluish with an olive tint.

Out of a number of Salmon parr or smolts caught by me on the 16th. of April, 1878, with a fly—of course I had the permission from the Severn Board of Conservators—the largest specimen measured six inches and seven tenths from end of the snout to the point of bifurcation of the tail; the smallest caught was four inches and two fifths in length. The dorsal fin of the larger example was dark clouded in the upper portion, the margin of the first ray nearly black, on the lower portion there were four or five dark spots; the pectorals were streaked longitudinally with dark lines, very dusky; the ventrals and anal nearly white; the marginal extremity of the caudal fin was dusky; the lateral line slightly descending at first, then straight to the middle of the tail; adipose fin membranous, dusky, quite free from a red tinge. Above the lateral line the whole colour of the back steel blue with purplish tinge, below lateral line silvery white; above and below the lateral line were a number of small round red spots; but these spots are variable in different individuals. In the smaller specimens the parr marks were broad and distinct; in large ones they were less apparent. The specimens of all I examined were full of insect and larval food.

If the reader would form any idea of the beautiful colour of a male Salmon in the breeding state, he should consult plate vii. in Sir William Jardine's *Illustrations of Scotch Salmonidæ.*

A Salmon in its young state, from one to two years old, is commonly called a parr, pink, smolt or smelt, and samlet; it has, however, many more names, such as brandling or brondling, fingerling, black-tip, blue-fin, scad, shed, gravelling, last-brood, hepper, last-spring, spawn, skirling or scarling, fry; many of these however include the young of other migratory *Salmonidæ*. In some parts of Ireland, as at Lough Melvin, a Salmon parr is called a jenkins. The term grilse or Salmon-peal denotes a fish on its first return from the sea; the former word is probably a corruption of the Swedish *graelax*, "a grey lax," *i.e.* "a grey Salmon." *Kelt* applies to a Salmon, whether male or female, after spawning, but the male is also specially distinguished by the term *kipper;* the female is called *shedder* or *baggit*.

The fin-ray formula of the Salmon is

> Dorsal 14.
> Pectoral 14.
> Ventral 9.
> Anal 11.

The figure of the adult male fish is from a specimen which weighed twenty-four pounds and three quarters.

The Grilse, or young Salmon, is from a specimen weighing seven pounds.

The figure of the Parr is on the plate with the Smelt.

# SALMON TROUT.

*(Salmo trutta.)*

| | |
|---|---|
| *Trutta salmonata, The Scurf* or *Bull Trout*, | WILLUGHBY, Hist. Pisc. p. 193. |
| *White Salmon*, | PENNANT, Brit. Zool. iii. p. 396, ed. 1812. |
| *Salmo trutta*, | FLEMING, Brit. Anim. p. 180; JENYNS' Man. p. 423; |
| | YARRELL, ii. p. 77; PARNELL, Fish. Firth of Forth (Mem. |
| | Wern. Nat. Hist. vii. p. 293); GÜNTHER'S Cat. vi. p. 22. |
| *Trutta trutta*, | SIEBOLD, Süsserwasserf. p. 314. |

THE Salmon Trout, or, as it is also called, the Sea Trout, is, perhaps, next to the Salmon, the most valuable of all the migratory species. It is most abundant in the rivers of Scotland, but it occurs also in those of Ireland. In England and Wales it would seem that this species is represented by the closely allied, if really distinct species, of the Sewen, or *Salmo cambricus*. Dr. Günther states that all the British specimens of *Salmo trutta* which he has examined, with the exception of the Fordwich Trout, were from Scotland, and those obtained from the rivers of Wales and Southern England belonged to *Salmo cambricus*.

The Fordwich Trout is mentioned by Izaak Walton, who says, "There is also in Kent,

SALMON TROUT (VAR.)

near to Canterbury, a Trout called there a Fordidge Trout, a Trout that bears the name of the town where it is usually caught, that is accounted the rarest of fish; many of them near the bigness of a Salmon, but known by their different colour; and in their best season they cut very white; and none of these have been known to be caught with an angle, unless it were one that was caught by Sir George Hastings, an excellent angler, and now with GOD; and he hath told me, he thought THAT Trout bit not for hunger, but wantonness; and it is the rather to be believed, because both he, then, and many others before him, have been curious to search into their bellies, what the food was by which they lived, and have found out nothing by which they might satisfy their curiosity."—(*Complete Angler*, i. p. 145, ed. Hawkins.) Yarrell says that the ancient right to the fishery at Fordwich was enjoyed jointly by two religious establishments; and that it is now vested in six or seven individuals, who receive a consideration for their several interests. It was formerly the custom to visit the nets at Fordwich every morning to purchase the fish caught during the night. "I have seen," he adds, "specimens of the Salmon Trout from the Sandwich river exposed for sale in the fish-mongers' shops at Ramsgate." The specimen in the British Museum from Fordwich is very fine, being a female, nineteen inches long.

There seems to be no doubt that in some localities the term Bull Trout is applied to this species under consideration; Dr. Günther identifies the *Salmo eriox* of Yarrell and other writers with the Salmon Trout, and thinks that no distinct species is designated by the name of Bull Trout, which, is applied to different species at different localities and by different persons. I am inclined to think that the *Salmo eriox*, as described by Yarrell, is a distinct species; it will, however, be considered separately in the course of this work. The White Trout of the angler—the Peal, or Salmon-peal, as it is also called—is the grilse state of this species *(S. trutta)*, as well as that of the Sewen *(S. cambricus)*.

In Scotland the Salmon Trout is equally abundant with the Salmon, and large quantities find their way to the London fish dealers. When I was in Belfast in July, 1878, I saw numbers of these fish in the markets, but it appears to be less widely distributed in Ireland than in Scotland, though said by Thompson to be common round the coast. Sir William Jardine, in his *Illustrations of Salmonidæ*, says that in approaching the entrance of rivers, or in seeking out, as it were, some one they preferred, shoals of this fish may be seen coasting the bays and headlands, leaping and sporting in great numbers, from about one pound to three or four pounds in weight; and in one of the smaller bays the shoal could be traced several times circling it, and apparently feeding. "In these bays," he continues, "they are occasionally taken with a common hang-net, stretched across; and when angled for in the estuaries, with the ordinary flies which are used in the rivers of the south for grilse, rose and took so eagerly that thirty-four were the produce of one rod, engaged for about an hour and a half. They enter every river and rivulet in immense numbers, and when fishing for the Salmon are annoying from their quantity. The food of those taken with the rod in the estuaries appeared very indiscriminate; occasionally the remains of some small fish which were too much digested to be distinguished; sometimes flies, beetles, or other insects, which the wind or tide had carried out; but the most general food seemed to be the *Talitrus locusta,** or common sandhopper, with which some of their stomachs were completely crammed. It is scarcely possible to arrive with any certainty at the numbers of this fish. Two hundred are frequently taken at a single draught of the net, and three hundred have occasionally been counted." The rivers most noted for Salmon Trout in Scotland are the Tweed, Spey, Don, and the Tay.

To the fly-fisherman the Salmon Trout affords great sport. Mr. Francis says, "The white Trout is one of the gamest fish that swims. Like a champion of the light weights, he is all activity. When hooked, he is here, there, and everywhere, now up, now down, now in the water and now out: indeed an hour or two's White-Trout fishing, when the fish are

---

The *T. locusta* is a terrestrial amphipod, and never voluntarily seeks the water; if this was the species, they must have been carried out by the tide.

in the humour, is about as lively and pleasant a sport as the angler can desire; and as Salmon Trout often take the fly well, up to six and seven pounds weight, where they *are* found of that size, the sport is little inferior to the best grilse fishing. They also take a spinning-bait well while still in salt water, and on the west coast of Scotland it is common to fish for them thus. As to where they are to be sought, that experience alone will determine. They abound in many lakes to profusion, and take nobly in them. I have myself caught a hundredweight of them in a day in a lake in Ireland. They are found in most Salmon rivers, and in smaller streams which are too shallow for Salmon. The smallest mountain beck will often, when in state, give good sport. They also, as I have shown, take in salt water, and are quite as likely to be found in the mouth of the river as they are in the highest pool up amongst the mountains, for they are great and pertinacious travellers. You may catch them in Salmon pools, in dull eddies, and in sharp streams; so I can give no advice which would be of any value on that score. They are at times very false risers, and come very short at the fly when making apparently a capital rise. This is very trying to the temper." Mr. Francis concludes that the White Salmon Trout "is the most sporting and game fish which the angler meets with."—(*Book on Angling*, p. 331-332.)

As to the colour and quality of the flesh, it is generally of deep pink or red, and of excellent flavour; its price is usually the same as that of a Salmon. The flesh of the Bull Trout of the Coquet is said by some to be invariably very light, with scarcely a tinge of pink about it, and to be inferior in quality. I have, however, been informed by Mr. Christie that sometimes the Salmon Trout of the Beauly is also white, and not very good. According to Günther the *Salmo trutta* attains to a length of about three feet, and the female is mature when from ten to twelve inches long.

In a specimen I received in May, 1878, which weighed three pounds and a half, the total length was twenty-one inches, the breadth above the origin of the dorsal fin about five inches; length of head to body as one to four; præoperculum with a distinct lower limb; hind margin of gill-cover obtusely rounded; the suboperculum not projecting or scarcely projecting beyond the end of the operculum. In the Sewen the suboperculum does thus project, but not in all cases; the maxillary is thin and feeble, and extends to below the hind margin of the orbit. In the Sewen the maxillary is strong and solid. Colour of the body above lateral line dark bluish, lighter on the sides; belly silvery white; the black X-shaped spots on this fish are generally very distinct; for the most part they are above the lateral line; but occasionally there are a few below; the gill-cover is usually marked with a few round black spots; adipose fin dark, free from any red tinge; the scales are round and small, and easily detached; tail nearly square.

Sir William Jardine (*Illustrations, &c.*, pl. x, fig. 2,) has figured a brown or sand-coloured variety of the Salmon Trout, which the fishermen of the Solway call "Sandbacks;" our figure (Salmon Trout var.) was taken from a specimen caught at the mouth of the Tweed: it weighed eight pounds. In a specimen I opened I found no trace of any kind of food; the stomach, pyloric cæca, and intestine were full of *tæniæ* and some other active entozoon, a species of *Ascaris*; there was some orange-coloured mucus accompanying these contents.

The fin-ray formula is

> Dorsal 12—13.
> Pectoral 14.
> Ventral 9.
> Anal 10—11.

According to Dr. Günther there are fourteen or fifteen scales in a transverse series running from behind the adipose fin obliquely forwards to the lateral line.

The specimen figured is from the Tweed.

RIVER SCENE, ABERGLASLYN.

Order IV.
PHYSOSTOMI.

Family
SALMONIDÆ.
Sub-generic Group—SALMONES.

# SEWEN.

*(Salmo cambricus.)*

*Salmo cambricus,*      DONOVAN's British Fishes, iv. pl. 91; GÜNTHER's Cat. vi. p. 34.
*Sewen,*      COUCH's Fish. Brit. Isl. iv. pl. 213, p. 208 (Grilse state).
*Blue Poll (Salmo albus,* Flem.),      COUCH, iv. p. 219.

THE Sewen is a species closely allied to the Salmon Trout; it occurs chiefly in Wales, and hence it was named *cambricus* by Donovan, who has given a tolerable figure of this fish in its grilse state; it is also found in the rivers of the South of England, as in Devonshire and Cornwall, and is said to occur in Ireland. There are continental specimens in the British Museum from Denmark, Norway, and Jutland. In the South of England this fish is known to the angler as the Peal or Salmon-Peal, which terms in Scotland are also applied to the Salmon Trout. Like this last-named species, the Sewen is migratory in its habits, ascending rivers from the sea for the purpose of depositing its spawn. In colouration this fish is subject to considerable variety, more so, I think, than occurs in any other migratory Salmonoid. When taken fresh from the salt water, or from an estuary, or indeed from a river, if it has not long sojourned therein, the colour is a beautiful blue, and greenish on the head

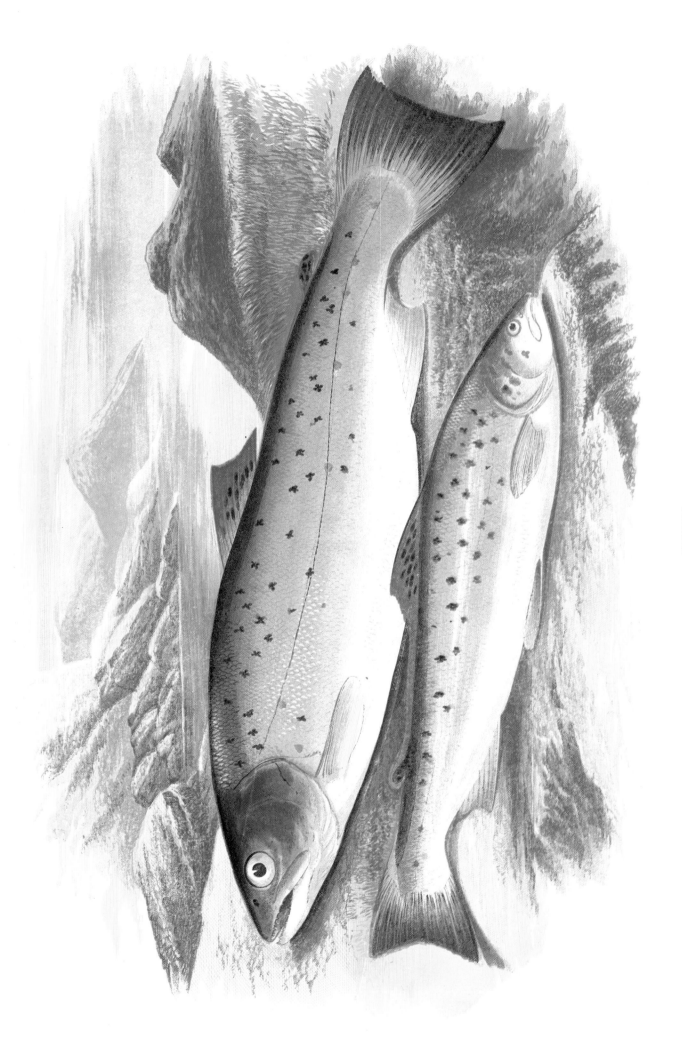

SEWEN

and shoulders; the X-shaped spots distinct and separate, sometimes occurring only sparingly. After the fish has been some time in the water of a river, the colouration is much more like that of the Common Brown Trout, for which indeed, in this respect, it might be mistaken if hastily examined. Commercially the Sewen is not nearly so important a fish as the Salmon Trout; not, however, because its flesh is a whit inferior in quality, but because it is less abundant than its Scotch relative, and does not find its way much into the markets of our large towns. In South Wales the Sewen is taken by nets in the bays and estuaries early in the year, as in March and April; they are generally from one to four pounds in weight at that time, and are delicious eating. These fish make their way up some of our rivers for a great distance; but, according to some observers, the Sewen is a less muscular fish than the Salmon, and has greater difficulty in ascending the weirs and obstructions. I have seen a large quantity of these fish caught by a net in the Dee, close to the residence of my friend Mr. Bigge, at Min-yr-Afon, near Ruabon, and have had an opportunity of noticing the difference in colour to which I have already alluded.

As a sporting fish the Sewen competes with the Salmon Trout. I am told by the Hon. Henry Butler, an excellent angler, that the best time to fish for Sewen is quite late in the evening, when it is dusk: a small fly and fine gut he recommends as the most successful apparatus. Dr. Günther says that the *Salmo cambricus* attains to a length of about three feet, and that the female is mature at a length of from twelve to thirteen inches, weighing occasionally as much as sixteen pounds; but such a size and weight is, I suspect, unusual. It seems that the term "Bull Trout" is sometimes applied to specimens of this fish, as it is to the Salmon Trout and perhaps to other species of *Salmonidæ*. This will be considered when I come to speak of the Bull Trout of the Coquet.

The following is a description of a specimen of Sewen I procured at Machynlleth in June, 1878:—Total length was sixteen inches and a half; its weight was two pounds; the greatest depth was four inches and a quarter; length of head three inches and a quarter; the maxillary strong, longer than snout, and reaching beyond the posterior orbit of the eye; mandible strong and broad; præoperculum with distinct lower limb, its posterior margin waved; gill-cover with a few round dark spots, sometimes iridescent with pink; suboperculum generally projecting beyond the operculum; dorsal fin smoky, with a few darker spots; adipose fin thick and fleshy, with two or three black spots; pectoral fin white, with dark narrow longitudinal lines; ventral white and immaculate; anal ditto; tail slightly emarginate, light smoke-colour, and dark at extremity; the head and upper parts of the back tinted with olive green; general colour of the body above lateral line bluish, with lighter shades of blue on the sides, spotted with numerous dark X-marks more or less distinct, the spots sometimes confluent; below lateral line there were a few indistinct spots; belly silvery white; scales small and rounded.

The number of rays in the fins is

> Dorsal 14.
> Pectoral 16.
> Ventral 9.
> Anal 11—12.

The specimen figured was caught in the Dovey near Machynlleth.

RIVER SCENE, LANGDALE.

Order IV.
*PHYSOSTOMI.*

*Family*
*SALMONIDÆ.*
*Sub-generic Group—*SALMONES.

# BULL TROUT.

*(Salmo eriox.)*

The Scurf, *Trutta salmonata,* and Bull *Trout, etiam dicta,*
*Salmo eriox, Grey Trout, Roundtail,*

WILLUGHBY, Hist. Pisc. p. 193.
YARRELL, Brit. Fish. ii. p. 71.

"NO distinct species," says Dr. Günther, "is designated by this name (Bull Trout); at all events the name is applied to different species at different localities, and by different persons. We have received numerous examples of *S. trutta* under this denomination; I have also seen stuffed examples of 'Bull Trout,' each of them of a peculiar aspect, but without any characters by which the species could be determined. It would appear that many examples somewhat differing in general aspect from *S. trutta* are named Bull Trout."— (*Catalogue,* vi. p. 23, note.) In his Addenda (p. 356) the same learned ichthyologist thus writes of a fine male sterile specimen of *Salmo salar* three feet long, caught in the Beauly at the beginning of April, and presented . by Lord Lovat as "Bull Trout:"—"Whilst this sheet was passing through the press, Lord Lovat's kindness afforded me an opportunity of seeing other specimens of 'Bull Trout,' at the moment when taken out of the water. It is his opinion that at least some of the fish are hybrids between the Salmon and Sea Trout (*S.*

*trutta*), an opinion confirmed by external appearance, and by the varying number of pyloric appendages, which in one specimen was found to be as low as fifty-four; yet the relative size of the scales on the tail is in all these Bull Trout the same as in the Salmon. Captain H. Fraser believes that other specimens of Bull Trout are true Salmon, which, having gone down to the sea as kelts, return to fresh water before having attained to the condition of well mended fish. Thus, as regards the river Beauly at least, fishes named 'Bull Trout' do not constitute a distinct species, but this name would appear to comprise—

1. Hybrids between Salmon and Sea Trout.
2. Specimens of Salmon returning from the sea before being well mended.
3. Sterile specimens—as, for instance, the specimen mentioned above.

The differences between 'Bull Trout' and Salmon are sometimes so slight as to be scarcely perceptible by an inexperienced eye. From what I have seen on the Beauly in the month of August, I should say that the numbers of Salmon, Bull Trout, and Sea Trout are as 30 : 3 : 1.

I may also add here that I have seen specimens of *Salmo brachypoma* in the same river, and that they are named there 'Phinok,' a name used for the grilse state of *S. trutta* on other rivers."

A gentleman, Mr. R. S. Congreve,—writing from Balmaghie, Castle Douglas, N.B.,—who has considerable experience as a Salmon-fisher, believes the Bull Trout of Scotland to be the Common White Trout *(Salmo trutta)*. He thinks "that at a certain unknown age they cease from breeding, and also that they cease from going down to the sea in the spring, and from coming up into the rivers in the autumn; that they then grow to a large size; in Loch Awe they are frequently caught of a great size, but never are of the silvery white colour characteristic of the Sea or Salmon Trout that ascend and descend the rivers annually; the scales are imbedded in the skin." He adds, "I myself have caught one of sixteen pounds weight, and have known them caught over twenty pounds."

Mr. Gillone, of Tongueland, Kirkcudbrightshire, considers the Bull Trout of the Dee to be simply a diseased Salmon. He says as a rule the flesh is not quite so good for eating as the Salmon; that in seven cases out of ten it will cut white and eat dry; but that exceptional cases occur in which the flesh cuts as red as that of a Salmon.

Thus it is certain that various species of *Salmonidæ* are sometimes designated as Bull Trout. Is there, however, no distinct species to which the name should be applied? There is one river in the north of England, the Coquet, where these so-called Bull Trout abound, to the exclusion of other migratory *Salmonidæ*. Through the kindness of Sir Walter Riddell, Bart., I have been fortunate enough to procure from Mr. Jacob Douglas, the keeper at Hepple, Rothbury, four fine specimens of these Bull Trout—three males and a spent female. (Nov. 18-29, 1878.) I have also a few young specimens in their parr state, obligingly given me by Mr. Frank Buckland.

Whether this Coquet fish is really a distinct species I will not take upon myself to determine, but it most decidedly deserves a separate plate and description. Certainly it does fairly well answer to Dr. Günther's description of *Salmo trutta;* but it is said that there is this remarkable peculiarity about the Coquet Bull Trout—it is almost white in the colour of its flesh, and very inferior as an article of diet. Mr. Dunbar, in a letter he has been good enough to write to me, says that the flesh is "very poor in flavour, and cuts nearly as white as a Cod; in fact they are not half so good as Cod." He adds that there are very few rivers in Scotland where there are not some of these Bull Trout; but of all the other rivers in the kingdom the Coquet may be said to be a pure Bull Trout river, for there are at least one hundred of these fish to every Salmon, and they run up to twenty-five pounds in weight. "I have taken," he says, "over a ton weight in a morning, and not one Salmon in the lot." Of

BULL TROUT

course this question is of great importance, for in the Coquet this inferior Salmonoid has nearly exterminated the Salmon. These fish are stronger than the Salmon, and, as Mr. Buckland says, "arising simultaneously with the Salmon at a weir, both species endeavour to ascend, and if there was no weir, both would equally ascend. The Bull Trout is the stronger animal of the two, and as there happens to be a weir, the chances are in favour of the Bull Trout as against the Salmon. A pair of Salmon and a pair of Bull Trout arrive at a weir at the same time; the Bull Trout by their superior strength get over the weir; the Salmon remain behind. If this operation be repeated time after time, the consequence will be that the Bull Trout arrive first at the best spawning places and deposit their ova, while the Salmon remain miles away down the river, and possibly do not get over the weir at all."—(P. 311.) Mr. Buckland's testimony as to the flesh of this fish coincides with that of Mr. Dunbar,—"the flesh is white and without the pure Salmon flavour, to which it is far inferior."

This fish is more frequently found upon the east coast of England than upon the west. "There are Bull Trout in the Tweed," writes Buckland in 1873, "the Coquet swarms with them, and the Tyne reports an increase." In order to restore the Salmon, the Home Secretary has given the Duke of Northumberland and the Board of Conservators permission to destroy the Bull Trout when they are running up the river in September, October, November, and December. The Bull Trout thus possesses the very unenviable distinction of being the only Salmonoid which is of inferior quality as food; as to its value as sport opinions differ. Some of the proprietors on the sides of the Coquet, I learn from Mr. Dunbar, of Brawl Castle, Halkirk, consider that the Bull Trout is a good sporting fish, and on this account they wish it to be protected by law. Lord Home, in a communication made to Mr. Yarrell (vol. ii. p. 73) some years ago, writes of this fish as follows:—"The Bull Trout has increased in numbers prodigiously within these last forty years, and to that increase I attribute, in a great measure, the decrease of Salmon Trout, which formerly abounded when I was a boy.* It is now a rare thing to see a Salmon Trout or Whitling, —for the Whitling in the Tweed is the Salmon Trout, not the young Bull Trout, which now go by the name of Trouts simply. The Bull Trout take the river at two seasons. The first shoal come up about the end of April and May. They are then small, weighing from two to four or five pounds. The second, and by far the more numerous shoal, come late in November. They then come up in thousands, and are not only in fine condition, but of much larger size, weighing from six to twenty pounds. The Bull Trout is an inferior fish, and is exactly what is called at Dalkeith and Edinburgh, Musselburgh Trout. Mr. Yarrell is mistaken when he says that these fish afford good sport to anglers; quite the contrary: a clean Bull Trout in good condition is scarcely ever known to take fly or bait of any description. It is the same in the Esk at Dalkeith. I believe I have killed as many, indeed I may venture to say I have killed more Salmon with the rod than any one man ever did, and yet put them all together I am sure I have not killed twenty clean Bull Trout. Of Bull Trout kelts thousands may be killed. The great shoal of these Bull Trout, not taking the river till after the commencement of close time, are in a great measure lost both to the proprietor and the public." Mr. F. Buckland was informed by Mr. Dunbar that the weight of Bull Trout caught between February and August, 1871, was seventeen thousand seven hundred and thirty-seven pounds, and only two Salmon were taken; from the 1st. of September to December, 1871, the weight of Bull Trout destroyed was forty-five thousand nine hundred and forty-two pounds, but only thirteen Salmon, and the same number of Salmon grilse.

Bull Trout are, in their grilse state, very destructive of Salmon eggs; but, doubtless, this is more or less true of the *Salmonidæ* generally, which are always ready to take ova with

---

* It appears from this statement that Lord Home regarded the Bull Trout as a distinct species from the Salmon Trout.

avidity. Sergeant Harbottle, officer of the Tyne Salmon Fishery, Tynemouth, states that as he was taking Salmon for the sake of procuring ova in December, 1871, he caught two Bull Trout, which disgorged Salmon eggs. "By a slight pressure of the hand," he adds, "I squeezed out of their stomachs nearly three wine-glassfulls of Salmon eggs, which would be about two or three thousand in number. These specimens weighed about one pound and a half apiece. It thus becomes a very important question practically to determine in what way the Salmon laws, with regard to this fish, may be altered; because what has happened in the Coquet, where Salmon have been nearly exterminated, and the Bull Trout have increased, may happen in other rivers, and thus a valuable source of food be diminished. It is also important to determine to what species this Bull Trout belongs. If, as Dr. Günther thinks, the Tweed Bull Trout, which I suppose is identical with the Coquet fish, is only the Salmon Trout, or *Salmo trutta;* then we have this rather curious anomaly, that the same species is both commercially of great value, and at the same time comparatively worthless. No doubt the quality of the flesh of some of the *Salmonidæ* varies considerably, even in specimens taken out of the same water; but there is a much greater difference when the fish inhabit different waters. Let us take the Trout, for instance; often in the same river one fish may be white in colour, and inferior in quality; another may be pink and well-flavoured. There is not a finer fish perhaps in the whole world than a good-sized Trout from Lough Neagh, with its red flesh and layers of white curd abundant; but a Trout from another water, where food is scant, is a very poor thing, and its flesh pale and insipid. But what causes should combine to render the Coquet and Tweed fish so very inferior in the quality of, and so different in the colour of its flesh from the ordinary *Salmo trutta*, it would indeed be difficult to say.

Mr. Buckland says, "It has been supposed by some that the Sea Trout and Bull Trout are identical. I know the Bull Trout very well indeed, and could pick him out among a thousand other kinds of *Salmonidæ.* I am certain, therefore, that there is a difference between the ordinary Sea Trout and the Bull Trout."

Mr. Dunbar, in a letter to me, says, "they are certainly a distinct species; they go by themselves, and breed by themselves." Dr. Günther writes, "Yarrell's collection of these fishes was chiefly composed of English and Welsh specimens, and he promiscuously named a part *S. trutta*, and another *S. eriox*, generally applying the former name to females (with a shorter head), and the latter to males (which have the head more elongate). However he was perfectly right in directing attention to the shape of the gill-cover, which is very characteristic for the two species, at least in most of the individuals. But he was not aware that numerous variations occur, and that there are specimens of *S. trutta* and *S. eriox (cambricus)* which have the gill-covers of precisely the same shape."—(P. 28.) Dr. Günther, therefore, is of opinion that the *S. eriox*, or Bull Trout of Yarrell, may be either the *Salmo trutta* or the *S. cambricus.*

I may mention, with regard to the gill-cover, that Yarrell is certainly in error as to its shape in this fish. In all the four specimens before me the line of junction of the operculum and suboperculum is not "nearly parallel with the axis of the body of the fish," as represented in the vignette at page 5, central figure, but oblique; I can see no difference between the gill-cover of the Bull Trout and that of the Salmon Trout, excepting that perhaps the posterior or vertical margin of the præoperculum is more distinctly waved. I think also that the maxillary, which reaches far beyond the posterior orbit of the eye, is longer than in the Salmon Trout. However, leaving the matter as to species, scientifically considered, undecided, I have thought it right to give a prominent place to this fish; for whether it be *S. trutta*, or, as I was at first inclined to think, a distinct species, the *S. eriox* of Yarrell, for all practical purposes it must be regarded, especially in the quality of its flesh, as different from any other of the *Salmonidæ.**

* This was written before I had received Mr. W. R. Pape's letter, which will be found further on.

The following is a description of a male Bull Trout received on the 18th. of November, 1878. For distinction's sake I shall call this fish "The Bull Trout or Pale-fleshed Salmon Trout of the Coquet."

Total length from snout to the end of the tail twenty-eight inches and a half; girth of body twelve inches and a half; length of head seven inches; præoperculum with distinct lower limb; vertical margin sinuous; posterior margin of operculum rounded; sub-operculum not extending beyond operculum; line of union between operculum and sub-operculum oblique; length of maxillary two inches and a half, greatest breadth half an inch; teeth on the maxillaries and mandibles strong; a few only, two or three, on the head of the vomer; body of vomer destitute of teeth; mandible hooked, fitting in a recess in the upper jaw; lateral line distinct, and for nearly all its length straight; dorsal fin greyish pink, with several round black spots; pectoral reddish brown, short, and very broad, margin dark; ventral short and broad; anal purplish grey; tail broad, margin somewhat rounded; adipose fin large and very fleshy, brownish pink with darker spots; the tip of the margin pink; head brownish pink; gill-cover with ten or eleven dark spots; whole colour of the body brownish pink, with a great number of round or obscurely shaped X marks. The whole appearance of this fish is that of a large Trout, being utterly destitute of the silvery colour of Salmon. This specimen had not parted with all its milt.

Description of a spent female from the Coquet, received November 29th., 1878:—Total length twenty-six inches and a half; girth eleven inches and three quarters; length of head five inches and three fourths; length of maxillary two inches and a quarter; breadth half an inch, reaching beyond orbit of the eye; snout rounded; distance between the end of snout and posterior orbit two inches and five eighths; sub-operculum rounded, and extending beyond the margin of the operculum; tail square; colour of the top of the head olive brown; gill-cover lighter; back dark, with bluish tinge and numerous dark spots, not very distinctly X-shaped; fins broad and short; colour below the lateral line silvery grey. The whole appearance of this female fish is more that of a Salmon than a Trout; there is great difference in colour between the male and the female; the head of the female, moreover, is less elongate than that of the male.

In a head of a male fish which measures thirty-two inches, just the size of that described by Yarrell—whose description, with the exception of the form of the gill-cover, already alluded to, is very accurate—the maxillary is narrow but of great length, extending considerably beyond the orbit of the eye; its length is two inches and four fifths; greatest breadth two fifths of an inch; the maxillary of the female is shorter and broader; the operculum and the maxillary in the male resemble those of the *Salmo trutta;* the same parts in the female are more like those of the Sewen, or *Salmo cambricus.**

Young specimens, obligingly sent to me by Mr. F. Buckland, which were hatched in February, 1878, attained the length of about three inches in November; but there is difference in this respect, some being less, others more than three inches; the parr marks number about eleven. These little fish are much spotted with brown, and are destitute of any red marks; the dorsal fin is strongly marked with dark brown oblong spots; the other fins are colourless, except the adipose, which is tinged with red.

The evidence with regard to this fish is in some respects most conflicting. Since the above has been in type I have received two more letters, one from Mr. W. R. Pape, of Newcastle, and the other from Mr. Dunbar. Both these gentlemen have had great opportunities of observing the Bull Trout. The former says, "The Coquet Salmon Trout is, I think, identical with all the Scotch Salmon Trout which I have seen. No fish varies so much in colour according to the sea weed and shades of the rocks where they feed; this is easily seen in

---

* There is difference in the comparative length and breadth of the maxillary; one male in my possession has this organ strong and broad, as in *S. cambricus.*

varieties the fishermen get from various parts of our coast. The Duke of Northumberland tried to kill out the Trout in the river, from the year 1868 to 1871, but the attempt gave general dissatisfaction to all classes, and destroyed the fishing on the sea coast so much, that the fishermen had almost to give up the Trout fishing; about seven or eight licences only were taken out; now, I think, there are thirty-five, since the preservation of the Salmon Trout during the last six years. The Duke of Northumberland, for that reason, is now of the general opinion, that we can get no better fish into the river, and that we must increase and preserve the Salmon Trout, and make the best of them as a food supply. The fishermen now kill twenty times the quantity they could a few years ago. When in season, the flesh of this Trout is pink; in June, July, and August, they get a very high deep pink."

Mr. Dunbar on the other hand writes, "The Coquet grilse of the Bull Trout is far from being anything like so good as the grilse, or, as it is called in the north, the *finnock of the Sea Trout;* the Bull Trout grilse is of a very pale pink, and very dry, with little or no flavour, while the grilse of the pure Sea Trout, *Salmo trutta*, is of a rich pink red and of excellent flavour, equal to, if not better, than the grilse of *Salmo salar*. The Bull Trout is decidedly the *Salmo eriox*, and is distinct from the *S. trutta*. I know several rivers in Norway, where they are plentiful; they seldom take a fly, though they will take the spinning bait well. It is the same in the Coquet, they seldom take a fly, excepting when they are returning to the sea as kelts."

The opinion of various observers with respect to this Bull Trout is now before the reader. The testimony as to the quality of its flesh, its character as a sporting fish, and its claim to be considered a distinct species, is conflicting. Structurally it is not easy to find any important difference between this fish and the *Salmo trutta;* and so high an authority as Dr. Günther would lead one to accept his verdict.

The fin-ray formula is

Dorsal 12.
Pectoral 14.
Ventral 9.
Anal 11.

The specimen figured was caught in the Coquet near Rothbury, Northumberland.

ON THE PARGLE.

*Order IV.*
*PHYSOSTOMI.*

*Family*
*SALMONIDÆ.*
*Sub-generic Group*—SALMONES.

# GALWAY SEA TROUT.

## *(Salmo gallivensis.)*

*Salmo gallivensis,*          GÜNTHER'S Cat. vi. p. 88.

I AM indebted to Mr. William Haynes, of Patrick Street, Cork, for some specimens of this interesting species of Salmon Trout from Galway. For the knowledge of this species zoological science is indebted to Dr. Günther, who first pointed out its characters. This fish grows to the length of eighteen inches or more; but the specimens so obligingly sent me by Mr. Haynes are about eleven inches in length; others are smolts or parrs with about nine or ten transverse dark markings. As an article of diet it is as good as the ordinary Salmon Trout, from which, indeed, it would not be distinguished by ordinary observers.

The most characteristic peculiarity of this Salmonoid is the small size of the pyloric appendages; in a specimen before me, eleven inches long, these stomachal cæca in their greatest length are not much more than half an inch, and about the diameter of a line; as Günther says, "not thicker than the quill of a pigeon." The largest specimen before me measures eleven inches and a half; the greatest breadth is not quite three inches; the head is small, more pointed than in *S. trutta;* the maxillary is feeble, extending slightly beyond the posterior orbit of the eye: in the smolt or parr stage this organ does not extend beyond a line level with the centre of the eye; the præoperculum has a distinct lower limb; the teeth are feeble; the pectorals are long, generally pointed, and streaked with black; the dorsal is spotted; tail more or less forked: in young parrs and smolts this organ is deeply incised; the scales are small and round, those near the tail are very perceptibly larger than the front body scales; general colour above lateral line dark blue with purplish tinge, thickly marked with many X or XX dark spots, and silvery below the lateral line; gill-covers with several round black spots.

The fin-ray formula is

> Dorsal 13.
> Pectoral 15.
> Ventral 9.
> Anal 11—12.

The specimen figured was procured for me by Mr. William Haynes, as already stated.

ON THE DEVON. SCOTLAND.

# SHORT-HEADED SALMON.

### (*Salmo brachypoma.*)

*Salmo brachypoma,* GÜNTHER'S Cat. vi. p. 87.

THIS is another well-marked species, for which we are again indebted to Günther. My efforts to procure specimens of this fish, I am sorry to say, failed; I have, however, been able to examine this species, through the kindness of Dr. Günther, in the British Museum. It is a migratory Salmonoid, like the rest which have at present come under our consideration: and is found in the rivers of the Tweed, Forth, and Ouse. "It is one of the best marked species of *Salmo;* its remarkably short head, and the extremely short præoperculum, (see woodcut on page 81,) renders it one of the easiest of determination; it is evidently nearly allied to the non-migratory species."—(P. 88, *Cat.*)

The fins in this Salmon are very short and rounded, the tail is truncate in specimens ten inches long, but never becomes convex; the maxillary is not so strong as in *S. fario* (Trout), and extends a little beyond the posterior orbit of the eye; the sides of the body have

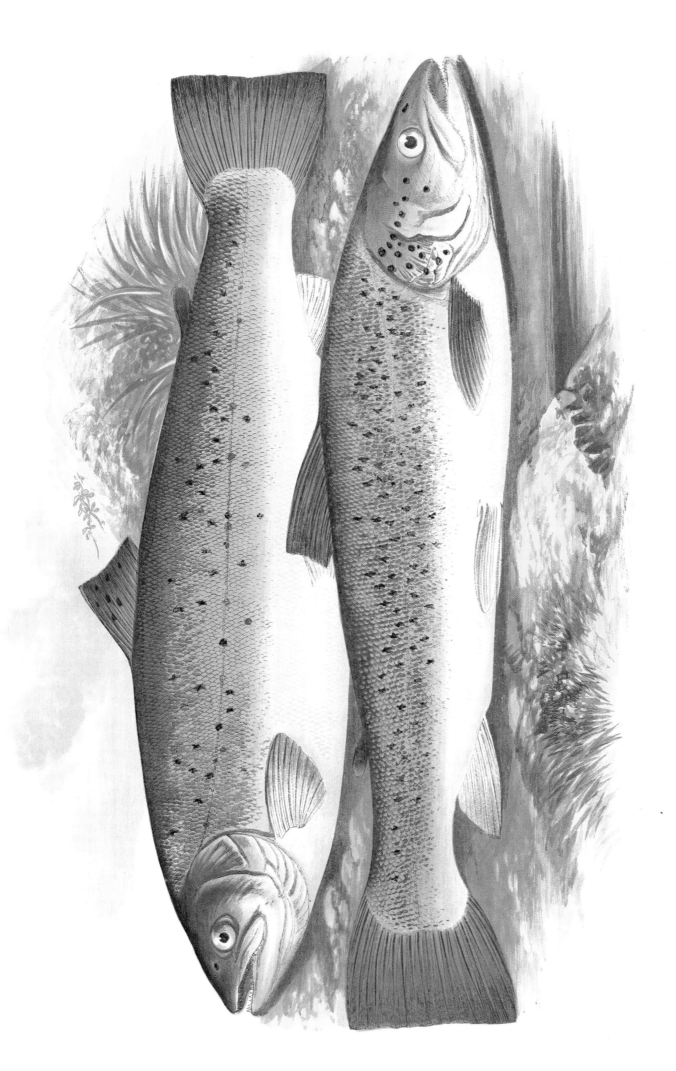

SILVERY SALMON

SHORT-HEADED SALMON

numerous X-shaped marks or ocellated black spots, with red ones along and below the lateral line; the dorsal fin has round black spots; the teeth are strong.

The term *brachypoma* from βραχυ, "short," and πωμα, "a lid or cover," has reference to the small size of the gill-cover.

This fish grows to a considerable size, the largest specimen in the British Museum is thirty inches long.

Whether this species is abundant or not I cannot say; nor do I know anything as to the quality of its flesh. I applied to the authorities at the museum in Edinburgh for information as to this species, but nothing apparently was known about it; and there was not a specimen in the collection. I hope to be more successful another year.

The number of rays in the fins is

Dorsal 13.
Pectoral 14.
Ventral 9.
Anal 10—11.

The figure is from a specimen twenty-seven inches and a half long, now in the British Museum.

---

*Order IV.*                                                      *Family*
*PHYSOSTOMI.*                                          *SALMONIDÆ.*
                                            *Sub-generic Group*—SALMONES.

# SILVERY SALMON.

### (*Salmo argenteus.*)

| | |
|---|---|
| *Fario argenteus, La Forelle argentée,* | CUV. AND VALENC., Histoire Naturelle des Poissons vol. xxi. p. 294-297, ed. 1828. |
| *Salmo argenteus,* | GÜNTHER'S Cat. vi. p. 86. |

THIS species is described by Cuvier and Valenciennes as having the form of a Salmon, and being in colour greenish, approaching olive grey on the back; the sides and the belly have a beautiful silvery brilliancy; the size of the specimens shown in the Paris markets is sometimes as much as two feet and a half, and it is not uncommon to see specimens two feet long. The Silvery Salmon is a migratory species of the Atlantic rivers of France, occasionally occurring on the coast of England. There is a specimen of a female twenty-six inches long now in the British Museum; it came from the river Rhymney, in Montgomery-shire, and had been kept for a short time in a fresh-water pond. It is a well-marked species, having a remarkably long head, being a fourth of the total length, without caudal; the præoperculum has a distinct lower limb, and its posterior margin waved; the maxillary is very broad and strong, and extends beyond the orbit of the eye; the fins are well developed; the pectorals are very broad and strong, and somewhat pointed at the extremity; the tail is truncate in specimens above twenty inches in length; the teeth are of moderate strength; there are conspicuous radiating striæ on the lower and posterior margin of the operculum, which has some round black spots more or less numerous; the sides are marked with dark X-shaped spots, and both the sides and the belly are brilliantly silvery.

The fin-ray formula is

> Dorsal 14.
> Pectoral 15.
> Ventral 10.
> Anal 11.

The drawing was made from a specimen in the British Museum.

ON THE TROUT STREAM, DRIFFIELD.

*Order IV.*
*PHYSOSTOMI.*

*Family*
*SALMONIDÆ.*
*Sub-generic group—*SALMONES.

# COMMON TROUT.

## *(Salmo fario.)*

| | |
|---|---|
| *Salar,* | AUSONIUS, Id. x. l. 88. |
| *Trutta fluviatilis,* | GESNER; RONDELETIUS; BELLON; WILLUGHBY, p. 199. |
| *Salmo, maxilla inferiore paulo longiore,* | |
| *maculis rubris,* | ARTEDI, Spec. Pisc. p. 23, No 3. |
| *Salmo fario,* | LIN., Sys. Nat. p. 509; DONOV., Brit. Fish. iv. pl. 85; FLEM., Brit. Anim. p. 181; JENYNS' Man. p. 424; YARRELL, ii. p. 85; GÜNTHER'S Cat. vi. p. 59. |
| *River Trout Salmon,* | PENNANT, Brit. Zool. iii. p. 408, ed. 1812. |
| *Common Trout,* | COUCH, Fish. Brit. Isl. iv. p. 225. |
| *Trutta fario,* | SIEBOLD'S Süsserwasserf. p. 319. |

"IT is a matter of surprise," says Pennant, "that this common fish has escaped the notice of all the ancients, excepting Ausonius; it is also singular that so delicate a species should be neglected at a time when the folly of the table was as its height, and that the epicures should overlook a fish which is found in such quantities in the lakes of their neighbourhood, when they ransacked the universe for dainties. The milts of *Murænæ* were brought

COMMON TROUT

from one place; the livers of *Scari* from another, and oysters, even from so remote a spot as our Sandwich; but there was, and is, a fashion in the article of good living. The Romans seem to have despised the Trout, the Piper, and the Doree; and we believe Mr. Quin himself, would have resigned the rich paps of a pregnant sow, the heels of camels, and the tongues of flamingoes, though dressed by Heliogabalus' cooks, for a good jowl of Salmon with lobster sauce."—(P. 399-400, ed. 1812.)

Ausonius is very brief in his notice of the Trout; he merely mentions its beauty, and makes no allusion to the quality of its flesh as an article of food—

> "Purpureisque Salar stellatus tergore guttis."
> "With purple spots the Salar's back is starred."

Ausonius makes use of the term *Fario*, but it is not easy to determine what species he intended—

> "Teque inter species geminas, neutrumque et utrumque
> Qui nec dum Salmo, nec jam Salar, ambiguusque
> Amborum, medio Fario intercepte sub ævo."     (128—130.)

> "Salmon or salar, I'll pronounce thee neither
> A doubtful kind, that may be none, or either,
> Fario, when stopt in middle growth."

Under the name of *Fario*, Ausonius may be referring to the grilse state of the *Salmo trutta*, but it is not possible to speak with any degree of certainty.

If the Salmon be rightly called the King of Fresh-water Fish, the Common Trout may, I think, fairly claim the second place of dignity; for whether we regard the Trout in respect of form and beauty of colouring, or in that of affording most excellent sport, or as a most nourishing and delicious fish for the breakfast or dinner table; in all respects the Trout is eminently good.

The earliest notice of the art of fly-fishing occurs in the writings of Ælian, who lived about the middle of the third century of the Christian era. In his chapter *De peculiari quodam piscatu in Macedonia*, he gives the following account, which I will translate from the Greek version of Jacobs' edition of the *Natura Animalium*. I think the fish he mentions are Trout.

"There is a river called Astræus, flowing midway between Berea and Thessalonica, in which are produced certain spotted fish (ιχθυες την χροαν καταστικτοι)—the Macedonians must give their name—whose food consists of insects which fly about the river. These insects are dissimilar to all other kinds found elsewhere; they are not like wasps, nor would one naturally compare them with the flies called *ephemera*, nor do they resemble bees, but they possess characters common to all these creatures; for they are as impudent as flies, as large as the *anthedon*, of the same colour as wasps, and they buzz like bees. The natives call this insect the *hippurus*. As these flies float on the top of the water in pursuit of their food, they attract the notice of the fish, which swim upon them. When a fish spies one of these insects on the top of the water, it swims quietly underneath it, taking care not to agitate the surface, lest it should scare away the prey; so approaching it, as it were under its shadow, it opens its mouth and gulps it down, just as a wolf seizes a sheep from the flock, or an eagle a goose from the yard; and having done this it swims away beneath the ripple. The fishermen are aware of all this; but they do not use these flies for bait, because handling would destroy their natural colour, injure the wings, and spoil them as a lure. On this account the natural insect is in ill repute with the fishermen, who cannot make use of it. They manage to circumvent the fish, however, by the following clever piscatorial device: they cover a hook with red wool, and upon this they fasten two feathers of a waxy appearance, which grow under a cock's wattles, (δυο πτερα αλεκτρυονος υπο τοις καλλεοις πεφυκοτα); they have a reed six feet long, and a fishing line about the same length; they drop this lure upon the water, and the fish being attracted by the colour, becomes extremely excited, (οιστρουμενος) proceeds to meet it, anticipating from its beautiful appearance a most delicious repast; but, as with extended mouth it seizes the lure, it is held fast by the hook, and being captured meets with a very sorry entertainment."

"The practice of fishing with a fly," says Couch, "has been thought almost peculiarly English, and of ancient date in this country, and Duhamel in France copies all that he has got to say of it from Walton and Cotton; but in both these particulars there is reason for doubt. The *Book of St. Albans* gives some directions for what it terms 'dubbing,' a practice referred to by Izaak Walton, and which in some distant degree bears a likeness to the modern method of fly-fishing. But neither does this dubbing with a fly obtain a principal place in this old treatise, the very title of which appears to limit it to 'fysshynge with an angle' or earthworm; nor was the patriarch of the art, Izaak Walton, much better versed in it; for it is to his friend Charles Cotton we are chiefly indebted for what afterwards grew to be a new phase in the art."

"The Common Trout," as Yarrell says, "is too widely diffused and too generally known to make any enumeration of particular localities necessary." This is no doubt generally true, nevertheless Trout are subject to great variety, especially in colouration, and some localities are infinitely superior to others as Trout-feeding waters. The Thames Trout are rightly justly celebrated; those of Lough Neagh are not to be surpassed by any fish in the world; the flesh is firm and brick-red, the layers of curd abundant, and I do not think any one can have a good idea of what a Trout is, unless he has handled and eaten the speckled beauties from Lough Neagh. Of the Thames Trout Mr. Manley shall speak:—"I hold," he says, "that a well-conditioned fish of this class is one of the most beautiful objects in animated nature. His symmetry and his colour are unexceptional. He is more beautiful both in form and colour than the most beautiful Salmon that ever ran up fresh from the sea, and when contemplated by his captor immediately on being 'banked,' is a richer feast for the eyes than the prettiest *Salmo salar* that Hampshire Avon, Severn, Tay, Tyne, Thurso, or Shannon ever produced. *Salmo fario* of the Thames v. *Salmo salar* all the world over; the latter charmingly symmetrical and silvery as you will, and beyond compare more beautiful than all silvery fishes; but the former resplendent with all the hues of the rainbow, and others to boot; yet not a mere gaudy creature, like the brilliant fish of the Mediterranean, but with a harmony of bright colours which subdue but do not extinguish one another, and such as no artist could have conceived and few can imitate."—(*Notes on Fish and Fishing*, p. 131.)

What Mr. Manley thus enthusiastically but rightly says of the Thames Trout, is every whit true of the Lough Neagh fish of Ireland.

The Trout, though a bold and voracious fish, is at the same time excessively shy, cautious, and cunning; hence great skill and patience are required to insure success on the part of the angler.

The River Trout is, as I have already said, subject to much variation as to colour as well as to small structural differences. Two forms deserve particular attention. One form, with fifty-seven or fifty-eight vertebræ, is found in Central Europe and the southern parts of England; the other, which has fifty-nine or sixty vertebræ, occurs in the northern parts of Europe, some parts of Scandinavia, Scotland, and Ireland. Now these two forms, the one more decidedly northern, the other southern, are thus distinguished by Dr. Günther as *Salmo fario gaimardi*,* and *Salmo fario ausonii*.† In Cumberland, however, as Dr. Günther tells us, at least

* From the name of a writer, P. Gaimard, author of a work entitled *Voyages de la Commission scientifique du Nord pendant les Années* 1835-6, 1838-40.

† From the Latin writer Ausonius, who would be acquainted with the southern form.

in some of the rivers, as the Caldew and Eden, the southern form occurs, whilst the northern one is found in the river Liddel. "However, the latter extends as far southwards as Shropshire, where both forms are met with. Both are subject to the same amount of variation; but the northern form appears to remain within smaller dimensions. The coincidence of the difference in the number of vertebræ with the geographical distribution appears to be remarkable enough to distinguish the two forms; but whether they be regarded as species or varieties is a matter of minor importance."—(P. 59.)

The *S. fario gaimardi* is thus described by Günther:—"Sides with numerous round or X-shaped markings; the upper surface and sides of the head, the dorsal, adipose and caudal fins generally with crowded round black spots; dorsal, anal, and ventral with a black and white outer edge." This form is the one generally met with in Iceland, Scandinavia, North Britain, Ireland, and Scotland. The Trout of the Clyde is said to form a very well-marked variety, being distinguished by a short body, very short snout, broad maxillary, strong vomerine teeth, small anal fin, and numerous fine X-shaped markings on the body; the spots on the dorsal fin are small, ovate, and numerous.

*S. fario ausonii* has the "body, head, and dorsal fin with numerous red and black spots; a part of the latter have generally a light edge; the black spots are either round or more irregular in shape, composed of X-shaped marks. The anterior margin of the dorsal and anal, and the outer one of the ventrals generally yellowish. This form inhabits the numerous fresh waters of Central Europe, Sweden, and England, and the rivers of the Maritime Alps."

In Shropshire we certainly meet with both these forms, as well as forms intermediate between them; the margins of the fins being sometimes white and sometimes yellowish.

Trout are inhabitants of fresh water, brackish water, and salt water; as Dr. Günther says, "the water has a marked influence on the colours. Trout with intense ocellated spots are generally found in clear rapid rivers and in small open alpine streams; in the large lakes with pebbly bottom the fish are bright silvery, and the ocellated spots are mixed with or replaced by X-shaped black spots. The brackish or salt water has the effect of giving them a bright silvery coat, without or with comparatively few spots, none of which are ocellated. Now some of the species, like *S. fario*, inhabit all the different waters indicated, even brackish water, and therefore we find an immense variation of colour in one and the same species."

There seems to be no doubt that the Common Brown Trout, though normally a non-migratory species, is frequently migratory in its habits, and descends to the sea, where the ordinary brown spots and trout colouration are exchanged for X-spots and a silvery hue. This leads me to notice a Trout, which I think is merely a variety of the *S. fario*, the Slob Trout, or Tidal Trout, occurring in some localities. I have not had an opportunity of examining these Slob Trout, and have only seen specimens of heads. Mr. Haynes, of Patrick Street, Cork, who knows them well, has sent me a short account of them, which I shall here transcribe.

"With regard to the habits of the 'Tidal' or 'Slob' Trout, of which numbers are to be had on the estuary of the Lee and Bandon rivers, I have for very many years been in habit of killing lots of them, and during that time I have never seen, or heard of one being taken above where the tide ebbs and flows. The best, and indeed almost the only time they are to be killed, is from the month of January to that of May; they will not rise readily to the fly, and are very seldom killed except at night; and then they are taken in good numbers. The best baits known for these fish is the Eel-fry or *Elvers*, as they are more generally called, also live shrimps, and best of all slob-worms commonly called 'rag-worm;' the best places to fish for the Slob Trout are off the bridges in the city of Cork, just under the gaslights, where they can be seen rising at the elvers, which always run on the surface of the water in great numbers, all night long, during the months of January, February, March, and April. When you catch one of these Trout, you could squeeze a handful of these young Eels out of him, the stomach being distended with them to an unnatural size. The Slob Trout is in its primest condition in January and February, and is then more the shape of a Roach than an ordinary Trout, having a singularly small head, and suddenly swelling out at its base; in fact, a two-pound Slob Trout, in good condition, seems just as if the head of a half-pound fish had been fixed to it, so unnaturally small does it look. My impression is, that this Trout is a species in itself, and not a cross breed between the White and the Brown Trout; if it were a cross breed, I feel certain it would partake of the migratory habits of both these fish. The colour of the Slob Trout is quite different from that of the Brown Trout; it is a sort of opaque or dirty cream-colour, and a very handsome fish to look at, being spotted with large black and red spots, very much larger than those of the Brown Trout. Where they migrate to in the summer I do not know, for neither are they taken in the nets nor with rod and line. The flesh of the fish may be either a delicate pink or pure white colour, but in either case it is equally well-flavoured, and far superior to either Brown or Sea Trout, or even to the primest Salmon. They give wonderfully hard play when hooked, and consequently very frequently get away from the angler, for it is absolutely necessary to use nothing but the finest tackle even when you are fishing on a pitchy dark night. Their weight varies from half a pound up to four pounds."

I am much obliged to Mr. Haynes for this extremely interesting account, and hope that I may be yet able to get hold of a few specimens, through the kindness of Mr. Haynes, who will, I know, do his best for me, and I trust I may be able to insert a short notice before this work is entirely printed off. I am inclined to think this Slob Trout is a variety, but a well marked one, of *S. fario;* for it is well known that the common river Trout is an inhabitant of brackish water, and also of sea water. Couch has rightly said that the Trouts of our own streams have been noticed many times in the month of May to be quitting the river for the deep Atlantic. "To satisfy myself of this," Mr. Couch adds, "I have procured an opportunity of having them taken in the salt water with a net; and a well-grown Trout has been brought to me that was caught at a considerable distance from a river or fresh water. Under such circumstances a material alteration takes place in the colour of the fish, which becomes of a rich dark brown, with an aggravation of the other characteristic tints. It is believed that these migratory examples in no long time return to their native river; at which season again their appearance is so changed that they have been judged a distinct species; and we believe that they are the same which Dr. Knox has denominated the Estuary Trout."—(*Fish. Brit. Isl.* iv. p. 230-231.)

Where difference in the colouration alone of the Common Trout is concerned, one would have considerable hesitation in accepting such differences as indicating specific distinction. Sir William Jardine has figured some of these varieties in his large work, *Illustrations of Scotch Salmonidæ*, where the reader may see differences in colouration; he draws attention to the fact that a variety of distinct colouring or spotting is confined sometimes to only a single loch of moderate size, while in others it ranges through a series of lochs adjoining each other. "In waters of greater extent again, the varieties in different parts of the same loch are very remarkable. Sometimes, almost every bay has its kind of Trout, and the opposite sides of an island, a few acres in extent, oftentimes afford Trout very different in markings and in quality." It is clear, however, that in some cases, Sir William Jardine has regarded the *S. nigripinnis* as a mere variety; a Trout which has, besides a very marked difference in colouration, certain structural peculiarities, which have been justly regarded by Dr. Günther as pointing to a distinction in the species. The figure No. 1, from Loch Awe, for instance, plate ii., is, I think, *S. nigripinnis*, and Sir William's description agrees well with that species.

The culture of Trout, by the artificial impregnation of the ova, and by the preservation of the young fish in small reservoirs of pure water, is now quite an institution in this country, and is most successfully carried on by many private individuals, as well as professional dealers.

Who was the first to institute the artificial breeding of Trout and other *Salmonidæ*, I know not; but it was successfully pursued by a German gentleman of the name of Jacobi some-time about the year 1763, as may be seen on reference to a translation of that gentleman's paper, which has been given in full by Yarrell, (vol. ii., p. 87—96.) His plan was a very simple one, and in its main features it is in use at the present time. Jacobi had some long wooden boxes constructed with fine gratings at the top and ends; these were partially filled with gravel, and having procured the ripe ova from a female Trout, and impregnated them by mixing them up with the milt of the male, he placed them in the gravel; the box was then put in pure running water, and nature performed the task of incubation. For many years nothing more was heard of Jacobi's piscicultural art, and it was not till the years 1848 and 1851 that the art was revived. In 1848 Gottlieb Boccius wrote "A Treatise on the Production and Management of Fish in Fresh-water by Artificial Spawning, Breeding and Rearing; shewing also the Cause of the Depletion of all Rivers and Streams," (Van Voorst). A short time after this date there appeared a paper in the *Journal des Travaux de l' Académie nationale*, (Paris, 1851), entitled *Fécondation artificielle des Poissons*, by two French fishermen, M.M. Géhin and Remy. The matter was shortly afterwards taken up by M. Coste, Member of the Institute, and Professor in the College of France, whose valuable work, *Voyage d' Exploration sur le Littoral de la France et de l' Italie*, (Paris, 1861), is in my own library and before me as I write. This work was published by order of the Emperor, and treats of pisciculture, oyster culture, and other kindred subjects. The result of the whole was that the government granted the sum of several thousand francs, and the establishment at Huningue arose. I need do no more than merely mention a few of the names of persons who have published treatises on the artificial rearing of fish, both on the Continent, in America, and in this country, such as Filippi, Fry, Haxo, Millet, Quatrefages, Sivard de Beaulieu, Marquis de Vibrage, Karl Vogt, W. Wright, Francis Francis, and though last, certainly not least, the indefatigable inspector of our English and Welsh Salmon Fisheries, Mr. Frank Buckland. As a practical breeder of Trout, I know no one more successful than my father-in-law, Mr. Masefield, of Ellerton Hall, Shropshire, who annually rears several thousands of fry, and, with his charac-teristic generosity, distributes to those requiring them.

The development of the ova is greatly influenced by the temperature; Mr. Bartlett, of the Zoological Gardens, hatched Salmon ova in the short space of thirty days after impreg-nation, the eggs usually taking from one hundred and fifteen to one hundred and forty days, according to the temperature of the water. The proper temperature of the water should range from 40° to 45°; Trout eggs at such a temperature would take about sixty days to develope into young fry ready to burst the membranes. Mr. Buckland says, "Lay it down for an axiom that the higher the temperature for the egg, the weaker the fish produced from that egg; everything above 50° is weakening."—(*Fish Hatching*, p. 102, London, 1863.)

Trout spawn, as a rule, in November and December, but the spawning time varies, both according to season and locality. Trout eggs have been taken from the fish as late as February; and the lateness in spawning must be taken into account in estimating the age of young fish at a certain time of the year. It appears that Trout do not always mature their ova; that they may miss a year or so. Sterile examples are known to occur, and have frequently been taken. In such cases the Trout are in season in January and February, being excellent food.

It is not easy to ascertain the age to which a Trout may attain. Daniel, in the sup-plement to his *Rural Sports*, mentions a case in which a Trout lived in a well at Dumbarton Castle for twenty-eight years, having been a pound in weight when placed there, and never having increased in size the whole time. As a rule, Trout in such confined places do not grow; but the following narrative, also given by Daniel, shows that a moderate degree of confinement will not limit the growth of a Trout. A certain gentleman had made a stew, in which he fed many Trout, one of which, weighing three pounds and a half, had been caught in a river not far distinct; its size and strength soon enabled it to become the master of all the other fish that were in the stew before him. "In about a year this fish, which had received the name of Fuller, and was an object of particular attention, had grown to about nine pounds, five of which had been added to his weight between March and October, at which date its length was twenty-seven inches. Its appetite was great, as was its activity; and the body was beautifully spotted. The food, which was not always abundantly bestowed, was worms, minnows, or the entrails of a calf, finely chopped; but unless much pressed by hunger, it neglected them by day. It is an hour before dark that it begins to move about, and then Fuller begins to exercise his tyranny over the rest. He chooses to feed alone on the food thrown to him, and not at all in haste; but when he looks round all the smaller Trout dart off into their hiding places, at which time he sails round to see that they have all withdrawn, and he repeats the circuit at every little interval of his feeding. About one hundred and twenty-five minnows formed the complement of a meal, and in devouring these, woe be to any one of the smaller tribe that ventured to intrude, except, indeed, a single favourite, which he appeared to have selected for a companion. It was only when the feast was ended that others were permitted to scramble for what was left. The greatest amount of activity was when the wind was brisk. Fuller's fate was at last unfortunate, in being stolen from the stew."

The Common Trout sometimes attains a large size. Thames fish have been caught which weighed fifteen to sixteen pounds, and more. Weybridge, Sunbury, Marlow Weir, and Richmond are mentioned as some of the best localities for Thames Trout. I have alluded before to the Lough Neagh fish; having been caught in the deep waters of the lake in nets, they are brought during the season in great quantities, in boats, to Toome Bridge, County Antrim, and thence are despatched, packed with ice in large boxes, by the railways and steamboats to London, Liverpool, Manchester, and many other large towns. Trout of twelve, eighteen, and twenty pounds are not unfrequently taken.

What produces the beautiful pink or red flesh of a Trout in good condition is at present a matter of conjecture. "Chemistry," as Dr. Günther says, "has not supplied us yet with an analysis of the substance which gives the pink colour to the flesh of many Salmonoids; but there is little doubt that it is identical with, and produced by, the red pigments of many salt- and fresh-water crustacea, which form a favourite food for these fishes."—(P. 3.) I confess I do not myself feel at all certain on this point.

Monstrosities in Trout sometimes occur. We meet with young fish with two heads, with humped backs, with their bodies twisted round their umbilical vesicle; Siamese-twin fish, with one tail, and one umbilical bag between them, etc. Generally these "monstrosities" live but a short time. The deformed Trout, however, whose figure-head is given by Yarrell, sometimes grow to half a pound in weight. The head is short and round, and the upper jaw is apparently absent; the lower jaw projects considerably beyond the truncated upper, causing the fish to have a very unsightly appearance. Mr. Yarrell's specimen was from Loch Dow; I learn from Mr. Haynes, of Cork, that similar deformed Trouts have been killed by him in County Cork and County Clare; he has sent me an ink sketch, which exactly resembles Yarrell's woodcut, only the upper jaw is still more elongated; Mr. Haynes has seen three specimens of these fish.

The two forms of *Salmo fario* have already been mentioned.

The fin-ray formula is, according to Günther,—

*S. fario gaimardi.*—Dorsal 13—14.
Pectoral 14.
Ventral 9.
Anal 11—12.

The pyloric cæca are 33—46. Vertebræ 59—60.

*S. fario ausonii.*—Dorsal 13 (—14.)
Pectoral 13.
Ventral 9.
Anal 10—11.

The pyloric cæca are 38—47 (—51.)  Vertebræ 57, counting the last rudimentary caudal, 58.

The specimen which afforded the illustration was taken in the Trout streams at Driffield.

BLACK-FINNED TROUT

On the Llugwy, North Wales.

*Order IV.*
*PHYSOSTOMI.*

*Family*
*SALMONIDÆ.*
*Sub-generic Group*—Salmones.

# Black-Finned Trout.

*(Salmo nigripinnis.)*

Salmo nigripinnis,                    Günther's Cat. vi. p. 96.

THIS well-marked species of non-migratory *Salmonidæ* appears to have escaped the observation of naturalists, as being specifically distinct from the Common Brown Trout *(S. fario)*,
until Dr. Günther brought it into notice.   It is clearly distinct from *fario* in some important
structural points; the maxillary in the Black-Fin is feeble, that of the Common Trout is strong;
the vomerine teeth are in a single series, in the Trout they are biserial; the pectorals are
very long and pointed, the tail is forked or more deeply incised than in specimens of *fario*
of the same size.   In colour, moreover, there is great difference between the Black-Fin and
the Common Brown Trout; the pectorals, especially in specimens of about seven or eight
inches long, are very black, as is also the caudal fin.

    I first made my acquaintance with this very interesting and beautiful species on my visit
to Lough Melvin in July, 1878.   The Black-Fin is the ordinary Trout of the Lake, where it

occurs in greater numbers than the Common Trout; at least my brother-in-law, Lieutenant-Colonel Masefield, and myself caught a great many more Black-Fins than Brown Trout, during our week's visit at Garrison. It was quite easy to fill our baskets with these fish, though a great number were rather small, about eight inches in length. They rise most freely at the fly, are very plucky, and fight strongly to get free; are beautiful in shape and colour; have deep pink flesh, and are unsurpassed as an article of diet for the breakfast or dinner table. I would advise any one who cares more for numbers than size to visit Garrison, where he will be well attended to, in every respect, by Mr. Scott, of the Hotel, and have opportunities of excellent sport with this lively little Salmonoid. The Black-fin occasionally grows to the length of fifteen or sixteen inches, but we seldom took a specimen above ten or eleven inches in length. This species is also found in the mountain pools of Wales, and I have in my possession specimens caught with the artificial fly from a river near Bala Lake, Merionethshire. Dr. Günther mentions the following additional localities for the Black-Fin:—Llyn Beguilin, Merionethshire, Llyn Gadr, Cader Idris, and probably the River Towey, from whence some sterile specimens had been transferred to a fresh-water pond.

The following is a description of a specimen caught by myself in Lough Melvin, Fermanagh, on the 16th. of July, 1878. The length was eight inches and a half, the greatest breadth two inches; the length of head was nearly two inches; length of maxillary seven eighths of an inch, breadth a little more than one eighth of an inch; eye large, three eighths of an inch in diameter; irides white; the præoperculum with a rounded indistinct lower limb; maxillary reaching to the hind margin of the orbit of the eye; in larger specimens the maxillary reaches beyond that orbit; teeth sharp, but not so strong as in *fario*; the teeth of the vomer, as seen in the mouth, appear to be arranged in a double series, but on dissection this apparently biserial arrangement is seen to be owing to the zig-zag disposition of a single series. The pectorals are long and pointed, the outer and inner margins dark; in young specimens, when taken immediately out of the water, they are always almost entirely black. The tail is largely developed and deeply forked, the lobes pointed, and smoky black; adipose fin finely tinged with pink; the dorsal has numerous large oval black spots. Colour of the head on the sides golden yellowish or olive, with several round dark spots on the gill-cover, which sometimes has an elongated silvery blotch: in some specimens these silvery marks are very indistinct or quite absent. The whole length of the back dark with purplish hue; spots large, dark, and reticulated; there are small red spots, sometimes faint in colour, on the lateral line, and a few above and below that line; the scales are small and round, margined with black, silvery in the centre; body full and thick, belly with a yellowish tinge, or white; some specimens have the colour of the body more golden than others. The length of the pectoral is always considerably more than half the distance of its base from that of the ventral; in *S. fario* the length of pectoral is not more than half that distance.

The fin-ray formula is

> Dorsal 12—13.
> Pectoral 13.
> Ventral 9.
> Anal 11—12.

I think this species is the one described by Sir William Jardine in his *Illustrations;* he says that when hooked these fish are very strong and lively, and frequently spring out of the water, that the flesh when dressed is pink and highly flavoured. (See pl. ii. fig. 1.) He gives Loch Awe as a locality. I am not sure, however, about this; but in my note-book I have this memorandum made when Sir William's figure was before me, "surely this is *nigripinnis.*" I am unable to refer again to the *Illustrations* while writing these remarks.

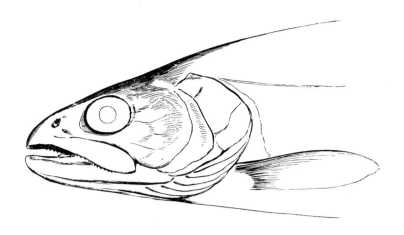

*Order IV.*
*PHYSOSTOMI.*

*Family*
*SALMONIDÆ.*
*Sub-generic Group*—SALMONES.

# LOCH STENNIS TROUT.

*(Salmo crcadensis.)*

*Salmo orcadensis,*  GÜNTHER'S Cat. vi. p. 91.

THIS species is said to be very similar to *S. nigripinnis*, "but distinguished from it by a broader and stronger maxillary, larger scales on the tail, and a greater number of pyloric appendages." It is thus described by Günther:—"Head well proportioned in its shape, and rather short when compared with the body; body rather slender......Præoperculum with the lower limb very indistinct; snout short, conical. Maxillary as broad and as strong as in *S. fario;* in specimens nine inches long it does not extend to below the posterior margin of the orbit. Teeth moderately strong; those of the vomer form a single series, and are persistent. Fins well developed: pectoral somewhat rounded, its length being more than one half of its distance from the ventral. The caudal fin is distinctly emarginate in specimens nine inches long, but nearly perfectly truncate in specimens twelve inches long: it has the lobes pointed. Scales on the hinder half of the tail considerably larger than on the sides of the trunk: there are about thirteen in a transverse series descending from behind the adipose fin obliquely forwards to the lateral line. Sides with more or less numerous black reticulated spots, between which a few red ones are interspersed. Dorsal with black spots.

Probably a non-migratory species, from Loch Stennis, in the Orkney Islands."

The fin-ray formula is

Dorsal 13.
Pectoral 14.
Anal 11.

The woodcut is from a specimen in the British Museum.

LOCHLEVEN TROUT

*Order IV.*
*PHYSOSTOMI.*

*Family*
*SALMONIDÆ.*
*Sub-generic Group*—SALMONES.

# LOCHLEVEN TROUT.

### (*Salmo levenensis.*)

| | |
|---|---|
| *Salmo levenensis,* | WALKER, Wern. Mem. i. p. 541; YARRELL, ii. p. 117; GÜNTHER'S Cat. vi. p. 101. |
| *Salmo cæcifer,* | PARNELL, Fish. Firth of Forth, Wern. Mem. vii. p. 306. |
| *Lochleven Trout,* | RICHARDSON, Faun. Bor.-Amer. Pisc. p. 143; YARRELL, ii. p. 117; COUCH, Fish. Brit. Isl. iv. p. 243, pl. 220. |

THE Lochleven Trout takes its name from the lake, on which stands the ruined castle in which the unfortunate Mary Queen of Scots was imprisoned; but, though this lake is the one most noted for this fish, the Lochleven Trout occurs also in Loch Scone, the river Forth, and a branch of Loch Lomond; the Lake of Windermere and the Rothay river are also mentioned as localities by Dr. Günther. "It has been supposed," says Couch, "that this is one of the many varieties in which the Common Trout is prone to appear, as influenced by differences in water and food; but observers who have been well qualified to form an opinion, such as Dr. Parnell, Mr. Yarrell, and Sir John Richardson," (to which names I may add that of Günther), "have confidently decided that it is a distinct species. From several particulars which they have brought forward in support of this conclusion, we feel no hesitation in adopting their decision; and so much the rather as it is shown that there are abundance of the ordinary Trout in the same waters, exposed to the same influences, but from which the species above mentioned is readily to be distinguished."

The Lochleven Trout, so long justly celebrated, are stated by Dr. Parnell to have fallen off in their general flavour and condition, owing, it is said, to the partial draining of the loch having destroyed their best feeding ground, by exposing the beds of fresh-water shells, which form the greater portion of their food. Parnell's prize essay was published in 1837; so his remarks may not be applicable now as to the condition of the Trout. Some years ago Lochleven Trout occasionally found their way into the markets and fish-shops of our large towns; but this is not the case now. Accounts of the results of fly-fishing in Lochleven frequently appear in the pages of *The Field* and *Land and Water*, the well-known weekly periodicals, and it appears that considerable numbers of Trout are taken with the fly; but as the Common Trout is also found in this lake, one cannot learn what proportion the Lochleven species forms of these captures. The Trout-fishing on this loch is, I believe, now reserved for anglers, and netting is not allowed; consequently none of these fish find their way into the English markets.

According to Dr. Parnell they spawn in January, February, and March. The flesh is said to be of a deep red in colour, and so far as I remember they are excellent in flavour; but I have not tasted a Lochleven Trout for many years. I believe it is a lively fish, and gives excellent sport.

The following are the principal points in which this species differs from *S. fario*:—The cæcal appendages are more numerous, varying from sixty to eighty in number; the body is much less stout than in *fario*, and the hinder part of the body is more tapering; the maxillary is much narrower and more feeble than in the Common Trout (see woodcut on page 81); the pectoral fins are more pointed; the caudal is more deeply incised, and has the lobes more pointed than in specimens of the same size of *fario*. There is difference in colour: in *levenensis* the upper parts are generally olive-green, and the sides, both above and below the lateral line, are marked with a great number of dark spots, some of which are round, and many X or XX-shaped; there are no red spots, which in *fario* are general and numerous; the adipose fin has a few brown spots, and is never tipped with red: according to my observations, in the Common Trout this red tip is universal. Mr. Francis Day, who, as is well known, is engaged on an important work on the Fishes of India, has kindly sent me a reprint from the *Linnean Society's Journal* (vol. xii.) of his paper on "The Introduction of Trout and Tench into India." He says that it may be assumed that the *S. levenensis* and the Tench have bred in the rivers and tanks on the Neilgherry Hills, in the Presidency of Madras, and thinks that this may eventually prove a success. Specimens of Lochleven Trout, received from Mr. H. S. Thomas, of the Madras Civil Service, by Mr. Day, showed bright red spots on the body. Mr. Day remarks very truly "that the colour of the water, and the soil through which streams flow, exercise great influence on the colours of fishes. The spots alluded to are now black; this is probably due to the fish having been bred in a clear mountain stream, but the result in this instance is most interesting."

This is a non-migratory species, inhabiting Lochleven and other Scottish lakes; also occurring in Windermere, and possibly in other north of England lakes.

The fin rays are

Dorsal 12—13.
Pectoral 14.
Ventral 9.
Anal 11.

Specimens sometimes attain to the length of twenty inches.

LOCH AWE.

*Order IV.*
*PHYSOSTOMI.*

*Family*
*SALMONIDÆ.*
*Sub-generic group*—SALMONES.

# GILLAROO TROUT.

*(Salmo stomachicus.)*

| | |
|---|---|
| *The Gillaroo,* | BARRINGTON, Philosoph. Trans. 1774, vol. lxiv. p. 116; WATSON, Ibid, p. 121; HUNTER, Ibid, p. 310; OWEN, Cat. Phys. Ser. Coll. Surg. i. p. 141; Anat. of Vertebrates i. p. 418; THOMPSON, Nat. Hist. Ireland iv. p. 154-156; COUCH, Fish. Brit. Isl. iv. p. 240, pl. 249. |
| *Salmo stomachicus,* | GÜNTHER'S Cat. vi. p. 95. |

THE Gillaroo Trout is an extremely interesting species of the non-migratory *Salmonidæ*, and beyond all doubt is distinct from the Common Brown Trout, or *Salmo fario*, in some important particulars. This fish occurs in some of the Irish lakes, as in Lough Neagh, Lough Melvin, Lough Corrib, and Lough Mask, also in the Shannon and the Galway lakes, according to the testimony of Thompson in his work on the *Natural History of Ireland*. Outside of the Green Island I believe there is no record of its occurrence. I believe the first notice of this Trout occurs in the *Philosophical Transactions* for 1774.

The thick muscular stomach—on which account Günther has very appropriately bestowed the specific name of *stomachicus* upon this fish—has been commented upon by that eminent

GILLAROO TROUT

physiologist, John Hunter. The muscular walls of the Gillaroo are so strong that they have been supposed to perform to a certain extent the function of a gizzard. Though such a function was denied by Watson and by Hunter, I think that this organ, with its thickened membrane is, to a small extent, a quasi-gizzard, analogous to that of birds; this is rendered probable from the fact that, in another genus of fishes (*Mugil*) there exists a modification of the stomach which seems to give it the true character of a gizzard. The essential characters of a gizzard are mainly these two: first, a power and motion fit for trituration, and secondly a cuticular horny lining. Now, Professor Owen has shown that in the Mullets (*Mugil*) this latter structure does exist in the stomach of the Mullet, as a distinct layer of rough and separable cuticle. "The modification which gives the stomach the true character of a gizzard, is best seen," writes Professor Owen, "in the Mullets, (*Mugil*). The cardiac portion here forms a long *cul-de-sac;* the pyloric part is continued from the cardiac end of this at right angles, and is of a conical figure externally; but the cavity within is reduced almost to a linear fissure by the great development of the muscular parieties, which are an inch thick at the base of the cone, and this part is lined by a thick horny epithelium."—(*Anat. of Verteb.* vol. i. p. 418.) With regard to the first essential point—triturating power and motion—there seems to be no doubt that such does exist in the stomachs of some, probably most, fishes. I here quote our great anatomist again. "The muscular action of a fish's stomach consists of vermicular contractions, creeping slowly in continuous succession from the cardia to the pylorus, and impressing a two-fold gyratory motion on the contents; so that, while some portions are proceeding to the pylorus, other portions are returning towards the cardia. More direct constrictive and dilative movements occur, with intervals of repose, at both the orifices, the vital contraction being antagonized by pressure from within. The pylorus has the power, very evidently, of controlling that pressure, and only portions of completely comminuted and digested food (chyme) are permitted to pass into the intestine."—(P. 419.) The food of the Gillaroo Trout consists for the most part of various molluscs, which it picks off the rocks and stones in the lakes inhabited by these fish, and there can be little if any doubt, that the strong muscular parieties of the stomach act in breaking up the shells of some of the molluscs on which they feed; and although the inner cavity of the stomach of the Gillaroo is destitute of a thick horny epithelium as seen in the Mullet—for the whole cavity is lined with a fine villous coat—still I doubt not that this organ does possess some power of grinding.

I have caught in company with Lieutenant Colonel Masefield, several of these fish in Lough Melvin, in July, 1878; they are a very plucky fish, and when hooked fight hard to get away. The beautiful bright peach and light orange colour of their sides reveals the species, as it approaches to seize the fly. The Gillaroo proceeds more leisurely and apparently more cautiously than either the Common Trout or the Black-Fin; it seems at first to hesitate at the fly, but turning itself on its side, and at length being satisfied all is right, it rises vigo-rously, and generally gets well hooked; and if the angler has a good fish, of two pounds or so, on his line, I can assure him, a Gillaroo will give most excellent sport, and where there are weeds, such as the *potamogetons* with their tough stems, unless the tackle be good, the chances are the fish will succeed eventually in avoiding the landing-net.

The boatmen at Lough Melvin say that the Gillaroo spawns on the shallower parts of the lake, and does not ascend the rivers for that purpose. As to size, the Gillaroo in the Irish lakes often weighs three, four, or five pounds. Thompson was informed that specimens weighing twelve pounds are sometimes taken at Lough Neagh, and Couch states that they have been known to attain the size of nearly thirty inches, with a weight of about twenty pounds. The largest I succeeded in taking did not weigh more than two pounds, but a fish of even a pound weight is quite an angler's prize, owing to the sport which it is able to afford. In memoranda of Mr. Walsh, F.R.S., (*Philosoph. Transact.*, quoted above, p. 119), dated Killaloe, Oct. 1st., 1773, "Innkeeper's account," it is stated that "the gizzard of a Gillaroo Trout is of the size of a large chicken, that it is white and excellent eating, is vastly broader than a Trout of the same length, and that some of the fish are three feet long; some from twelve to eighteen (inches) long; that the Trout itself is bad eating."

The stomach is often much distended with the quantity of molluscous food therein contained, and one can feel the shells within grating against each other, on pressure with the fingers. Besides molluscs, its favourite diet, the Gillaroo will feed on flies of various kinds, such as the *Ephemeridæ* and *Phryganidæ*, etc., in their perfect or imago state, and also the larvæ of various aquatic insects of these and other families of insects. Sometimes the stomach is full of only one species of shell-fish. In the stomachal contents before me, taken from a two-pound Lough Melvin fish, caught by myself with a fly, there is only one species of mollusc in any appreciable quantity, and that is the *Limneus pereger*, with young specimens of which the stomach was absolutely crammed; in other fish I have found a variety, as *Bythinia tentaculata, Ancyclus fluviatilis, Limneus pereger*, two or three species of *Planorbis*, and the curved sand-cases of some of the *Trichoptera* (the *Mystacida* and *Sericostoma* of Pictet).*

The flesh of the Gillaroo is as pink as a Trout in good condition, but neither Lieutenant Colonel Masefield nor myself considered them as nice eating as the Common Trout or the Black-Fin. We thought there was a decidedly molluscous flavour about the flesh; and certainly the examination of a Gillaroo's stomach is, as I know from experience, by no means an agreeable task, owing to the very strong odour exhaled from the swallowed and partly digested shell-fish. "Very hot, Sir," was the remark elicited from one of the boatmen, on my mentioning this fact to him. Thompson, too, says that the fishermen consider the Gillaroo inferior to the other *Salmonidæ* for the table. Barrington says that the stomachs of these fish were in his time sometimes served up at table in Ireland under the name of gizzards; I do not know whether such a dish is ever now served up in any part of Ireland.

The following is the description of a specimen caught by Lieutenant Colonel Masefield on July 17th., 1878:—Total length ten inches and a half; length of head two inches and one eighth; greatest breadth of body two inches and five eighths; snout short and convex; maxillary longer than snout, broad and flat, extending a little below the posterior orbit: in smaller specimens it does not extend beyond the middle of the eye; præoperculum with lower limb rounded off; dorsal fin with large oval dark spots, occasionally mixed with a few red ones; pectoral pointed, its length being about one half the distance of its base from that of ventral; caudal fin emarginate: in young specimens this fin is more deeply incised; adipose fin tipped with red; head rather small; gill-cover with numerous round black spots, and with a yellowish tinge; back glossy bluish black; sides of a beautiful apricot above lateral line, shading into a delicate yellow below that line; body covered with numerous large clear black and vermilion reticulated spots; belly white; colour of pectoral and ventral fins deep vivid pink; eye large, irides white. The teeth are feeble: those on the vomer are arranged in a double series, and are persistent through life. The whole body of the fish is full and deep; the hinder part of the tail is also deep.

The fin-ray formula is

> Dorsal 13—14.
> Pectoral 13.
> Ventral 9.
> Anal 13.

The specimen figured was caught by Lieutenant Colonel Masefield on July 17th., 1878, in Lough Melvin.

* Molluscs are frequently found in the stomachs of other species of *Salmonidæ* without this peculiarity of that organ; but there is this difference, that in the Gillaroo shell-fish is the usual diet, in other species it is an occasional one.

Order IV.
PHYSOSTOMI.

Family
SALMONIDÆ.
Sub-generic Group—SALMONES.

# GREAT LAKE TROUT.

### (*Salmo ferox.*)

| | |
|---|---|
| *Salmo lacustris,* | BERKENHOUT, Synopsis of the Natural History of Great Britain and Ireland, 1789, vol. i. p. 79. |
| *Salmo ferox,* | JARDINE AND SELBY, Edinb. New Philosoph. Journal, 1835, xviii. p. 55; JARDINE'S Illustrations of Scotch Salmonidæ pl. iv.; YARRELL, ii. p. 110; RICHARDSON, Faun. Bor.-Amer. Fish. p. 144; GÜNTHER'S Cat. vi. p. 92. |
| *The Great Lake Trout,* | JENYNS' Man. p. 425; THOMPSON'S Nat. Hist. of Ireland iv. p. 156; GÜNTHER'S Cat. vi. p. 92. |
| *Lake Trout,* | COUCH'S Fish. Brit. Isl. iv. p. 222, pl. 217. |
| *Salar ferox,* | CUV. AND VALENC., xxi. p. 338. |

ONE of the first observers to draw attention to the Great Lake Trout appears to have been John Birkenhout, who gave to it the name of *Salmo lacustris*, as may be seen in his *Synopsis*, (quoted above); but his description is very brief. He simply writes, (p. 79), *Salmo* No. 3, "*Lacustris*, Lake Trout. Sometimes fifty or sixty pounds weight (?). Probably a distinct species. In the North." If this is our Great Lake Trout, then his specific name has the claim of priority; but as the term *lacustris* is applied to other *Salmonidæ* by conti-

GREAT LAKE TROUT

nental writers, it is well to retain the name of *ferox*, as proposed by Jardine and Selby. "The large Trout," writes Sir W. Jardine, "to which the above specific designation *(ferox)* was applied by myself and Mr. Selby, had been long previously known and incidentally mentioned by various writers, but it was at the same time confounded with the large Trouts of the lakes of Central Europe, and the distinguishing characters between it and *S. fario* had not been pointed out. In Scotland it occurs in many of the large lochs, but at the same time it is rather local in its haunts."

The Great Lake Trout is a non-migratory species inhabiting the lochs of the north of Scotland, as Loch Shin and Loch Awe, Loch Laggan, Lochs Loyal and Assynt; it is found also in some of the Irish lakes, as in Lough Neagh, Lough Melvin, Lough Eske, and Lough Erne; in Wales it occurs in the Lake of Llanberris; it is found also in Derwentwater, Ullswater, and perhaps other lakes of the north of England.

This fish is essentially a deep-water species, and only ascends the rivers in connection with the lakes for a short distance for the purpose of spawning, which takes place late in September and in October. The efforts of my brother-in-law and myself, when at Garrison, to obtain a specimen of *ferox* were fruitless, though we trolled through many miles of water, using a young trout as the bait. It may be that we did not allow the bait to sink deep enough; I am rather confirmed in this opinion by what I have, since my visit to Ireland, read in Mr. Cholmondeley Pennell's work, *The Angler Naturalist*. As I think his remarks may be useful, I will here quote what he says.

"The only way of taking the larger fish is by spinning with a small parr or other glittering bait towed behind a boat, for which purpose very powerful tackle is required, as the fish is of immense strength, and its teeth as sharp as those of a Pike. As a rule, however, not much success attends the troller for the Great Lake Trout—a circumstance which may possibly be in some measure attributable to the general ignorance of all its habits, and of the manner in which it is to be fished for.

The secret of success lies in four points—time, depth, speed, and place.

*Time.* As a rule, *begin* fishing at the time when other people are *leaving off*—that is, about six o'clock p.m. Up to this hour the fish are rarely in a position from which they can by any accident see your bait. From six o'clock until midnight Lake Trout may be caught. These fish are essentially night feeders. During the day they lie hid under rocks and in holes, in the deepest part of the extensive lakes which they generally inhabit, and only venture into fishable water at the approach of evening.

*Depth.* Instead of weighing your tackle to spin at from three to four feet from the *surface*, lead it so as to sink within about the same distance from the *bottom*, be the depth what it may.

*Speed.* Let your boat be rowed *slowly*, rather than at a brisk lively pace, as a large Lake Trout will seldom trouble himself to follow a bait that is moving fast away from him; consequently your bait must possess the speciality of spinning at all events moderately well, or it will not spin at all.

*Place.* The place to spin over is where the bank shelves rapidly into deep water, say at a depth of from fifteen to thirty or forty feet, according to the nature of the basin; a much greater or much less depth is useless. This a rather important point, as thereupon it depends whether your bait is ever seen by the fish you wish to catch. The food of the Lake Trout consists of small fish. These are not to be found in any great depths of water, but on the contrary on the sloping shores of the lake, up which, therefore, the Trout comes in search of them, stopping short of the shallows."—(P. 335-336.)

I feel sure that the whole of this advice is most admirable, and I shall certainly put it in practice when I next visit Ireland.

The *Salmo ferox* will occasionally take a fly, and must therefore sometimes swim not very far from the surface; a specimen which weighed six pounds and a half was killed on the 21st. of September, 1874, in Lough Eske, on a fly by Mr. Arthur Wallan; its length was twenty-two inches and a half. Mr. Arthur R. Wallace took last season (1878) on a fly a young *Salmo ferox*, one pound and a half in weight, in Lough Eske. In the landing-net he ejected from his stomach a small Trout five or six inches in length, partially digested. It was a large fish for its captor to swallow, and had been doubled up in the stomach, for which it was evidently too long. Young fish, from one to two pounds in weight, are said to rise more freely to the usual Trout flies; but neither my brother-in-law nor myself succeeded in catching even a young Lake, or as it is called at Garrison, a Black Lough Trout; and I do not think we ever rose one.

When I was at Lough Melvin, the boatmen were particularly desirous that I should secure a *Salmo ferox*, knowing that I had come not simply for sport, but chiefly for specimens. After many hours' fruitless trolling, at last the line from the reel ran out briskly, and I had "great expectations" that the fish would turn out to be the Great Lake Trout. "Shure, Sir," said one of the boatmen, "it is a Black Loch," on the fish being landed and seen by him. It was really nothing but the Common Brown Trout of about two pounds in weight. "The wish was father to the thought," and I suspect that fish are often taken in Lough Melvin which the non-scientific angler is led to believe to be *Salmo ferox* by the sympathetic boatmen. This feature in the character of the Irish fishermen, for whom I have the greatest respect for their sterling worth, honesty, and good nature, is well illustrated by Charles Kingsley, in his book *The Water Babies*.

"You must not believe all that Dennis tells you, mind, for if you ask him,

"'Is there a Salmon here do you think, Dennis?'

"'Is it Salmon, thin, your honour manes? Salmon? Cartloads it is of thim, thin, an' ridgmens, shouldthering ache out of water, an' ye'd but the luck to see thim.'

"Then you fish the pool over, and never get a rise.

"'But there can't be a Salmon here, Dennis! and if you'll but think, if one had come up last tide, he'd be gone to the higher pools by now.'

"'Shure, thin, and your honour's the thrue fisherman, and understands it all like a book. Why, ye spake as if ye'd known the wather a thousand years. As I said, how could there be a fish here at all, just now?'

"'But you said just now they were shouldering each other out of water.'

"And then Dennis will look up at you with his handsome, sly, soft, sleepy, goodnatured, untrustable, Irish grey eye, and answer with the prettiest smile:

"'Shure, and didn't I think your honour would like a pleasant answer.'"—(P. 130.)

*Salmo ferox*, as its name implies, is a most formidable fish, both from the size to which it attains, as well as from the very formidable armature of its mouth: next to the Pike it is perhaps the most ferocious of the fresh-water inhabitants of our lakes and rivers. Mr. Couch mentions that the Earl of Enniskillen has taken Lake Trout of the weight of twenty-eight and even thirty pounds in Lough Eske. Thompson was informed by a fish vendor that he had frequently in his possession for sale specimens that weighed thirty pounds. In a note Thompson says, "In Sampson's *Londonderry*, the Great Trout of Lough Neagh is said to reach fifty pounds." The fish of this last named lake, I have little doubt, feed extensively on the Pollan, or Fresh-water Herring, so abundantly occurring there. The largest Common Trout ever caught in Lough Neagh, was taken with a night-line, and a Pollan as a bait; if I remember right, it weighed thirty-three pounds. In Loch Lomond there is a Trout which the people call *Powan-eater;*—the Scotch Powan is the same as the Irish Pollan (*Coregonus pollan*)—this Powan-eater is probably *S. ferox*. In Ireland the term *Buddagh* is sometimes applied to this fish. Swift, in *A Dialogue in Hibernian Style between A and B*, makes *A* inquire, "What kind of a man is your neighbour Squire Dolt? *B*. Why, a mere *Buddagh!*

He sometimes coshers with me; and once a month I take a pipe with him, and we shot it about for an hour together." The word *Buddagh* is said to mean a "big fat fellow." (See Thompson's *Natural History of Ireland*, iv. p. 158.)

I have never had an opportunity of tasting the flesh of *S. ferox*, and can give, therefore, no opinion as to its quality. The colour is said to be orange-yellow, and the flavour to be coarse and indifferent.

Like some other *Salmonidæ* the colour of this fish is found to vary; I do not think, however, that there is a great difference in this respect in the case of individuals inhabiting the same large lake; but where they have been transferred from their natural habitations to small and circumscribed ponds, then there is a marked difference in colouration. A specimen obligingly sent to me by Mr. A. Scott, of Garrison, caught in Lough Melvin, was a handsomely marked fish, as may be seen by the accompanying illustration, while another specimen, which I saw and handled alive in October, 1878, taken out of a small stew in the occupation of Mr. John Parnaby, of Troutdale, Keswick, was quite free from any purplish tint: the back and body were yellowish brown with darker brown round spots, and the belly yellow with a slight tinge of gold. This specimen had been caught in Derwentwater, and had been two years in this little pond, in which weeds grew abundantly; it was occasionally fed with chopped horse-flesh, and was thin and in bad condition; it was twenty-one inches in length.

The following is a description of a young male fish I received from Lough Melvin in October, 1878:—Total length sixteen inches; greatest depth three inches and five eighths; length of head four inches; the maxillary one inch and five eighths, narrow, and extending beyond the posterior orbit; the præoperculum is crescent-shaped, the descending portion rounding itself off, with scarcely a trace of a lower limb. The pectoral fins in this specimen are long and somewhat pointed, the length is two inches and three eighths, and is more than the half of the distance of its base from that of the ventral; the tail is emarginate; the snout is long; eye long; the whole aspect of the head giving the fish a fierce expression. The colour of the back is dark purplish brown, becoming lighter purple on the sides above lateral line, below this line the sides are silvery, the sides marked with numerous black and brown reticulated spots; there are spots on the gill-cover and on the dorsal fin, the gill-cover slightly tinged with pale yellow; the teeth are strong and sharp; vomerine teeth in a single series, and arranged in a zig-zag form; these teeth are persistent, for in the specimen of a head belonging to a fish which weighed twenty pounds, these vomerine teeth are well seen.

The number of rays in the fins are

Dorsal 13—14.
Pectoral 15.
Ventral 9.
Anal 11.

Mr. Alexander Scott, of the Hotel, Garrison, Belleek, Ireland, supplied the specimen from which the drawing was made.

# CHARR.

---

*Characters of the Sub-generic Group* SALVELINI.—"Teeth on the *head* of the vomer only from the earliest age of the individuals."—GÜNTHER.

THE British fresh-water species of fishes which belong to this sub-generic group, comprise the Charrs, the Smelt, the Pollan, Gwyniad, Vendace (*Coregonus*), and the Grayling. The three species of the genus *Coregonus*, however, are destitute of teeth on the vomer, and indeed of any teeth at all. Commercially, this sub-generic group is, comparatively speaking, of little importance; for the Charr are very local, and being inhabitants of deep water, excepting at the spawning season, when they approach the shores of the lakes inhabited by them—at which time they are now protected by the Salmon Fisheries Laws—they are difficult to capture; the Pollan is caught in considerable numbers in Lough Neagh during the spring and summer months, and sent to the markets of Liverpool and other large towns. The Gwyniad and Vendace are known only to a few, and the Grayling is food only for the angler. The Smelt, however, is an exception, and large quantities of this delicate and delicious fish find their way into the markets of all our towns.

Of this group, the Charrs come nearest, both in form and habits, to the non-migratory *Salmones*. Often beautiful in colouration, and always elegant in shape, the Charrs at once attract the attention and admiration of the beholder.

Much obscurity has hung over the history of these fish, and little was known of either their habits or of the different species which occur in the lakes of Great Britain and Ireland, until Dr. Günther set himself to work out the problem. In a series of valuable papers published in the years 1862, 1863, and 1865, in the *Proceedings of the Zoological Society of London*, Dr. Günther has contributed a great deal to our knowledge of the British Charrs. From his investigations it appears that there are at least six different species found in the lakes of this country. All these species I have been fortunate enough either to examine or to get possession of. I have also had the pleasure of seeing many living specimens of the Charr of Windermere, swimming about in the large tanks, belonging to Mr. John Parnaby, at Troutdale, near Keswick, and the opportunity of handling and taking notes of these fish. I have received specimens, in a beautiful condition and perfectly fresh state, of the two Irish species, the *Salmo colii* from Lough Eske—thanks to the kindness of Mr. T. Brooke, Mr. Arthur R. Wallace, and Mr. Alex. Scott—and the *S. grayi* from Lough Melvin.

From the secluded habits of the Charr, which frequent the deepest parts of the waters inhabited by them, it is no wonder, perhaps, that little was for a long time known of them Willughby is the first naturalist who has given an account of Charr. The Llanberris Charr, which he mentions under the name of Torgoch, "red-belly," he identifies with the Windermere species; from which, however, it is clearly distinct.  But Willughby also mentions a fish, which he calls the Gilt Charr, as occurring in Windermere; and says that this fish is very different from the Red Charr, both in colour and in the vomerine teeth; for the Gilt Charr has a white belly.  What this Gilt Charr may be I know not, but I think it probable it may be the fish which has occasionally been supplied to Mr. Parnaby, under the name of Silver Charr, which is said to be found in Lake Windermere.  Pennant, Donovan, Thompson, Yarrell, and others, have given us notices of Charr, but, as I said before, scarcely anything was definitely known, until Dr. Günther turned his attention to these interesting fish.

I will now proceed to a consideration of the different species.

Order IV.
*PHYSOSTOMI.*

*Family*
*SALMONIDÆ.*
*Sub-generic Group—*SALVELINI.

# WINDERMERE CHARR.

*(Salmo willughbii.)*

| | |
|---|---|
| *Torgoch Wallis, Westmorlandis, The Red Charre, lacus Winandermere,* | WILLUGHBY, Hist. Pisc. p. 196. |
| *Charr,* | PENNANT, Brit. Zool. iii. p. 407, (confused with other species); YARRELL, ii. p. 121 (similarly confused). |
| *Willoughby's Charr,* | COUCH, Fish. Brit. Isl. iv. p. 262, pl. 222 (good). |
| *Salmo alpinus,* | DONOVAN, Brit. Fish. iii. pl. lxi. |
| *Salmo umbla,* | THOMPSON, Ann. and Mag. Nat. Hist. 1840, vi. p. 439, (confused with other species,) or Nat. Hist. of Ireland, iv. p. 160-167. |
| *Salmo Willughbii,* | GÜNTHER, Proc. Zool. Soc. 1862, p. 46, pl. v. and 1863, p. 11; Cat. vi. p. 131. |

THE Charr of the lake of Windermere is the species which is most generally known. It is mentioned by Willughby, Pennant, Donovan, and other writers, as being caught in nets—"retia *Trammels* Anglice dicta," says the first named authority,—as, being much esteemed for the table, and very delicate when potted. Although Windermere is the lake where this species appears to have its head-quarters, it is found also in other north of England lakes.

Mr. Parnaby tells me that during the season Charr are taken in Buttermere, Ennerdale, Coniston Water, and Wast Water; but he does not say definitely whether this Charr is the Windermere species. The same species, or one very closely allied to it, is found in Loch Bruiach in the north of Scotland, as mentioned by Günther. Mr. Parnaby tells me that there are two species of Charr in Windermere, called by the fishermen the Red Charr and the Silver Charr; that they spawn at different times, and under different circumstances. It is possible that this Silver Charr may be the "Gilt Charr" which Willughby says is found in Windermere; but I have been unable to see a specimen of this fish.

Before the application of the Fishery Laws to the capture of Charr, these fish used to be taken in considerable quantities in nets, in the months of October and November, when the Charr seek the shallower portions of the lake for spawning. A few are taken in the summer months by anglers; a writer in *Land and Water*, a few years ago, speaks thus of the Windermere Charr:—"Though the Charr exists in other lakes of Westmoreland, Windermere is doubtless its head-quarters. The largest Charr I have ever seen exceeded two pounds in weight. Half a pound may be set as about its average full-grown size, though a fish of three ounces will often take the bait. They are bold biters at either the artificial fly or spinning minnow, or the spinning spoon. Though this implies a habit of feeding on the surface, the conjecture that they feed chiefly at the bottom of the water is not thereby refuted, for a practice has lately been introduced of trailing a revolving bait from a plummet sunk deep in the water, the revolution being kept up in the depths, as on the surface, by the motion of the boat. This fishing for Charr by bait, though the best during spring, is carried on successfully through the whole of the summer. The favourite fishing places are the deepest parts of the lake; an odd fish or two may be occasionally picked up elsewhere, but the knowing hands confine themselves to constantly passing and repassing over the shoal. The Charr come into shallow water to spawn during the autumn, and being then within reach of the nets are destroyed sacrilegiously. They also run up into the rivers to spawn; or, as it would be more correct to say, into a river—for though two rivers fall into Windermere at its head, forming a junction half a mile above the lake, the Charr never go up the Rothay, though myriads turn off at the fork into the Brathay.* Any cause for this preference has hitherto been sought in vain. The rivers run through two neighbouring valleys, the geological formation of which is the same—the ordinary slate-stone of the country. The course of the rivers is of about the same length, and lakes are to a certain extent the feeders of both."

The flesh of Charr, when fried like a Trout, is pink, and I should not know the difference in flavour between Trout and Charr. Potted Charr at Windermere has been an institution for a very long time; the writer in *Land and Water*, just quoted, says on this subject:—"As for any resemblance between the Charr and Trout, the nearest I know of is in the taste, and the public would probably be of the same opinion, if they knew which they are eating under the denomination of potted Charr. The flesh of the Trout may be of as pink a colour as that of the Charr. Both may be alike in season, and of equal flavour, without showing any of that colour. And the red external colour, which the belly of the Charr assumes at the breeding season—the only time at which they are sold for potting—has no colouring influence whatever upon the flesh. The only perceptible difference between their respective flavours must be that imparted by the silver or the gold which they have cost."

Charr, when in perfect condition, and when taken fresh out of the water, are splendid fish, but a correct idea of their beautiful colour can only be formed when seen just out of water. Moreover these fish, when kept in confinement, lose much of their colour. The specimens which Mr. Parnaby has in his tanks at Troutdale, though fine healthy-looking fish, are almost destitute of the brilliant red, characteristic of the fish in their natural habits,

* The same is the case at Ullswater, as I am informed by Professor Busk; Charr invariably ascend one river and invariably avoid the other.

1. WINDERMERE CHARR   2. COLE'S CHARR   3. GRAY'S CHARR

and when in best condition.    The plan adopted by Mr. Parnaby at his fish-breeding establishment, is to place the ova after impregnation, not with gravel in boxes, but between the
spaces of slips of glass fitted into an oblong framework, as below, the whole being in a trough,

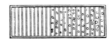

through which fresh water constantly but quietly flows.    The advantages of this method are:
(1) facility in counting the eggs; (2) easy detection and ready expulsion of blind or unfertilized
eggs; (3) the rough edges of the glass enable the young fish to extricate themselves more
readily from the egg membrane.    In this way Mr. Parnaby succeeds in rearing many thousand
young Charr every season; as well as large numbers of that lovely American Charr, *Salmo
fontinalis*, one of the most beautiful of all the species, and one which highly deserves cultivation in our own country.

The Windermere Charr is thus described by Dr. Günther—the two most important points
in which this species differs structurally from the allied Welsh species I print in italics.—"Body
compressed, slightly elevated, its greatest depth being one fourth of the distance of the snout
from the end of the middle caudal rays.    Head compressed, *interorbital space convex*, its width
being less than twice the diameter of the eye.    Jaws of the male of equal length anteriorly;
teeth of moderate strength, four in each intermaxillary, twenty in each maxillary.    Length
of the pectoral less than that of the head, much more than half the distance between its root
and that of the ventral; *the base of the pectoral is entirely free, and not overlapped by the gill-
cover apparatus; the nostrils are situated immediately before the eye; the posterior is the wider, and
the cutaneous bridge between the two is not developed into a flap.*    The scales are thin and small,
those on the back rudimentary and hidden in the skin.    The colour on the sides of the back
is a dark sea-green, passing into blackish on the back, on the greater part of the dorsal and
caudal.    Sides with a slight silvery shade, passing into a beautiful deep red on the belly.
Pectoral greenish, passing into reddish posteriorly, the upper margin being white; ventral red,
with white outer margin, and with a blackish shade within the margin; anal reddish, with a
blackish shade over the whole of the middle, and with white anterior margin; sides of the
head silvery, lower parts minutely dotted with black."    I may remark that the white margins
of the pectoral, anal, and ventral fins are very conspicuous in living specimens of these Charr
as seen when swimming in the water.

I am indebted to my friend Mr. T. J. Moore, Curator of the Museum, Liverpool, for a
female specimen, eleven and a half inches long; and to Mr. John Parnaby for a male specimen of the same length.    Perhaps this 's about the ordinary size, but I have seen specimens
in Mr. Parnaby's tanks which measured as much as seventeen inches in length.    One specimen of about this size had been in confinement eight years; it seemed in good health, but
was blind.

Charr love cold water; which, for their successful breeding, should not exceed a temperature of 37° Fahr.

The fin-ray formula is

> Dorsal 12—13.
> Pectoral 13—14.
> Ventral 9—10.
> Anal 12.

*Order IV.*
*PHYSOSTOMI.*

*Family*
*SALMONIDÆ.*
*Sub-generic Group*—SALVELINI.

## COLE'S CHARR.

*(Salmo colii.)*

| | |
|---|---|
| *Salmo colii, Charr of Lough Eske,* | GÜNTHER, Proc. Zool. Soc. 1863, p. 12, pl. 11; Cat. p. 138. |
| *Cole's Charr, Enniskillin Charr,* | COUCH, Fish. Brit. Isl. iv. p. 269, pl. 225. |

THIS is one of the smallest, if not the smallest of the British Charrs. I am indebted to Mr. Thomas Brooke, of the Castle, Lough Eske, as well as to Mr. Arthur R. Wallace, of Dublin, for several specimens of this fish, received in November, 1878. Mr. Wallace tells me that he has occasionally taken this Charr with the artificial fly, as when they come from the deep water towards the shore as the spawning season approaches they show in small shoals on the top of the water, somewhat like Mackerel. This species is mature when about five or six inches in length; none of the specimens so obligingly sent to me from Lough Eske exceeded eight inches, and according to inquiries made by the Earl of Enniskillin it never attains to a greater size.

The only known localities for this Charr are the lakes of Eske and Dan. "Lough Eske (Eske or Yesk meaning Fish)," writes Mr. Brooke, whose family have resided near the lake for more than two centuries, "was the crater of an extinct volcano, as suggested by Dr. Wilde, of Dublin; a high mountain range runs close to the north-east shores. In the season Salmon, White Trout (*S. trutta*), and the Common Lake Trout are in abundance. The Commissioners of Fisheries have decided that the Charr of Lough Eske are the *Salmo alpinus*, thus placing them in the same Act as Salmon; so that, except for scientific purposes, we are not permitted to take them after August. Formerly, in the months of October and November, the fish were taken in large quantities by the country people, without any apparent diminution of their number. Now, at the permitted season of fishing, they remain in such deep waters that the people have not nets sufficiently large to take them."—(*Proc. Zool. Soc.* 1865, p. 14.) The Salmon Acts are now applicable to all the species of Charr, which, so long as they continue in force as at present, can never furnish food supply to the people. The extension of the Salmon Acts to Charr is, I think, a great mistake. The only time—and that time is of short duration—when Charr can be taken in any numbers, is in October and November, when they leave their deep-water haunts for the shallower parts of the lakes. The destructive agency of man, limited as it was to one or two month's duration, could have but little effect in causing a diminution of the species, in the extensive depths of our great lakes, which for five sixths of the year provide safe and unassailable harbour.

The trivial name assigned to this species is intended as a mark of respect to the Earl of Enniskillin, whose family name is Cole, to whom zoological science is considerably indebted for many interesting specimens of natural history which may now be seen in the British Museum. I have to thank the same nobleman for writing me a letter containing information which proved of value to me on my visit to Ireland in July, 1878. It is much to be regretted that the Earl has now become so blind that he is quite unable to procure specimens of fish as he once was able to do, both for Dr. Günther and Mr. Couch, in times gone by.

The only localities for this species given by Günther are Lough Eske, County Donegal, and Lough Dan in the county of Wicklow.

The following is a description of a male specimen I received on the 30th. of October, 1878:—Total length, from end of snout to bifurcation of the caudal fin, eight inches and a half; greatest depth one inch and seven eighths; length of head one inch seven eighths; maxillary rather feeble, extending to the posterior orbit; pectoral fin free from the operculum, acutely pointed, inner margin streaked with vermilion, length one inch and a quarter, considerably shorter than the head; ventral fin red, with distinct outer white margin; anal reddish, with outer white margin; adipose slightly tinged with red; tail deeply incised, lobes pointed and of a reddish tinge; eye large; scales small. Colour of the head deep olive black; back dark, with several small inconspicuous round Salmon-coloured spots above the lateral line; spots below lateral line more distinct; sides brownish pink, or deep roseate hue over silver; under part of jaws whitish; gill-covers somewhat silvery; belly a delicate pink; scales small, but conspicuous. In this specimen the dark parr marks characteristic of the young of the Salmonidæ were visible.

The fin-ray formula is

Dorsal 14.
Pectoral 13.
Ventral 9.
Anal 12.

*Salmo colii* is readily distinguishable from *S. grayi* by the comparative shortness of the pectoral fin.

---

<table>
<tr><td>*Order IV.*<br>*PHYSOSTOMI.*</td><td>*Family*<br>*SALMONIDÆ.*<br>*Sub-generic Group*—SALVELINI.</td></tr>
</table>

## GRAY'S CHARR.

*( Salmo grayi.)*

| | |
|---|---|
| *Salmo umbla,* | THOMPSON, An. and Mag. Nat. Hist. 1840, vol. vi. p. 439; Nat. Hist. of Ireland, iv. p. 160. |
| *Salmo grayi, The Fresh-water Herring of Lough Melvin,* | GÜNTHER, Proc. Zool. Soc. 1862, p. 51; Cat. vi. p. 136. |
| *Gray's Charr,* | COUCH, Fish. Brit. Isls. iv. p. 267, pl. 224. |

I AM indebted to Mr. Alexander Scott, of Garrison, Lough Melvin, for several excellent specimens, both male and female, of this beautiful Charr. They were caught in the month of November; the males had not parted with all their milt, and in the ovaries of the females a few eggs still remained. Little is known of the life history of this species; it appears that the female matures early, and when only five inches long has fully developed eggs of the size of a pea. These fish were known to Thompson, who referred the species to the *Salmo umbla*, Linnæus, and *S. salvelinus* of Donovan. Dr. Günther, however, has clearly shown that the species is distinct, and he named it after the late kind-hearted Dr. Gray, of the British Museum. When Günther published his account of this species in the Zoological Society's Proceedings, the female fish was known only by a short notice of Mr. Thompson. I received six female specimens nearly all with a few ova within them, on the 29th. of November, 1878, from Mr. Scott; the ova I examined were two lines in diameter. On the 19th. of November, I received from the same source, five specimens which proved to be all males. Of the young of this species I believe nothing is known. Like the other kinds of Charr, the Melvin species is an inhabitant of the deep parts of the lake; a few are now and then caught with a fly in the summer months, but little is seen of them until their spawning instincts lead them to seek the shallower parts of the lake, at which time they have been taken in cartloads. Mr. Scott had considerable difficulty in procuring me the specimens; he had to send to a man at the other end of the lake, who, owing to the storms, had great trouble in setting his nets.

The following is a description of a male specimen received by me from Lough Melvin on the 19th. of November. Total length ten inches and three quarters; greatest depth two inches and three quarters; length of head two inches and a quarter; pectoral fin two inches and a quarter, not covered by the operculum; greatest height of dorsal one inch and seven eighths; length of ventral and anal one and five eighths; length of the pointed lobes of the caudal fin two inches and one eighth, shortest caudal ray one inch. Maxillary feeble, extending to the posterior orbit; teeth small. In colour the head is brown; shoulders and back glossy purplish brown down to the lateral line, which rises from the top of the gill-cover, slightly descending, then straight to the middle of the caudal fin, towards which the brown changes to silvery; belly delicate roseate. Above the lateral line there are a number of very small round pink spots, very indistinct. Below lateral line these Salmon-coloured spots are larger and more distinct. Eye large; irides white; præoperculum crescent shaped, rounding off into a lower limb; suboperculum extending beyond operculum; dorsal fin brown; inner base of pectoral tinged with red; ventral reddish brown, inner rays red; anal brown; tail brown, with tinge of olive. Adipose fin membranous, brown; pectoral acutely pointed, a little longer than the head in some examples, and extending as far as, or even slightly beyond the origin of the dorsal fin. I can discover no difference externally in the female from the male of the same size, and caught about the same time. This is a beautiful fish, both in delicacy of colouring and in symmetry of form; the scales are more conspicuous than in other species of Charr. Though somewhat similar, both in form and colour, to Cole's Charr, the species last described, it is readily distinguished from it by the excessive length of the pointed pectoral fin, which in Cole's fish does not nearly equal the length of the head; there is another important difference in the form of the pyloric cæca: in Gray's Charr, the specimen before me, these appendages measure about three eighths of an inch; in Cole's they are about one eighth of an inch, some of them being merely small cylindrical capsules.

The fin-ray formula is

Dorsal 13.
Pectoral 13.
Ventral 9.
Anal 12.

RIVER SCENE AT PONT-Y-CYFFING.

*Order IV.*
*PHYSOSTOMI.*

*Family*
*SALMONIDÆ.*
*Sub-generic Group*—SALVELINI.

# TORGOCH, OR WELSH CHARR.

### *(Salmo perisii.)*

| | |
|---|---|
| *Torgoch Wallis, Westmorlandis, The Red* | |
| *Charre lacus Winandermere,* | WILLUGHBY, Hist. Pisc. p. 196. |
| *Salmo salvelinus,* | DONOVAN, Brit. Fish. vol. v. pl. 112; JENYNS' Man. p. 428. |
| *The Charr,* | YARRELL, (3rd. ed.) i. p. 241, fig. p. 245. |
| *Salmo cambricus,* | GÜNTHER, Proc. Zool. Soc. 1862, p. 49, pl. 6. |
| *Salmo perisii,* | GÜNTHER, An. and Mag. Nat. Hist. 1865, xv. p. 75; Cat. vi. 133. |
| *Torgoch of Llanberris,* | COUCH, Fish. Brit. Isls. iv. p. 264, pl. 223. |

THE Welsh word Torgoch, from *tor*, "a belly," and *coch*, "red," not unaptly describes this fish, which, as we have seen, has been described by Willughby (born 1635) in his *Historia Piscium.* That naturalist thought that this species of Charr is identical with the Charr of Windermere; but Günther has demonstrated that the two species are distinct. Donovan, who was acquainted with this fish, says it differs from the Charr of Wynandermere, "and can be no other than the true *Salmo salvelinus*," a continental species, from which, however, it is distinct. According to Donovan, the Torgoch, at one time an inhabitant of Llanberris Lake, had disappeared entirely, on account, it was said, of the noxious waters of a neighbouring copper mine flowing into the lake and destroying the brood; in his day this Charr was confined to the waters of Llyn Quellyn, on the west side of Snowdon. "Llyn Quellyn (Cwellyn) is a vast lake of unknown depth, sheltered on one side by an abrupt mountain, which rises immediately out of the water; and in the deep recesses at the base of which the Torgoch is supposed to pass the milder seasons of the year in perfect security." Whatever may have happened about the time of Donovan, the Torgoch is now and has for some time been an inhabitant of the lake of Llanberris. Dr. Günther originally applied the specific name of *cambricus* to this Charr, but on his discovering that the *Salmo cambricus* had already been used by Donovan to denote the Sewen, he changed the name to *perisii*.

Donovan speaks with enthusiasm of the beauty of the Torgoch. It is "of an elegant and somewhat slender shape, the head long and rather pointed, and its colour splendid beyond all example among the indigenous fishes of this country. Nothing can exceed the fervid aspect of its colours when first taken; the scarlet of the belly may be truly said to emulate the glowing redness of the fiery element. The upper part of the head and back is of a deep purplish blue, blending into silvery in approaching the lateral line, beneath which the sides are tinged with yellow, passing into orange, and the orange into fine scarlet as it descends towards the belly; the whole of the back and sides are spotted in a most beautiful manner with fine red; the lower fins are also red, except the first ray of the ventral and anal which are white." Donovan's description on the whole is good, and much better than the figure he gives of this fish.

The Torgoch is a smaller species than that found in Windermere and other North of England lakes, seldom exceeding twelve or thirteen inches in length; though its size may be very probably influenced by food and water, and depends, moreover, on the constitutional vigour of the individual fish. Mr. Mascall, writing in 1835, in *The Magazine of Natural History* for April, says that the males of the Charr of Ennerdale Lake, in Cumberland, are superior in colour to the females. The fish from Ennerdale which I have seen and handled belong not to the Welsh Charr but to the Windermere species; but these Ennerdale individuals appear to grow to a larger size than is attained by the same species in Windermere. If I have not made a mistake, one of these Ennerdale Charr, which I measured on the 25th. of October, 1878, at Troutdale, which had been three years and a half in confinement in a tank, measured as much as twenty-two inches in length. These Charr are said to rise more freely at the fly than the same fish in Windermere. Mr. Parnaby feeds his fish on chopped pieces of horse-flesh, or other procurable food; it is likely that an abundant supply of nutritious food influences their size to a considerable extent.

The Torgoch is found in Llanberris and some other lakes of North Wales; it is not known to occur in the North of England, or in Scotland or Ireland. I give Günther's description, and mark by italics those points in which the Torgoch chiefly differs specifically from its Windermere relative:—"Body slightly compressed and elongate; the length of the head is considerably more than one half of the distance between the snout and the vertical from the origin of the dorsal. Head rather depressed; *interorbital space flat*, its width being less than twice the diameter of the eye; males with the lower jaw longest; teeth of moderate strength; *gill-cover overlapping the root of the pectoral*. Length of the pectoral less than that of the head, much more than one half of the distance between its root and that of the ventral. The nostrils are situated midway between eyeball and end of snout; *the anterior is round, open, surrounded by a membrane, which posteriorly is developed into a small flap entirely covering the smaller oblong posterior nostril*. By this character alone the Torgoch may be distinguished from the Charr (*S. willughbii*), and the Fresh-water Herring (*S. grayi*). The back is sea green, which colour becomes lighter on the sides, assuming a yellowish shade, and gradually passing into the bright red of the lower parts; sides with numerous reddish orange-coloured dots. Pectoral greenish, passing into reddish posteriorly, the upper margin being white; ventral and anal red, with white anterior margin; dorsal and caudal blackish, with broad lighter margins. Cheeks and operculum with numerous black dots."

The number of the rays in the fins are

> Dorsal 13.
> Pectoral 12.
> Ventral 9.
> Anal 12.

---

*Order IV.*
*PHYSOSTOMI.*

*Family*
*SALMONIDÆ.*
*Sub-generic group*—SALVELINI.

##  ALPINE CHARR.

*(Salmo alpinus.)*

| | |
|---|---|
| *Salmo alpinus,* | LIN., Faun. Suec. p. 117, No. 310; Syst. Nat. i. p. 510; NILSS., Skand. Faun. Fisk. p. 426; GÜNTHER, Proc. Zool. Soc. 1863, p. 8; Cat. vi. p. 127. |
| *Salmo umbla,* | PARNELL, Fish. Firth of Forth, Mem. Wern. Soc., vii. p. 308. |
| *Alpine Charr,* | COUCH, Fish. Brit. Isl. iv. p. 272, pl. 226. |

I KNOW nothing whatever of this species beyond having seen specimens in the British Museum. It is an inhabitant of the Scandinavian peninsula and some waters of Scotland. The British Museum Scotch specimens are from Sutherlandshire and Invernesshire, and from Lake Helier in Hoy, Orkneys. Parnell says it is found in many of the lakes of England, Wales, and Scotland, but in all probability he is confusing this species with others. Couch has given a figure and description, as he says, "from undoubted examples of this fish, which he obtained through the kindness of Robert Embleton, Esq., from Loch Grannoch, where or in which neighbourhood alone it has hitherto been found in the United Kingdom." But this is clearly an erroneous statement. Mr. Cholmondeley Pennell mentions his having taken with a fly during a violent snowstorm in July, 1862, from Loch Roy, Invernesshire, a small specimen of a very beautiful Charr, which he thought would prove to be the young of the Northern Charr. This is doubtless the specimen now in the British Museum, presented by Mr. Pennell, who thus proved himself correct in his opinion as to the species. The Scotch specimens are said by Dr. Günther to differ from those of Lapland in some respects. They are considerably smaller in size at the period of its first maturity; the largest British Museum specimen is a mature male eleven inches long; it has a more elongate body than the males from Lapland. "The operculum is as high as long; the pectoral fin terminates at a considerable distance from the vertical from the origin of the dorsal, equals the length of the

TORGOCH     ALPINE CHARR

head without snout, and is contained once and a quarter in the distance between its root and that of the ventral. The females do not differ from the males. The immature specimens have the same short pectorals which are found in the young Lap Charr, but the operculum is much less elongate." With regard to the colouration this species is said not to differ from *S. willughbii;* but immature specimens have the sides silvery, and the red of the lower parts is replaced by a slight tinge of orange-colour.

The fin-ray formula is stated to be

Dorsal 13.
Pectoral 13.
Ventral 10.
Anal 9.

On the Wye.

Order IV.
PHYSOSTOMI.

Family
SALMONIDÆ.
Sub-generic Group—SALVELINI.

# Loch Killin Charr.

## (Salmo killinensis.)

Salmo killinensis,          GÜNTHER, Proc. Zool. Soc. 1865, p. 698, pl. 11; Cat. vi. p. 130.

THIS is a very well characterized species of Charr, first noticed by Thompson in his work on the *Natural History of Ireland* (iv. p. 164), and described by Dr. Günther, who has also given a good figure of this fish in the *Proceedings of the Zoological Society of London*, as quoted above. Thompson writes thus of this fish, "About fifteen miles from Loch Corr is Loch Killin, situated in the pastoral vale of Loch Stratherrick. Three specimens of Charr have thence been brought me. They are remarkably different from the Loch Corr example, are of a clumsy form, have very large fins like the Welsh fish, and are very dull in colour; of a blackish leaden hue throughout the greater part of the sides, the lower portion of which is of a dull yellow, no red appearing anywhere. So different indeed is this fish from the Charr of the neighbouring localities, that it is believed by the people resident about Loch Killin to be a species peculiar to their lake, and hence bears another name—'Haddy' being strangely enough bestowed upon it. This fish is only taken when spawning, but then in great quantities, either with nets or a number of fish-hooks tied together, with their points directed different ways. Those, unbaited, are drawn through the water where the fish are congregated in such numbers that they are brought up impaled on the hooks. The largest of my specimens is sixteen inches in length, and others of similar size were brought to my friend at the same time—on the 26th. or 27th. of September, when about a cart-load of them was taken. The flesh of some was white and soft. They contained ova the size of peas. On dissection my specimens were found to be male and female. Externally the sex could not have been told with certainty. Their stomach and intestines were empty. This fish bears a resemblance to the Lough Melvin Charr, but differs from it in some characters."

Dr. Günther speaks of this Charr as one of most remarkable form, which in the excessive development of its fins, differs from all the other species known to him from Great Britain and the continent of Europe. "Only *Salmo grayi* from Ireland, and *S. nivalis* from Iceland approach it in the length of the pectorals; but the former cannot well be confounded with it, having much larger scales, and the body compressed and rather elevated; from the latter it differs in several points of minor importance, and especially in the increased number of pyloric appendages, which besides are extremely narrow and slender. For specimens of this Charr I am indebted to Mr. Gould, to whom they were sent by Mr. Hanbury Barclay, and who informs me that they inhabit a very retired loch in Invernesshire, Loch Killin, about two thousand feet above the level of the sea. They are caught only in September and October, when they approach the edge of the lake to spawn."—(*Proc. Zool. Soc.*, 1865, p. 698.)

The only specimens of this interesting Charr that I have seen are those in the British Museum; and through the kindness of Dr. Günther I have had an opportunity of examining them. It would be impossible to confuse this well marked fish with any other known species. Günther thus describes it:—"Head and body thick, but slightly compressed; the greatest depth of the body equals the length of the head, and is two ninths of the total length (to the extremity of the central caudal rays). The length of the head is little more than one half of the distance between the snout and the vertical from the origin of the dorsal fin. The lower jaw is rather shorter than the upper; and the maxillary extends scarcely beyond the hind margin of the orbit in adult males. Teeth very small. Snout obtuse; eye of moderate size, much shorter than the snout, and about half the width of the interorbital space. Suboperculum very short and high. Fins excessively developed; pectoral not much shorter than the head; dorsal long and high, the longest ray being nearly as long as the head (without snout), or shorter than the pectoral fin. The ventral fin extends nearly to the vent; caudal very broad, slightly emarginate. Head, upper parts and fins brownish black; lower with an orange-coloured tinge in the male; sides with very small light inconspicuous spots. Anterior margins of the lower fins white or light orange coloured." The specimens are from ten to fifteen inches long.

The fin-ray formula is

Dorsal 14—15.
Pectoral 13.
Ventral 9.
Anal 13.

The illustration was taken from a specimen in the British Museum which was nearly fourteen inches long.

LOCH KILLIN CHARR

Dr. Günther sums up the results of his investigations with respect to the British Charrs as follows.   He shows that

1. Three very distinct species of Charrs are found in Great Britain, namely:—*S. willughbii* in the Lake of Windermere and in Loch Bruiach; *S. perisii* in Wales; and *S. alpinus* in certain parts of Scotland.
2. That those three species differ by most constant characters from the *S. umbla* and *S. salvelinus* of the Continent; but that *S. alpinus* of Scotland is closely related to the *S. alpinus* of Lapland, differing merely by its smaller size when first attaining to maturity, and by the number of vertebræ, there being sixty-two in the Scandinavian variety and fifty-nine in the Scottish.
3. That Iceland is inhabited by a distinct species *(S. nivalis)*.
4. That the Charrs of Ireland form a separate group by themselves, distinguished by the feeble development of their dentition; and that the Charr of Lough Melvin *(S. grayi)* is a distinct species from that of Lough Eske and Lough Dan *(S. colii)*.

The following synopsis of the species, showing *a few* of the principal characters by which the *mature* individuals of the different species are distinguished, will be found useful.

    *I.   Jaws well developed; teeth of moderate size.*

A. The length of the pectoral fin in the mature fish less than one half of the distance between the roots of the pectoral and ventral fins.
1. Thirteen dorsal rays. Intermaxillary teeth much stronger than those of the maxillary. L. lat. 185. Lower parts silvery. *S. umbla.*
2. Fourteen dorsal rays. Intermaxillary and maxillary teeth equal in strength. L. lat. 190. Lower parts red. *S. salvelinus.*

B. The length of the pectoral fin in the mature fish, more than, or equal to, one half of the distance between the roots of the pectoral and ventral fins.
1. The height of the body one fifth or one sixth of the total length; the height of the dorsal fin three fifths or one half of the length of the head. L. lat. 195—200. *S. alpinus.*
2. The height of the body one fifth of the total length; the height of the dorsal fin equals the length of the head, without snout. L. lat. 190. The gill-cover not overlapping the root of the pectoral. *S. nivalis.*
3. The height of the body one fifth or one sixth of the total length; the height of the dorsal fin two thirds of the length of the head. L. lat. 170. The gill-cover overlapping the root of the pectoral. *S. perisii.*
4. The height of the body one fourth of the total length; the height of the dorsal fin equals the length of the head, without snout. L. lat. 165. The gill-cover not overlapping the root of the pectoral. *S. willughbii.*

    *II.   Lower jaw very feeble; teeth minute.*

1. The pectoral extending to or beyond the origin of the dorsal fin. *S. grayi.*
2. The pectoral terminating at a considerable distance from the origin of the dorsal fin. *S. colii.*

Of course it is possible that other and hitherto undescribed species of Charr, besides the species already known, may be found to inhabit the lakes of this country, but it is to be feared that the operation of the Salmon Acts will greatly diminish the chances of further discoveries in this line.

ON THE DART, LOVER'S LEAP.

Order IV.
PHYSOSTOMI.

Family
SALMONIDÆ.
Sub-generic group—SALVELINI.

# GRAYLING.

*(Thymallus vulgaris.)*

| | |
|---|---|
| THYMALLOS, | ÆLIAN, Nat. Anim. xiv. c. 22, ed. Jacobs. |
| *Thymallus seu Thymus,* | GESNER, de Aquat. p. 978; WILLUGHBY, Hist. Pisc. p. 187. |
| *Coregonus maxilla superiore longiore,* | ARTEDI, Spec. Pisc. p. 20, No. 3. |
| *Salmo thymallus,* | LIN., Sys. Nat. i. p. 512; DONOVAN, Brit. Fish. iv. pl. 88. |
| *Coregonus thymallus,* | LACÉP., v. p. 254; FLEM., Brit. An. p. 181. |
| *Thymallus vulgaris,* | YARRELL, ii. p. 136; JENYNS, Man. p. 430; SIEBOLD, Süsserwasserf. p. 267; GÜNTHER's Cat. vi. p. 200. |
| *Grayling Salmon,* | PENNANT, Brit. Zool. iii. p. 414, ed. 1812. |
| *Grayling or Umber,* | WALTON, Compl. Angl.; SIR HUMPHRY DAVY, Salmonia; COUCH, Fish. Brit. Isl. iv. p. 280, pl. 228. |

*Characters of the Genus* THYMALLUS.—"Body covered with scales of moderate size. Cleft of the mouth small; maxillary short, broad, scarcely extending beyond the front margin of the orbit. Small teeth in the jaw bones, on the head of the vomer and the palatines; none on the tongue. Dorsal fin long, many rayed; caudal forked. Pseudobranchiæ well developed; air-bladder very large. Stomach horse-shoe-shaped, pyloric appendages rather numerous. Temperate parts of the Northern Hemisphere."—GÜNTHER.

THE only classical authors who have mentioned the Grayling are Ælian, to whom this fish was known under the name of *Thumallus*, and Ausonius, who appears to allude to this fish in his tenth Idyll, under the name of *Umbra*.

"Effugiensque oculos celeri levis Umbra natatu." (90.)

Ælian gives the following account of the Grayling:—"The river Ticinus, in Italy, produces the fish called Thymallus; it is about a cubit in length; in appearance it partly resembles the *labrax* (Sea Perch) and the *cephalus* (Grey Mullet). When captured it has a remarkable odour—not that other kinds are destitute of a fishy smell—so that you would say you had in your hands a freshly-gathered piece of thyme. In fact if you did not see the fish you would imagine you had the plant, which is the chief food of bees—whence the fish takes its name—in your hands, so fragrant is the smell. It is taken easily in a net, but not with a bait and hook, whether the bait be the fat of a pig, or a *serphus* (some two-winged fly), or a shell-fish (Xημη), or the entrail of another fish, or the neck of a strombus. It is taken only by a small gnat, the troublesome little beast, which day and night is a nuisance to men on account of its biting and buzzing: with this, which is the only food of which it is fond, is the Thymallus captured."

The association of the odour of thyme with the Grayling, noticed by Ælian, has been kept up ever since his time. It is referred to by Izaak Walton, who says, "Some think that he feeds on water-thyme, and smells of it at his first taking out of the water; and they may think so with as good reason as we do that our Smelts smell like violets at their first being caught, which I think is a truth." Walton also refers to the opinion of St. Ambrose—"Much more might be said of this fish's taste and smell; but I shall only tell you that St. Ambrose, the glorious Bishop of Milan, who lived when the Church kept fasting days, calls him the flower-fish, or flower of fishes, and that he was so far in love with him, that he would not let him pass without the honour of a long discourse." Willughby thinks that more modern writers are simply following in the wake of the ancients; he says Salvianus could detect no thyme flavour about the Grayling, but thinks the Grayling has a sweeter odour about it than fish in general. Pennant speaks of the "imaginary scent" like thyme, but he never could perceive any particular smell about the Grayling. Mr. Cholmondeley Pennell thinks that the odour rather resembles that of a cucumber than of thyme. Mr. Francis Francis writes, "he has a peculiar and strong fragrance when handled, which is said to be like thyme, and is so to some little extent." I must place myself among the number of persons who, as Mr. Manley says, "utterly fail to distinguish this thymy fragrance" about the Grayling; but I will not deny that to the olfactory nerves of some people, the association of the odour of this plant with the Grayling may be sufficiently striking.

The Grayling is found in the fresh waters of Central and Northern Europe, but though abundant in some streams, it is a local fish, much more so than the Common Trout. As to English localities, I cannot quote a better authority than Mr. Francis Francis, who justly has a very high opinion of the Grayling. "If the Trout," he says, "be the gentleman of the streams, the Grayling is certainly the lady." The rivers mentioned by Mr. Francis as containing these fish, are the Teme, the Lugg, and the Wye, with their tributaries wherever they are found to suit them; the Ure and the Swale, in Yorkshire. Of the Derbyshire streams, the Wye, Derwent, and the Dove. The Grayling is found in the Hampshire rivers, the Avon, Itchin, and Test, where it runs to a large size; Mr. Francis has taken Grayling, both in the Itchin and Test, up to four pounds weight. This fish has been brought into the Clyde, where it has thriven well; it is said to be increasing rapidly in the Tweed. "But there are very many other rivers—the tributaries of the Thames—where it could be naturalized; the

GRAYLING

GWYNIAD

VENDACE

two Colnes, the Windrush, parts of the Mole, the Darent, the Wey, the Brent, and others
—for it is not every river which will suit the Grayling; whereas almost any river, if not
already overrun with coarse fish, will suit the Trout, if there are any shallows at all for it
to spawn on. Grayling love deep eddies and quiet reaches, but they also like sharp and rapid
shallows—a weedy shallow which ends in a deep safe eddy, with a gravelly bottom, and loamy
hollowed-out banks, being the especial abiding-place of Grayling; and where these alternate
with sharp bends full of nooks and corners of refuge, the stream will suit Grayling to admiration."—(*Book on Angling*, p. 299—300.)

The spawning season of the Grayling is different from that of the *Salmonidæ* generally:
for it occurs in April and May; so that the Grayling is in the best condition about the time
when the Trout is in its worst, that is in October and November. Mr. Francis says the Grayling
should not be taken till August. At spawning time, and for long after, "the fish is scarcely
eatable, and until August is not worth a rush. Cut a Grayling in June and cut one in
November, and the difference is most remarkable. Although in June he may be a handsome
shaped and bright-looking fish, his play is unusually dull, and his flesh like that of an indifferent roach, soft, spongy, and flavourless. In November he has a blue bloom on him like
a rich plum......his black spots contrast brilliantly with the dazzling silver of his belly; and
as for his flesh, it is as hard, firm, and flaky, as a Trout's when in the best condition." Mr.
Francis is amusingly angry with any angler who would take Grayling in the early summer
months. "Throw him in again, then, brother fisherman, till at least the middle of July be
turned. Whereas, if you do take him in May or June, listen to my solemn anathema, and
let it lie heavy on your soul. May your rod-top smash at the ferrule, and the brazing stick
in tight, at the commencement of your 'crack day of the season,' and may you be unable to
beg, buy, borrow, or steal another rod within twenty miles. May you travel hundreds of
miles into a strange country, find the river in splendid ply, and then discover that you have
left your reel at home.......And now go and catch your Grayling in May and June, and much
good may they do you. I hope you'll eat 'em,—all of them—that's all; and that your wife
will have locked up the brandy, and gone out for a day or two; and please send for Dr.
Francis to administer consolation. Ha! ho! I hate a fisherman who slaughters kelts and ill-
conditioned fish, more than any other species of poacher going."—(P. 298.)

The Grayling passes its time entirely in fresh water, and I cannot understand how
Donovan, whose figure, bad as it is, shows itself to be this fish, says it is migratory, "passing
the winter season in the open sea, and the summer in fresh water."

The food of the Grayling consists of insects and their larvæ, small shell-fish (molluscs),
crustacea, etc. In a specimen I examined I found the stomach full of the *Ancyclus fluviatilis*.
I notice that Sir Humphry Davy states that its stomach "is very thick, not unlike that of
a Charr or Gillaroo Trout, and contains flies, gravel, and larvæ with their cases."—(*Salmonia*,
p. 183, Murray, 1869.) This is contrary to my experience; for in the Charr and Grayling the
walls of the stomach are not abnormally thick.

The Grayling of the Teme, near Ludlow, have the reputation of being the finest in
England. The scenery at Downton Castle, where Sir Humphry Davy wrote his charming
*Salmonia*, and where the river Teme flows, is remarkably beautiful. My own associations here,
however, are connected, not with the Grayling of that picturesque stream, but with the various
beautiful and curious, and some rare, funguses, found in the neighbourhood. Downton is a
favourite "meet" for the Woolhope Natural History Field Club, and many a pleasant day
I have had with the members of it. As I have gazed into the Teme, on these fungus
expeditions, in October, I have often thought how I should enjoy a day's fly-fishing, and
handle the Teme Grayling, in a month in which they are in the primest condition. "Just
taken out of the water," says Mr. Pennell, "the Grayling is certainly one of the most beautiful fish that can be imagined. At this time, the back is of a deep purple colour, with small

dark irregular spots on the sides; the stomach is brilliantly white, with a fringe or lacing of gold; and the tail, pectoral, and ventral fins, are of a rich purplish tint. The dorsal fin is very large—almost disproportionally so—and is covered with scarlet spots and wavy lines, upon a dark ground of reddish brown. The little velvet back fin, near the tail, is also dark brown or purple, and the whole body is shot with violet, copper, and blue reflections, when seen in different lights. Properly to appreciate this colouring, the fish should be laid horizontally upon the hand, to be looked at, in which position its varied tinting is seen to the greatest advantage."—(*Angler Naturalist*, p. 357.)

Grayling are taken like Trout with the artificial fly, but having tender mouths they often break away, so that a light hand is very necessary, if you would be successful. Mr. Francis says that "the most slaughtering way of fishing for Grayling is with the grasshopper. The grasshopper, so called, is not a grasshopper at all, and though actually an artificial bait, in no wise resembles a grasshopper; why it should have been called a grasshopper, any more than a gooseberry, which it much more resembles, I cannot conceive. No matter: this is the grasshopper. Take a No. 5 or 6 Trout-hook; lap round the shank some lead, enough to sink it pretty quickly; over this wind Berlin wool of various colours, chiefly green, with a few turns of yellow or red, or both. The method in which this curious lure is employed at Leintwardine, which is perhaps the head-quarters of it, and where I have killed many fine Grayling with it, is as follows:—Having saved as long into the winter as possible, a good store of gentles or maggots, you stick on the hook which protrudes from the green monstrosity, a good bunch of gentles, six or seven perhaps. Then dropping the bait into the stream to be fished, in order to see the depth, you fix, as if it was a float on the line, a bit of sliding quill. This is simply used to let you know how deep your bait is down, and when it touches the bottom; without it you could form no idea. Then coming to the pool, stream, or eddy, you cast in just clear of the heavy stream, letting the bait go to the bottom, and as soon as it touches, jerking it up and letting drop again in short jumps, and drawing it hither and thither while doing so, so as to search the entire water thoroughly, or all such parts of it as are likely to hold fish. You strike at every touch, tap, or nibble, that you may feel; and as the tackle is strong and hook big, you do not lose many fish when once fairly hooked. It is, indeed, a most destructive method, and kills all the largest and best fish; and it ought only to be tolerated when the Grayling get so far ahead as to want thinning down pretty freely, as is the case oftentimes at Leintwardine. To give some idea of the deadly nature of this bait on some streams, I have known instances where by the use of it large twenty-five or thirty pounds' baskets have been filled and emptied three times over, in one day's fishing, by a single rod. Its use is confined chiefly to the Worcester and Shropshire streams,—the tributaries of the Severn in fact."—(*Book on Angling*, p. 295—296.)

Unlike Trout, the Grayling never jumps out of the water, is unable to surmount obstructions or stem very rapid torrents, and is more prone to descend than to ascend the stream. Grayling rarely exceed three pounds in weight, though they are said to have been caught weighing four or even five pounds. In this country these fish are non-migratory, being permanent residents of fresh water all the year round; but in colder latitudes, as in Scandinavia, the Grayling is found in the North Sea, Cattegat, and Baltic, according to Nilsson; in Lapland they are taken in the high fell lakes, and are said to weigh as much as eight or nine pounds. Some of the Swedish fish remain all the year in fresh water, and some are found in the Baltic at all seasons. Sir H. Davy found that in this country Grayling will not live in brackish water, but he allows that in many successive generations animals may be fitted to bear changes which would have destroyed their progenitors. The northern species, the *Salmo thymallus* of Linnæus and Bloch, the *Thymallus vulgaris* of Nilsson, appears to be identical with our British species.

Grayling are said to grow rapidly, and to attain to the size of four or five inches in a few months' time.　Sir Humphry Davy (*Salmonia*, p. 188) goes so far as to believe that Grayling hatched in May and June become in September or October of the same year nine or ten inches long, and to weigh from five ounces to half a pound.　This I feel sure is a mistake.　Such fish would surely be quite a year old.　Grayling ova as well as fry may, I believe, be had from Mr. Parnaby, of Troutdale Fishery, Keswick, in the season.

The fin-ray formula in the Grayling is

Dorsal 2o— 23.
Pectoral 16.
Ventral 10—11.
Anal 13—16.

The specimen which supplied the illustration was caught by myself with a fly in the Severn ; it is a male fish.

---

*Order IV.*
*PHYSOSTOMI.*

*Family*
*SALMONIDÆ.*
*Sub-generic Group*—SALVELINI.

# GWYNIAD.

### *(Coregonus clupeoides.)*

| | |
|---|---|
| *Guiniad Wallis, piscis lacus' Balensis,* | WILLUGHBY, Hist. Pisc. p. 183. |
| *Gwyniad Salmon,* | PENNANT, Brit. Zool. iv. p. 419, ed. 1812, pl. 73. |
| *Coregonus clupeoides,* | LACÉP., v. p. 698; GÜNTHER's Cat. vi. p. 188. |
| *Coregonus lacepedei,* | PARNELL, Ann. and Mag. Nat. Hist. 1838, i. p. 162; YARRELL, ii. p. 151; COUCH, Fish. Brit. Isl. iv. p. 295, pl. 232. |
| *Coregonus lavaretus,* | FLEM., Brit. An. p. 182; JENYNS' Man. p. 431. |
| *Gwyniad, Schelly (Ullswater),* | YARRELL, ii. p. 142. |
| *Guiniad,* | COUCH, Fish. Brit. Isl. iv. p. 286, pl. 229. |

*Characters of the Genus* COREGONUS.—"Body covered with scales of moderate size. Cleft of the mouth small; maxillary broad, short or of moderate length, not extending behind the orbit. Teeth, if present, extremely minute, and deciduous. Dorsal fin of moderate length; caudal deeply forked. Pseudobranchiæ well developed; air-bladder very large. Stomach horse-shoe-shaped; pyloric appendages extremely numerous. Ova small."—GÜNTHER.

THE fishes belonging to the genus *Coregonus* are inhabitants of the northern parts of temperate Europe, Asia, and North America.　The three British species are found only in lakes, but there are many foreign kinds which periodically ascend from the sea, especially from the Arctic Ocean.

According to Dr. Günther the species of this genus are not less numerous than those of *Salmo*, some having a very extended geographical range, whilst others are confined to very limited localities.　They are less subject to variation than the Trout, and therefore more easily characterized and distinguished.　"Hence we find that naturalists who look with distrust on the different species of *Salmo* are quite ready to admit those of *Coregonus*.　The characters which are the most reliable are the shape of the snout, the development of the maxillary, the form of the supplemental bone of the maxillary, the length of the mandible, the height of the body and tail, the position of the dorsal, and the number of scales and vertebræ."

The Gwyniad, which in Welsh denotes "making white," "a white fish," from *gwyn*, "white," is a good name for this bright silvery fish. It is mentioned by Willughby, who seems to have thought that it is identical with *S. fera* (Cuvier and Valenc.) of the great lakes of Switzerland, the Tyrol, etc., a larger species than any of our British species. Willughby noticed the great number of cæcal appendages in the Gwyniad, its gregarious habits, and its whiteness. As to locality he says, "Invenitur in lacu *Pimblemeer* dicto, proprie oppidum *Bala*, in comitatu *Merionethensi Walliæ*, non autem in fluvio *Dea* qui eum perfluit." —(P. 184.) He is correct in identifying this fish with the *Schelly* of Cumberland, "qui in lacu Hulswater non procul ab oppido *Pereth* (Penrith) invenitur." Willughby mentions its similarity in form to a Herring, which is also true of the Irish species, the Pollan.

I owe much to the kindness of Sir Watkin Williams Wynn, Bart., who, with his well-known willingness to be of service, placed his pretty little steam-launch (which, by the way, bears the name of "Gwyniad,") at my disposal on the 28th. of September, 1878, for the express purpose of procuring me specimens of this Bala fish. I also have to thank Mr. Owen Wynne and Mr. Bigge for their kindness in accompanying me, and for the enjoyment of a very pleasant day with the nets on that beautiful lake. It is true that we succeeded in capturing only one Gwyniad, though we worked for a great part of the day;* nevertheless, it was an interesting sight to behold this brilliantly shining specimen, iridescent with the most delicate colours, as it lay on the grass just after it was taken out of the water. As these fish swim in shoals, there is often great uncertainty as to their falling within the parts of the lake swept by the net.

This fish, under the name of *Schelly* (from the scales), occurs, as has been said, in Ullswater, and in Haweswater. In Scotland it is found in Loch Lomond, where it is called a Powen. I believe the Gwyniad is still numerous in Ullswater. Pennant writes that he was informed, that during one day in the summer as many as seven or eight thousand were caught at one draught of the net. The Gwyniad is a delicate fish, and dies soon after it is taken out of the water. The flesh is said to be rather dry and insipid; but the poorer classes, who consider them as Fresh-water Herrings, preserve them with salt, and thus use them as food; indeed they are very bad-keeping fish, like the salt-water Herring, properly so called. The spawning time is towards the end of the year; the ordinary size is from ten to twelve inches in length. Little is known with respect to the habits of this fish; I believe it is not known what places they select for spawning, nor is there any published account of that proceeding. They do not run up the rivers out of the lakes for this purpose, but probably approach the shores, but whether the ova are deposited in the gravel or on water-weeds I do not know. Bala Lake is or was known by the names of Pemble-Mere, and the Welsh Llyn Tegid, meaning "fair lake,"—and rightly is it so called. "It has long ago been observed in Camden,". says Pennant, (*Brit. Zool.* iv. p. 421, ed. 1812,) "that these fish (Gwyniad) never wander into the Dee, or the Salmon ever ventures into the Lake; this must be allowed to be generally the case, but by accident the first have been known to stray as far as Llandrillo, six miles down the river, and a Salmon has now and then been found trespassing in the Lake."†

The specimen I procured from Bala is small, being six inches and a half in length, without the tail; depth of body one inch and five eighths; length of the head one inch and three eighths; snout truncated; upper jaw slightly longer than lower; the maxillary is broad

---

\* We secured, however, some Pike in glorious condition, quite pictures to behold.

† That Salmon sometimes enter Bala Lake from the Dee is certain. On my visit on the 28th. of September, one splendid female Salmon in spawning colours was taken out of the lake.

and flat to about the anterior margin of the eye; pectoral pointed, its length is more than half the distance between its base and that of the ventral fin. The colour above lateral line a beautiful glossy brown, slightly tinged with delicate pink; iridescent and silvery below lateral line; belly pure white; gill-cover bright silvery; eye large, irides white; tail deeply incised.

The fin-ray formula in this species—

Dorsal 14—15.
Anal 13—16.

---

*Order IV.*
*PHYSOSTOMI.*

*Family*
*SALMONIDÆ.*
*Sub-generic Group*—Salvelini.

# VENDACE.

(*Coregonus vandesius.*)

| | |
|---|---|
| *Vandesius et Gevandesius,* | Sibbald, Scotia Illustrata p. 26. |
| *Vangis* and *Juvangis of Loch Maben,* | Pennant, Brit. Zool. iii. p. 420, ed. 1812. |
| *Vendace,* | Knox, Transact. Roy. Soc. Ed. xii. p. 503; Yarrell, ii. p. 146; Couch, Fish. Brit. Isl. iv. p. 289, pl. 230. |
| *Coregonus marænula,* | Jenyns' Man. p. 432. |
| *Coregonus willughbii,* | Jardine's Illust. Scot. Salm. pl. 6; Yarrell, ii. p. 146. |
| *Coregonus vandesius,* | Richardson, Faun. Bor-Amer. iii. p. 213; Günther's Cat. vi. p. 194. |

THE only recorded locality for the Vendace is, I believe, Loch Maben, in Dumfriesshire, and the neighbouring waters. Sir William Jardine was the first to recognise this fish as a distinct species. His account of it I shall transcribe, as I know nothing of this fish excepting from specimens in the British Museum and in that at Liverpool. "The Vendace is well known to almost every person in the neighbourhood; and if among the lower classes fish should at any time form the subject of conversation, the Vendace is immediately mentioned, and the loch regarded with pride, as possessing something of great curiosity to visitors, and which is thought not to exist elsewhere. The story that it was introduced into these lochs by the unfortunate Mary Queen of Scots, as mentioned by Pennant in his description of the Gwyniad, and it is likely that his information was derived from this vicinity, is still in circulation. That the fish was introduced from some continental lake, I have little doubt;* but would rather attribute the circumstance to some of the religious establishments, which at one time prevailed in the neighbourhood, and which were well known to pay considerable attention both to the table and the cellar. Mary would scarcely prefer a lake so far from even her temporary residence, for the preservation of a luxury of troublesome introduction, and leave her other fishponds destitute of such a delicacy. An idea prevails that this fish, if once taken from the water, will die, and that an immediate return will be of no avail; and it is also believed that it will not exist in any other water except that of the Castle Loch. These are, of course, opinions which have gradually, from different circumstances, gained weight, and have at last

---

* This species is not, I believe, *known to occur* anywhere on the Continent; but one cannot say it does not exist there.

been received as facts. The fish is of extreme delicacy: a circumstance which may have given rise to the first notion; and the introduction of it must have taken place by means of the spawn, the fish themselves, I am confident, could not be transported alive even a few miles. As to the second opinion, they are not confined to the Castle Loch, but are found in several others, some of which have no communication with that where they are thought to be peculiar.

In general habits the Vendace nearly resemble the Gwyniad, and indeed most of the allied species of the genus. They swim in large shoals; and during warm and clear weather retire to the depth of the lakes, apparently sensible of the increased temperature. They are only taken with nets, a proper bait not being yet discovered; and the fact that little excrement is found in their intestines has given rise to another tradition, that they are able to subsist without food. They are most successfully taken during a dull day and sharp breeze, approaching near to the edges of the loch, and swimming in a direction contrary to the wind. They spawn about the commencement of November, and at this time congregate in large shoals, frequently rising to the surface of the water, in the manner of the Common Herring, and making a similar noise by their rise and fall to and from the surface. The sound may be distinctly heard, and the direction of the shoal perceived, during a calm and clear evening. They are very productive. The lochs abound with Pike, of which they are a favourite food; but their quantity seems in no degree to be diminished, notwithstanding that immense numbers must be destroyed. They are considered a great delicacy, resembling the Smelt a good deal in flavour; and though certainly very palatable, the relish may be somewhat heightened by the difficulty of always procuring a supply. During the summer fishing parties are frequent, introducing some stranger friend to the Loch Maben Whitebait; and a club, consisting of between twenty and thirty of the neighbouring gentry, possessing a private net, etc., meet annually in July to enjoy the sport of fishing and feasting upon this luxury." Mr. Yarrell tells us that in the autumn of 1840, when he was staying with Sir William Jardine, he saw some Vendace caught, and partook of some at dinner. He considered "the fish quite entitled to all their character for excellence."

The principal food of the Vendace appears to be the minute crustacea, as the *Entomostraca*, "for feeding on which," Sir William Jardine says, "the structure of the mouth is beautifully adapted." According to Dr. Knox, the females of the Vendace are more numerous as well as larger than the males, often measuring more than eight inches in length, the males being seldom more than seven inches.

To judge from the figure (pl. vi.) which Sir William Jardine has given, the Vendace, when fresh out of the water, must be a most beautiful fish. The specimen he has figured is thus coloured:—The back is olive, a little darker towards the shoulders; dorsal fin olive with pink tinge at the base; adipose fin olive, caudal lighter olive, brownish at base, and much forked. Near the lateral line are some pinkish specks; below lateral line the body is slightly yellowish for a short depth, then white iridescent violet reflections; gill-covers violet and pink; upper part of the pectoral fin tinged with yellow. Anal white, with violet tinge at the base; gill-cover with a violet patch gradually fading away. This species is said to be but little variable in colour. In the Vendace the under jaw is the longest; mouth small; maxillary short, but broad and flat, reaching half way to the eye, and bent. Scales of moderate size, easily detached; the eye is large and prominent.

The fin-ray formula is stated by Dr. Günther to be

Dorsal 11.
Anal 13.
Ventral 11.

I do not know whether the young of the genus *Coregonus* are barred like those of the genera *Salmo* and *Thymallus*.

THE WYE, FROM GOODRICH CASTLE.

<table>
<tr><td>*Order IV.*<br>*PHYSOSTOMI.*</td><td>*Family*<br>*SALMONIDÆ.*<br>*Sub-generic Group*—SALVELINI.</td></tr>
</table>

# POLLAN.

*(Coregonus pollan.)*

| | |
|---|---|
| *Coregonus pollan,* | THOMPSON, Proc. Zool. Soc. for 1835, p. 77; Nat. Hist. of Ireland iv. p. 168; JENYNS' Man. p. 432; YARRELL, ii. p. 156; COUCH, Fish. Brit. Isl. iv. p. 292. pl. 231; GÜNTHER'S Cat. vi. p. 194. |

OF the three British species of *Coregonus*, the Pollan of Ireland is the only one that may be said to have any commercial value. This species was first described by Thompson in the *Proceedings of the Zoological Society*, 1835, and the description reprinted in his *Natural History of Ireland*. "The earliest notice of this species," writes Mr. Thompson, "that I have seen is in Harris' *History of the County of Down*, published in the year 1744, as well as in the statistical surveys of the counties of Armagh and Antrim; it has subsequently been introduced as one of the fishes of Lough Neagh, under the name of Pollan; but as may be expected in works of this nature, little more than its mere existence is mentioned." Large quantities of Pollan are caught during the season by the fishermen in the vicinity of Lough Neagh, but they are not taken in such numbers as formerly, owing, it was told me when at Toome

POWAN

POLLAN

Bridge, to the enormous destruction of the fry of these fish, which a few years ago were caught in nets of small mesh. This, I believe, has been very properly stopped. The fishermen catch the Pollan in different parts of the great Irish lake, and pack them in boxes; they are then brought to Toome Bridge, and conveyed by rail to the coast, whence they find their way to Liverpool, Manchester, and other towns. Thompson mentions the greatest take of these fish he ever remembers as having occurred in September, 1834: it was at the bar mouth, where the river Six-mile Water enters the lake. "At either three or four draughts of the net one hundred and forty hundred (one hundred and twenty-three individuals to the hundred) or seventeen thousand two hundred and twenty fish were taken; at one draught more were captured than the boat could with safety hold, and they had consequently to be emptied on the neighbouring pier. They altogether filled five one-horse carts, and were sold at the spot at the rate of 3s. 4d. a hundred, producing £23 6s. 8d. They are brought in quantities to Belfast, and when the supply is good the cry of "fresh Pollan" prevails even to a greater extent than that of "fresh Herring," though both fishes are in season at the same period of the year."

The Pollan is said to deposit its spawn where the lake presents a hard rocky bottom; this occurs in December. The stomachs of those fish I examined last July contained the remains of the larvæ of insects and some small crustacea. Those which Mr. Thompson examined in June, 1836, were full of the larvæ of various aquatic insects, but chiefly of mature individuals of *Gammarus aquaticus* (fresh-water shrimp); some shells of the genus *Pisidium*, and one of the fry of the Three-spined Stickleback also were found. Besides inhabiting Lough Neagh, the Pollan occurs in Lough Derg, an expansion of the Shannon. Yarrell was supplied with a jar full of Pollan from Lough Erne, in County Fermanagh, by the Earl of Enniskillen; those specimens are said to be deeper in proportion to the length than those from Lough Neagh.

The following is a description of a female specimen I examined on July 11th., 1878:— Total length ten inches and a half; depth two inches and five eighths; length of head two inches; the maxillary, reaching to the middle of the eye, rather broad, but thin and short; præoperculum with distinct lower limb; snout short and obtuse; lateral line distinct, beginning from above the gill-cover, descending for about six scales, then going in a straight line to the middle of the caudal fin, which is deeply incised. Dorsal fin light, tinged with smoke colour, as also the tail; the anal, ventral, and pectoral fins white and immaculate. Colour of head and back bluish brown, the rest of the body bright silvery; pyloric cæca very numerous, densely crowded, covered with fat; the ovaries consisted of two lobes, four inches and five eighths long, of bright orange colour; and the contained ova were about the size of dust-shot. Air-bladder very large; teeth none, or extremely rudimentary. The whole fish was thick and fat, though the intestines were full of *tæniæ*.

The people at Toome and in the neighbourhood ascribe a soporific property to the flesh of the Pollan. "You must move about, Sir," a boatman said to me, "soon after eating them, or they may send you to sleep." Lieutenant-Colonel Masefield and myself had a dish of Pollan fried, and we thought them very fair food; we both thought they resembled in flavour and texture of flesh very good Dace. Neither of us felt inclined to go to sleep after eating them, but then the Colonel is more wide awake than most men.

The size of full-grown adult specimens is about ten to twelve inches long, and I do not think they often attain to a greater length.

The fin-ray formula of the Pollan is

> Dorsal 12—14.
> Pectoral 14.
> Ventral 11—12.
> Anal 12—13.

The specimen figured was taken in a net at Lough Neagh.

# POWAN.

THE fish of Loch Lomond which, under the name of Powen, or Powan, has been thought by some to be a species of *Coregonus* distinct from *C. clupeoides*, or the Gwyniad, appears to be identical with it. Parnell, considering it to be a distinct species, named it after the French naturalist, Lacépède, and this is retained by Yarrell in his second edition. "These fish," says Parnell, "are found in Loch Lomond in great numbers. They are caught from the month of March until September with large drag nets, and occasional instances have occurred in which a few have been taken with a small artificial fly; a minnow or bait they have never been known to touch. Early in the morning and late in the evening large shoals of them are observed approaching the shore in search of food, and rippling the surface of the water with their fins as they proceed. In this respect they resemble in their habits the Vendace of Loch Maben and the salt-water Herring. They are never seen under any circumstances in the middle of the day. From the estimation these fish are held in by the neighbouring inhabitants, they are seldom sent far before they meet with a ready sale, and are entirely unknown in the markets of Glasgow. In the months of August and September they are in the best condition for the table, when they are considered well-flavoured, wholesome, and delicate food. They shed their spawn in October to December, and remain out of condition till March."

There seems to be no doubt that the Powan is merely the Scotch representative of the Welsh Gwyniad. The *Coregonus microcephalus* of Parnell is also to be referred to the Gwyniad.

The food of the Gwyniad, and of the other British species of *Coregonus*, consists principally of insect larvæ, both those which swim in the water, as the *Ephemeridæ*, and those which are attached to stones, as some of the *Trichoptera*.

AT CLEVE, ON THE THAMES.

*Order IV.*
*PHYSOSTOMI.*

*Family*
*SALMONIDÆ.*
*Sub-generic Group*—SALVELINI.

# SMELT, SPARLING.

### (*Osmerus eperlanus.*)

| | |
|---|---|
| *Eperlanus,* | WILLUGHBY, Hist. Pisc. p. 202. |
| *Osmerus,* | ARTEDI, Syn. Nom. Pisc. p. 45; Spec. Pisc. p. 21, No. 1. |
| *Salmo eperlanus,* | LIN., Sys. Nat. i. p. 511; DONOVAN, Brit. Fish. ii. pl. 48. |
| *Smelt Salmon,* | PENNANT, Brit. Zool. iii. p. 416, ed. 1812. |
| *Smelt, Spirling and Sparling (Scotland),* | YARRELL, ii. p. 129; COUCH, Fish. Brit. Isl. iv. p. 276, pl. 227. |
| *Osmerus eperlanus,* | LACÉP., v. p. 229; FLEM., Brit. Anim. p. 181; JENYNS' Man. p. 429. |
| | PARNELL, Fish. Firth of Forth, Mem. Wern. Nat. His. Soc. vii. p. 312. |
| | YARRELL, ii. p. 129; SIEBOLD, Süsserwasserf. p. 271; GÜNTHER'S Cat. vi. p. 166. |
| *Eperlanus vulgaris,* | GAIMARD, Voy. Isl. et. Grœnl. pl. 18, fig. 2. |

*Characters of the Genus* OSMERUS.—"Body covered with scales of moderate size. Cleft of the mouth wide; maxillary long, extending to, or nearly to, the hind margin of the orbit. Dentition strong; intermaxillary and maxillary teeth small, much smaller than those of the mandible. Vomer with a transverse series of teeth, several of which are large, fang-like; a series of conical teeth along the palatine and pterygoid bones. Tongue with very strong fang-like teeth

SMELT

SALMON PARR

YOUNG TROUT

anteriorly, and with several longitudinal series of smaller ones posteriorly. Pectoral fins moderately developed. Pseudobranchiæ present, but rudimentary. Blind sac of the stomach of moderate length. Pyloric appendages very short, in small number; ova small. Atlantic coasts of the temperate parts of Europe and North America; periodically ascending rivers, and frequently permanent residents of fresh waters."—GÜNTHER.

THE Smelt or Sparling is, perhaps, one of the most delicate in flavour of all fish that swim, whether in salt or fresh water. It is one of the few fishes which possess any strong peculiar and decided flavour. Willughby's opinion is expressed in these words,—"Carne est molle et friabile, sapore delicato, gratissimum violæ odorem spirante."

The Smelt is an inhabitant of fresh water from August to May. They spawn in March and April, and about this time descend to the sea. Pennant, speaking of the peculiar odour,—which some compare to the cucumber, others to violets,—says, "They have a very particular scent, from whence is derived one of their English names, *Smelt, i.e.* smell it. That of *Sparling*, which is used in Wales and the north of England, is taken from the French *Eperlan*. There is a wonderful disagreement in the opinion of people in respect to the scent of this fish; some assert it flavours of the violet; the Germans, for a very different reason, distinguish it by the elegant title of *Stinkfisch*."* The derivation of the word *Smelt* is referred by Johnston to the *smelting* of metals, in allusion to the transparency and delicacy of this fish; this is obviously wrong, for the name of the genus *Osmerus*, as first used by Artedi, has reference to the smell, from the Greek word οσμηρης or οσμηρος. Yarrell states that the Smelt, as a British fish, appears to be almost exclusively confined to the eastern and western coasts of Great Britain. The Smelt is abundant in Scotland, not so common in Ireland, where it is local; Couch says that no Smelts have been recognized along the shores of England from the Thames westward to the Land's End. They formerly abounded in the Thames, from Wandsworth to Putney Bridge, and from thence to the Suspension Bridge at Hammersmith from thirty to forty fishing-boats might have been seen working together many years ago. Below Woolwich, where it is said they now alone appear in the Thames, the angler would scarcely be inclined to go and try his luck among Smelt.

Though the Smelt is a pearly and fragile-looking fish, it appears to be voracious in its habits. A writer in *Land and Water* found shrimps and small fish in quantities in their stomachs.

Dr. Günther states that Smelts are frequently permanent residents of fresh waters. Experiments have been occasionally made in this country to retain it in ponds, one of which, as recorded by Yarrell, was attended with complete success. "Colonel Meynell, of Yarm, in Yorkshire, kept Smelts for four years in a fresh-water pond, having no communication with the sea: they continued to thrive, and propagated abundantly. They were not affected by freezing, as the whole pond, which covered about three acres, was so frozen as to admit of skating. When the pond was drawn, the fishermen of the Tees considered that they had never seen a finer lot of Smelts. There was no loss of flavour or quality."—(ii. p. 131.) I do not know what further experiments have been made in this way, but I have often thought that modern pisciculturists might profitably turn their attention to the cultivation of a fish of such a peculiar and delicate flavour as the Smelt or Sparling.

In some parts of Sweden, as we are informed by Nilsson, Smelts are found in lakes with a sandy bottom all the year round. In the spring they leave the deep water and pass in thousands to the shallower shores of the rivers, where they are caught in numbers.

The finest Smelts I ever see come from the Conway, where they grow to the length of ten or even twelve inches; but the specimens usually exposed for sale in the fish-shops are much smaller. The Smelt is found in the Tay, the Frith of Forth, and the Ure on the

---

* Pennant in a note says, "And not without reason, if we may depend on Linnæus, who says there are two varieties in the Baltic; the one which is called *Nors, fœtidissimus, stercoris instar*, which in the early spring, when the peasants come to buy it, fills all the streets of Upsal with the smell. He adds that at this season agues reign there."

Yorkshire coast. Large quantities are taken by nets in the Humber, in the Yare of Norfolk, where they grow to a large size, the estuary of the Thames, and the Medway. On the western coasts they are found in the Solway Frith, the Mersey, Dee, the Conway, and Dublin Bay.

I have no specimen before me as I write; I shall therefore give Dr. Günther's description: —"The height of the body is much less than the length of the head, which is one fourth or two ninths of the total (without caudal). Snout produced, much longer than the diameter of the eye; young examples have the eye comparatively larger. Vomerine teeth and anterior lingual teeth large, fang-like; posterior mandibulary teeth larger than the anterior ones, which form a double series, the inner series containing stronger teeth than the outer one. The maxillary extends to, or nearly to, the vertical from the hind margin of the orbit. Back transparent greenish, sides silvery."

The Smelt, which is the only British species belonging to this small genus, is found on the coasts and fresh waters of North and Central Europe.

The number of rays in the fins is

Dorsal 11.
Pectoral 11.
Ventral 8.
Anal 13—16.

*Order III.*
*ANACANTHINI.*
A. Anacanthini Gadoidei.

*Family*
*GADIDÆ.*

# BURBOT, EEL-POUT.

*(Lota vulgaris.)*

| | |
|---|---|
| *Mustela,* | Pliny, Nat. Hist. ix. cap. 17. |
| *Lota,* | Gesner, De Aquatil. p. 599. |
| *Mustela fluviatilis, nostratibus, Eel-pout*<br>*nomine a Belgis mutuato, and Burbot*<br>*Gallico vocabulo dicta,* | Willughby, Hist. Pisc. p. 125, tab. H. 3, fig. 4. |
| *Gadus dorso tripterygio, ore cirrato,*<br>*maxillis æqualibus,* | Artedi, Spec. Pisc. p. 38, No. 13. |
| *Gadus lota,* | Lin., Syst. Nat. i. p. 440; Lacép., ii. p. 435; Donov., Brit. Fish. pl. 92. |
| *Burbot,* | Pennant, Brit. Zool. iii. p. 265. |
| *Lota vulgaris,* | Jenyns' Man. p. 448; Yarrell, ii. p. 267; Günther's Cat. iv. p. 359. |
| *Burbolt, Burbot, Eel-pout,* | Couch, Fish. Brit. Isl. iii. p. 93, pl. 146. |
| *Molva lota, Eel-pout, Coney-fish, Bird-Bolt,* | Flem., Brit. An., p. 192. |

*Characters of the Genus* Lota.—"Body elongate, covered with very small scales. A separate caudal; two dorsal fins and one anal; ventrals narrow, composed of six rays. Villiform teeth of equal size in the jaws and on the vomer; none on the palatines. The first dorsal with ten to thirteen well-developed rays. Chin with a barbel. Branchiostegals seven or eight. Fresh-water fishes of the temperate regions of the Northern Hemisphere."—Günther.

BURBOT

THE Burbolt, Burbot, or Eel-pout is the only British species of the family of *Gadidæ* that has its abode permanently in fresh water. This curious fish appears to have been known to, or at least to be mentioned by Pliny under the name of *mustela*, or "weasel-fish." He says, "The fish next (to the *scarus*) best for the table are the *mustelæ*, which, strange to say, the lake of Brigantia, in Rhætia, amongst the Alps, produces, rivalling the fish of the sea." According to some editions this fish was valued only for its liver; the Brigantine lake is the present Boden See, or Lake of Constance. In some parts of France it is said still to be called by the name of *motelle*, which I suppose is a corruption of *mustela*. The Lake of Constance still produces Burbots, and there are specimens now in the British Museum from that piece of water; there are also specimens from the Gotha River, Sweden, the river Elbe, Switzerland, and the south of Europe. American representatives of this fish are found in Canada and the adjoining parts of the United States. In our own country the Burbolt is rather a local fish. I have obtained, through the kindness of Mr. William Shelton, of the Grange, Wergs, Wolverhampton, specimens from the Penk, a tributary of the Trent, which river also produces it. According to Yarrell, the Nottingham market was, in his time, occasionally supplied with examples for sale. It is found in the rivers of Yorkshire and Durham, Norfolk, Lincolnshire, and Cambridgeshire. A good many years ago, Mr. Masefield, of Ellerton Hall, had numbers of these fish in the fishponds on his estate; he used to prize them highly for the table, for the flesh is rich and delicious. I believe that a long and hard frost was the means of killing a number; at any rate the Burbot has ceased to exist in the Ellerton waters. Mr. Masefield is desirous to introduce them again into his ponds; and being hardy fish, there would be no difficulty about the matter, excepting that as they are generally caught with hooks on night-lines, the specimens are usually too much injured to survive long after being taken.

The Burbot does not occur in Scotland, nor is it included by Mr. Thompson among the fishes of Ireland. It prefers slowly-running rivers, but will thrive in still waters. Like the Eel—to which it bears some resemblence, hence, doubtless, its name Eel-pout*—the habits of this fish are to conceal itself under stones and deep banks, and on this account it has been called the Coney or Rabbit Fish, from its lurking nature. May the name of *mustela*, mentioned by Pliny, refer to the same habits, associated in his day with those of the weasel? The spawning time is in March and April; but little, if anything, is known, I believe, of the young fry, or of the time required for the development of the ova. Bloch states that the spawning time is in December and January.

Pennant calls it a very delicate fish for the table, though of disgusting appearance when alive; says that it is very voracious, and preys on the fry and lesser fishes; that it will not often take a bait, but is generally caught in weels. Certainly the Burbot is a curious-looking fish, but Pennant was too much given to detect what he called the disgusting in nature.

In this country these fish seldom grow to a greater size than three or four pounds in weight; a more common size is about two pounds. According to Pennant, the largest British specimen he ever heard of was taken in the Trent by Sir Jervase Clifton, which weighed eight pounds; a fish of very unusual size. Lloyd is quoted by Couch as mentioning a Scandinavian specimen weighing twenty pounds.

The Burbot was known to Plot, who has some very quaint remarks about it. Of the fishes of this "inland county (Staffordshire) I could hear but of one," he says, "amongst them all that I think undescribed, and that one of the smooth sort without scales, and for its solitary way of living, of the σποραδικοι,† there having not above four of them been catch't, that I

---

*\* Pout*, I think, refers to a fuller form of the belly than is seen in the Eel, which to some extent reminds one of the belly of the Codfish, to which fish, indeed, it is related.

† A term used by Aristotle; σποραδικα ζωα, "solitary animals," or "animals living only here and there."

could hear of, within memory, and these all single and without any company, no, not so much as of their own kind." Plot's figure is as quaint as his language, but no doubt it is intended for the Burbot. He says, "However we may allow it to be a *Mustela fluviatilis*, though in Staffordshire, by some it is call'd a *Burbot*, or *Bird-bolt*, perhaps from that sort of Arrow, rounded at head, somewhat like these *fishes;* by others, from the oddness of the shape, and rarity of meeting them, the *Non-such;* there having never but four (that I could hear of) been found within memory."—(*Natural History of Staffordshire*, by Robert Plot, ed. Oxford, 1686.)

This fish is very deserving of cultivation, and I hope that pisciculturists will soon turn their attention to the Burbot.

I have no specimens before me as I write,—my own I presented to the Liverpool Museum, —I therefore take Yarrell's description, which I remember to be accurate. "The head depressed, smooth; jaws equal; chin with one barbule; the gape large, with small teeth above and below; eyes of moderate size; gill-opening large; the length of the head compared to that of the body as one to four; the form of the body cylindrical, compressed posteriorly. The first dorsal fin is small and rounded; the second elongated, reaching nearly to the tail; both dorsal fins nearly uniform in height; ventral fins placed very forward, narrow and pointed; the pectoral fins large and rounded: the anal fin begins on a line behind the commencement of the second dorsal fin, but ends very nearly on the same plane; the tail oval and slightly pointed.

The fin rays in number are

Dorsals 14.68.
Pectoral 20.
Ventral 6.
Anal 67.

The colour of the body is yellowish brown, clouded and spotted with darker brown, and covered with a mucous secretion; the under parts lighter; scales small; the fins partaking of the part of the body from which they emanate, those of the lower surface being much the lightest."

The word Burbot, probably, is to be referred to *barba* and *barbatus*, "beard," "bearded," in allusion to the barbule with which the under jaw is furnished. Continental names of this fish are *Die Quappe*, *Aalraupe*, *Treische*, *La Lotte*, etc.

The specimen which supplied the illustration was caught in the neighbourhood of Driffield.

ON THE DEE.

*Sub-class*—GANOIDEI.
*Order II.*
*CHONDROSTEI.*

*Family*
*ACIPENSERIDÆ.*

# STURGEON.

### (*Acipenser sturio.*)

| | |
|---|---|
| *Attilus,* | GESNER, De Aquatil. p. 109; WILLUGHBY, Hist. Pisc. p. 241, tab. P. 7, fig. 3. |
| *Sturio,* | GESNER, De Aquatil. p. 931; WILLUGHBY, Hist. Pisc. p. 239. |
| *Acipenser corpoıe tuberculis spinosis exasperato,* | ARTEDI, Spec. Pisc. p. 91, No. 1. |
| *Acipenser sturio,* | LIN., Sys. Nat. i. p. 103; LACEP., i. p. 411; DONOVAN, Brit. Fish. pl. 65; PARNELL, Mem. Wern. Soc. vii. p. 403; JENYNS' Man. p. 493; FLEMING, Hist. Anim. p. 173; YARRELL, ii. p. 475; SIEBOLD, Süsserwasserf. p. 363; GÜNTHER'S Cat. viii. p. 342. |
| *Sturgeon,* | PENNANT, Brit. Zool. iii. p. 164, ed. 1812; COUCH, Fish. Brit. Isl. i. p. 157, pl. 35. |
| *Acipenser latirostris,* | PARNELL, Mem. Wern. Soc. vii. p. 405; YARRELL, ii. p. 479. |

*Characters of the Genus* ACIPENSER.—"The rows of osseous scutes not confluent on the tail. Spiracles present. Caudal rays surrounding the extremity of the tail. Inhabitants of the temperate and arctic regions of the northern hemisphere, periodically entering rivers. Some species entirely confined to fresh water. The geographical distribution of the Sturgeons is nearly identical with that of *Salmo.*"—GÜNTHER.

STURGEON

A LL the British fresh-water species, which up to this place have occupied our attention, belong to the great sub-class TELEOSTEI, from the Greek τελεος or τελειος, "complete," and οστεον, "a bone," since all the individuals belonging to it possess an ossified skeleton, and completely separated vertebræ.

The Sturgeon comes under the sub-class GANOIDEI, in which the fishes have a skeleton more or less ossified. In this sub-class there are two orders—

*I. Holostei,* in which the body is covered with scales, and the skeleton bony, and

*II. Chondrostei,* in which the skin is naked, or with bony bucklers.

In the first order there are no British species of fish. To the second the Sturgeon family (*Acipenseridæ*) belongs; it is thus characterized by Dr. Günther:—"Body elongate, subcylindrical, with five rows of osseous bucklers. Snout produced, subspatulate, or conical, with the mouth at its lower surface, small, transverse, protractile, toothless. Nostrils double in front of the eye. Four barbels in a transverse series on the lower side of the snout. Vertical fins with a single series of fulcra in front. Dorsal and anal fins approximate to the caudal, which is heterocercal. Gill membranes confluent at the throat, and attached to the isthmus. Branchiostegals none; gills four; two accessory gills. Air-bladder large, simple, communicating with the dorsal wall of the œsophagus. Stomach without blind sac. Pancreas divided into pyloric appendages. Rectum with a spiral valve."—(*Catalogue,* viii. p. 332.)

The Sturgeon, occurring as it does in the Mediterranean, was in all probability known to the ancient Greeks and Romans; other species of the family may also have been known to them. The accounts, however, of the fishes called ακιπησιος, *acipenser,* ελλοψ, ονισκος, etc., are so unsatisfactory, than we can do little more than form a conjecture that some species of Sturgeon is intended by all these various names.

This fish is occasionally taken in Salmon nets on various parts of our coasts; generally speaking, in the estuaries, or not far up the rivers; sometimes, however, it ascends rivers to a considerable distance. A specimen, eight feet long, and weighing one hundred and ninety-two pounds, was caught in the Severn, in 1802, in a weir near Shrewsbury. It has been taken in the Trent, near Nottingham. The antiquarian Aubrey, records it as commonly reported, that before an heir of Clifton, of Clifton, in Nottinghamshire, dies, a Sturgeon is caught in the river Trent near that place.

The spawning time is in the winter and early spring, when the fish ascend the fresh water of the larger rivers. The spawn consists of roe or small grains shed in the same manner as that of the *Teleostei,* or bony fishes. This Sturgeon's roe is the *caviar* of commerce, a thing, in my opinion, disgusting in appearance, offensive to the smell, and horrible to the taste. The Sturgeons supply the greater part of this, so called, relish. It is prepared near the mouths of the Volga, Danube, Dnieper, and Don. "In the month of March, the Sturgeon arrives in great numbers for spawning at these places. The ovaria of the largest of these fish are estimated to contain three millions of eggs. The fish are caught both with nets and hooks. Caviar is prepared by removing from the roe all its membranes; it is then washed in vinegar or white wine, and dried by being spread on a board in the air. After this it is thoroughly salted, the salt being rubbed in with the hand; it is then put into a bag, and pressed in order to remove the liquour; finally it is packed in kegs, and is then ready for sale. The caviar made on the shores of the Caspian is for the most part sent up the Volga to Moscow; that shipped from the ports of the Black Sea and Sea of Azof, is bought at Astrakhan by the Armenians of Nakhitchivan and the Greeks of Taganrog. This caviar is not so good as that which is made on the Caspian. The principal exports are to Italy: very little is brought to England. The shipments altogether form only a small part of what is made, the consumption in Russia being very great, in consequence of the three seasons of fasting which occur in the year. There has been known to be as much as one thousand hundredweights of caviar shipped from Odessa in a single year; but this is far beneath the produce of the Caspian, which has in some years reached fifteen thousand hundredweights. When of good quality, caviar is dry and of a brown colour; it is commonly eaten with oil and lemon juice. A cheaper and less prized kind is obtained from the roe of the Grey Mullet, and from some species of Carp, which are common in and near the Black Sea."— (*English Cyclop.* Arts and Science Div. ii. p. 691.) According to M. Littré, the name *caviare* is derived from the Turkish *chouiar;* what that means I do not know. The word to me, when I see the substance on the breakfast table, always suggests *caution*, and I associate it, wrongly I know, but feelingly, with the Latin word *cave !*

The membrane of the air-bladder of the Sturgeon supplies isinglass, a substance known to the ancient Greeks and Romans under the name of *ichthyocolla*, "fish-glue." Russia supplies most of the isinglass of commerce. The thick air-bladder ("sounds") is washed in cold water, and exposed for a short time to the air, in order to stiffen. "The outer skin is then taken off and rejected, and the remainder cut out, and loosely twisted into rolls, according to the intended size of the pieces, which are called *staples*, and are known in commerce by the names of long and short staple, and of these the first is the best. These are dried in the air. The best sort of isinglass is used for the table and in confectionery; it is also largely employed in refining wine and beer."—(*Engl. Cycl.* iv. p. 998.)

I have never tasted a Sturgeon, and should not know how to cook it. Yarrell says it is generally stewed with rich gravy, and the flavour is considered to be like that of veal. Being a cartilaginous fish, the flesh is doubtless very nutritious.

The Sturgeon grows to a great size. One of the largest British specimens on record is mentioned by Pennant; it was caught in the Esk, and weighed four hundred and sixty pounds. In the aquarium at Southport, one of the best, if not the best aquarium in the kingdom, specimens of Sturgeons are often to be seen swimming about in the great tanks. In a letter from Mr. Jackson, the Curator, kindly written to me in October, 1878, I learn that there were then two Sturgeons living at the aquarium. "One was caught last summer; the other, a very fine specimen, seven feet long, was caught three years last August; it feeds freely on lugworms, and is in fine condition. The Sturgeons are always kept by us in salt water, which prevents fish in general from being attacked by parasitic epizoa, which is not the case in fresh water." Pennant's fish has lately been thrown quite into the shade, as will be seen from the following extract from the *Leeds Mercury* of February 1st., 1879:— "The largest Sturgeon ever delivered at the port was brought into Grimsby on Wednesday morning by the smack 'The Kitty,' (S. Shelton, master), Mr. Smethurst, Jun., owner. The Sturgeon was four feet eleven inches in circumference, eleven feet nine inches in length, and weighed forty-four stones and a half. It was sold to Mr. A. Clifton, fish merchant."

The mouth of the Sturgeon, which is in the form of a sucker, is situated on the under side of the head, not far from the feelers, or *cirri*, which, being well supplied with nerves, are able to point out to this fish the food with which it meets as it pokes about with its pointed snout.

"When caught in the Thames, within the jurisdiction of the Lord Mayor," says Yarrell, "the Sturgeon is considered a royal fish; the term being intended to imply that it ought to be sent to the king, and it is said that this fish was exclusively reserved for the table of Henry the First of England."

The fish thought by Parnell to be a distinct species, to which he gave the name of *Acipenser latirostris*, is by Dr. Günther referred to a variety of the Common Sturgeon, *A. sturio*. It appears, however, that the American species, *A. maculosus*, has been taken from the Firth of Tay. This is the *A. thompsoni* of Richardson, in the third edition of Yarrell's *British Fishes*, ii., 456, (see Günther's *Catalogue*, viii., p. 339, note). The *Acipenser sturio* is thus described:—"Snout pointed, produced, it being equal to, or but little shorter than, the remaining part of the head in examples to three feet long. Barbels nearer to the eye than to the extremity of the snout; in very large examples, especially those with a broad snout, the barbels are midway between snout and eye, or even nearer to the end of the snout. Osseous shields well developed: 11—13 along the back, and (34) 29—31 (in young examples sometimes 26 or 27) along the side. Skin with very small rough points in very young examples; in older ones these ossifications are broader, rough, substellate, and more or less regularly arranged in oblique series. Anal fin below dorsal. Dorsal 37—44." This species is found in the Mediterranean, western and northern Europe, and eastern North America.

The word Sturgeon is to be referred to the German *Stör*, the name of this fish; perhaps the term may be connected with the verb *stören* "to poke," "rummage about," in allusion to this fish seeking its food at the bottom with its pointed head.

# EELS.

---

" THERE are few animals," says a celebrated French naturalist, "whose image one must retrace with as much pleasure as the Common Eel......We have seen superior instinct in the enormous and terrible shark, but then it was the minister of an unsatiable voracity, a sanguinary cruelty, a devastating strength; we have found in electrical fish, a power which we may almost call magical, but beauty did not fall to their share. We have had to represent remarkable forms, but nearly always their colours were dull and dark. Glittering shades have struck our view; rarely have they been united with pleasing proportions, more rarely still have they served to adorn a creature of elevated instinct. And this kind of intelligence, this mixture of the glitter of metals, of the colours of the rainbow, this rare conformation of all the parts which form one whole joined in happy agreement, when have we seen all these bestowed where the habits are, so to speak, social, the affections gentle, and the enjoyments in some sort sentimental? It is this interesting union, however, which we are going to show in the Common Eel; and when we shall have comprised into one point of view its slender form, its delicate proportions, its elegant colours, its gracious flexions, its easy gyrations, its rapid springs, its superior swimming, its serpent-like movements, its industry, its instinct, its affection for its mate, its sociability, and the advantages which man is ever deriving from it, we shall not be surprised to find that some of the Greek and Roman ladies most famous for their charms have given its form to one of their most *recherchés* ornaments."* While allowing that the language "verges on the poetical," I must confess a partiality for Eels, and own that there is a great deal of truth in what the French naturalist has said. But then we must think of the Eel as a free and unmolested inhabitant of the water, and not as a writhing victim on the fishing-line of some disciple of Walton, when he certainly is a troublesome fellow, and when we may fairly say of him, "Nihil tetigit quod non *fœdavit.*" The Eel, however, has long enjoyed, and still deservedly enjoys, a wide celebrity. "It is agreed," says honest Izaak Walton, "that the Eel is a most dainty dish; the Romans have esteemed her the *Helena* of their feasts, and some the queen of palate pleasure." There are a few exceptions, however, to this general rule. The Jews—excellent cooks and judges of what is good—refuse to eat the Eel at this very day, though they are perfectly aware that it has scales.† Amongst

---

* *Œuvres du Comte de Lacépède,* vi. p. 457.

† It is an error to suppose that the Jews are unacquainted with the fact that Eels have scales. According to the popular belief, the celebrated Leuwenhoek was the first to record the existence of scales in the integument of the Eel. To this observant naturalist probably belongs the merit of having first published the fact to the scientific world of modern Europe; but that the Jews were long before aware of it is evident from a certain narrative in the Talmud (*Abada Sara,* fol. 39, a.), which relates that when Rabbi Aschi came to Tamdoria, some one placed before him an Eel-like fish (TSELOPEKHA, which Rashi explains by "anguille"); and that on his holding it to the light, he noticed some very fine scales, and thereupon did not scruple to partake of its flesh. That the Hebrew word denotes an Eel is further evident from the following quotation from the old work *Aruch*—"TSELOBEKHA, a fish

the Scotch there is a great antipathy to Eels; whence derived one cannot say, unless from an objection to their snake-like form.*    I have known Englishmen make this objection.    To a question in *Notes and Queries* (Sept. 26th., 1863), as to whether the Scotch have any definite reason for their dislike of this fish, the following reply is given:—"It would appear from Partington's *British Cyclopædia*, that the Scottish objection to Eels as an article of food, is mainly due to their supposed *unwholesomeness*.    In the northern part of Britain, in Scotland especially, the prejudice of the people runs very strong, not only against the form of the Eel, but against the *quality of its flesh* as an article of food."    And again, "Eels are held in small estimation in the North; and, even discounting their serpent-form, they are regarded as far from wholesome."    I shall refer by and bye to the supposed unwholesomeness of this fish.    I have been told of a Scotch lady who once tasted Eel inadvertently, and thought it excellent; but on finding out what it was, would eat no more, and has never tasted it since.

To the naturalist the Eel is a subject of particular interest, chiefly on account of the difficulty which has hitherto attended the study of its history; and although it is certain that Eels are produced after the manner of fish generally, *i.e.*, from deposited ova, much yet remains in obscurity.    To this point I must revert again.

The difficulty of holding an Eel has given rise to many proverbs.    "Every one knows who may have tried the experiment," happily observes Dr. Badham, "every one knows that to hold an Eel with the naked hand, is as abortive an attempt as detaining a pig by the tail, after it has been well soaped; or, in morals, to hold a knave to his word.    Hence the apophthegm,† 'Anguilla est, elabitur,' 'He's an Eel, and is off;' but both rogue and Eel may be held tight if we set about it in the right way."    The ancient method of retaining an Eel was by seizing it with some rough leaf in the hand.    The fig-leaf was usually employed: hence the proverb, τω θριω την εγχελυν, "an Eel with a fig-leaf."‡    Alciati has the following epigram upon a captured rogue:—

> "Jamdudum quocunque fugis te persequor, at nunc
>      Cassibus in nostris denique captus ades.
> Amplius haud poteris vires eludere nostras,
>      Ficulno anguillam strinximus in folio."—*Emb.* ed. 1540.

Modern fishermen know how to retain an Eel in the naked hand without any extraneous help.    There is, however, but one successful mode, viz. to grasp the slippery beast in the middle with the second and third fingers above and the first and fourth below.    He is thus held as in a vice.    Gesner quotes the Greek proverb, απ' ουρας την εγχελυν εχεις, "You've an

---

unclean amongst the Jews, thin, round, and like a serpent, which on account of its slipperiness can only be retained in the hand by being covered with sand or dust."    According to the *Aruch*, the Eel bears the same name in Arabic, though a more usual Arabic designation is ENKELIS, which is evidently the Greek εγχελυς.    The modern Jews, doubtless, still object to the Eel on account of its snake-like form.    See Buxtorf's *Lex. Talm. et Rabbin.* p. 1910; Lewysohn's *Zoologie des Talmuds*, p. 264.

\* Hence the Latin *anguilla*, from *anguis*, "a snake."    Compare Juvenal, Sat. v. 103.    "Vos anguilla manet longæ cognata colubræ."    Similarly the French, Italian, and Spanish words; also the English "snig" (snake), sometimes used to denote the middle-nosed variety, but often, in a general sense, any Eel.    "*Eel*," German and Dutch *aal*, according to Wedgwood, is from the Finnish *ilja, iljakka*, "slimy," or the Esthonian *illa*, "slime."

† Plautus Pseud. II. 4. 57.

‡ According to the *Hieroglyphica, sive de Sacris Ægyptiorum Commentarii*, of J. P. Valerian Bolzani, Basil, 1755, lib. xxix. De Anguillâ, the fig-leaf was used for this purpose by the ancient Egyptains; for when they wished to denote "certainty with regard to an uncertain object," *spes certa re super ambiguâ*, they depicted an Eel rolled up in a fig-leaf.    It is curious to note the correspondence of ideas, between the Egyptians and Greeks in this matter of the allegorical meaning of the Eel.    Bolzani states that the picture of "an Eel held by the tail" denoted "a man vainly pursuing a fugitive object;" and the representation of a man engaged in catching Eels, was meant to typify "one who was growing rich from civil discord," such as Cicero represents Catiline and his co-conspirators, when he speaks of them as men "qui, honores, quos quieta republica desperant, perturbata se consequi posse arbitrantur."    In L. Cat. ii. cap. ix.    See further on.

Eel by the tail," as expressing either a man "lubrica fide"—"a slippery fellow," or an object which it is impossible to retain. The same proverb has found its way into German, "Du hast den Aale bei dem Schwanz." The slippery nature and line-entangling propensities of the Eel are often the subject of much merriment. Who does not remember, as depicted by the pencil of John Leech, the disconsolate look of poor Mr. Briggs as he holds up on the end of his fishing-line a whacking Thames Eel, that has twisted that said line into the most inextricable conglomeration of worse than Gordian knots? Or who can ever forget the scene of the bursting of the aquarium—the conception of the same inimitable artist—and the vain efforts of the old lady to pick up her favourite Eel with a pair of tongs!

Eels were held in high, and indeed in very absurdly high, repute by the ancients. As to the Egyptians, they paid the Eel so great a compliment as to enrol it amongst their gods. Only another fish, if Herodotus is correct, shared this honour with the Eel, and that was known by the name of *lepidôtus,* some fish probably of the Carp family, and so called from the large size of its scales.* Antiphanes† ridicules the Egyptians for the honour they paid to Eels, and contrasts the value of the gods with the high price asked for this fish in the market of Athens. "In other respects men say that the Egyptians are clever, in that they esteem the Eel to be equal to a god; but they are far more valuable than the gods, for we can propitiate them by prayer; but as for Eels, we must spend twelve drachmas or more merely to get a smell at them." And Anaxandrides‡ thus amusingly contrasts the manners of the Egyptains with those of his fellow-countrymen. "I never could associate with you, for neither do our customs nor laws agree with yours, but differ widely. You adore an ox, I sacrifice him to the gods; you esteem an Eel as the greatest deity, we think him far the best of fish; you don't eat swine's flesh, I am particularly fond of it; you worship a dog, I beat him if I ever catch him devouring my victuals," &c.

The ancient Greeks carried their partiality for the Eel to a most ridiculous excess; now she is invoked "as the goddess of pleasure, sometimes as the white-armed goddess—and, finally, as the Helen of the dinner-table, because every guest strove, like Paris, to supplant his neighbour, and keep her for himself."§ The Eels from the river Strymon and lake of Copais appear to have been those generally most highly prized, though Sicily was also cele-brated.‖ Archestratus,¶ of Syracuse, who appears to have been a sort of ancient Soyer, and who travelled far and wide for the purpose of learning anything that might be useful in the culinary art—whose opinion, therefore, we may be content to take in this question— naturally gives the preference to Eels from his own shores. The Greeks, in the time of Aristophanes, used to serve up their Eels with beetroot, though sometimes they were boiled in salt and water, with marjoram and other herbs. Eubulus** is quoted as saying,—

> "then there came
> Those natives of the lake, the holy Eels,
> Bœotian goddesses, all clothed in beet."

The ancients sometimes captured Eels by means of hooks baited with large worms or small fish. Aristotle†† mentions a three-pronged spear (τριοδους)—probably similar to our

---

* ii. 72.                    † Apud Athenæus, vii. 55, ed. Dindorf.                    ‡ Ibid.

§ *Prose Halieutics,* p. 381.

‖ The Strymon is the modern Struma or Carasu, which flows through the Lake Prasias (now Takino). The Eels that formerly abounded there were doubtless an attraction to the numbers of cranes (Strymoniæ grues) frequently mentioned by ancient writers. Belon *(Les Observations,* p. 124) speaks of the large size of the Eels of the Strymon: "Les anguilles y sont d'une excessive grandeur." The Lake Copais (now Topolias) is still famous for its Eels. In the dark recesses of the subterraneous channels which form the outlets of the lake Eels would find a congenial habitation.

¶ Athenæus, vii. 53, Younge's translation.

** Athen. vii. 56.                    †† *Hist. Anim.* iv. 10, § 4.

common Eel-spear—which was used by the Greek fishermen to take the Flat-fish (*Pleuronec-tidæ*) on the sand. He also says that Eels in the Strymon were taken at the time of the rising of the Pleiades, when the stormy winds stirred up the mud, and that at other times it was useless to try to obtain them.* In modern days the best time for catching large numbers of Eels is after heavy storms and floods. Aristotle gives as a reason for their being caught at these times, that Eels having small gills are soon suffocated if the water is muddy. The following ingenious mode of angling as adopted by the Grecian youth is given by Oppian :—†

> "With ludicrous device, in slimy bays,
> Some boy the silver volum'd Eel betrays;
> A sheep-gut's humid length his hand protends,
> Below the perforated line descends.
> The Fish sucks down the bait with rav'nous joy,
> And gives the tugging signal to the Boy;
> To th' opposite Extream his lips adjoyn,
> And fill with crowded air the rounding Line.
> Swoln with the springy blast the entrail strains,
> And binds the captive's throat with airy chains;
> The imprison'd winds his straitened jaws dilate,
> And fill his heaving breast with bloated fate.
> Panting he rolls, and struggles all in vain,
> A floating captive to the youthful swain."

Eels were also taken in wicker baskets with narrow necks,‡ as with the moderns; they were sometimes decoyed into earthenware vessels covered with colander-shaped lids, and baited with bits of cuttle-fish or other tempting morsels;§ they were kept by the Romans in their fish-ponds (*vivaria*), ready at hand for the table when required. Pliny states that immense numbers of Eels used to be taken in the lake Benacus (Lago di Garda), in the territory of Verona,—through which lake the river Mincius flows,—generally in the month of October, when the waters were disturbed, and that masses of more than a thousand in number were often taken by the traps *(excipulis)* placed in the stream. Eels were sometimes caught by stirring up the mud of the ponds and lakes in which they were found;∥ hence the Greek proverb, εγχελεις θηρασθαι, "to fish for Eels," or, as we should say, "to fish in muddy waters," with the political meaning of disturbing a state for the sake of gain; thus the sausage seller addresses Cleon, "Yes, for it is with you as with Eel-catchers, when the lake is still they take nothing, but if they stir up the mud they have good sport; so have you when you disturb the state."

It is well known that the mode of procreation of Eels has for ages been a puzzling question; and there is still something wanted to complete our knowledge of the general subject. Aristotle, after asserting that Eels are not produced from ova, or, as some persons have stated, from the metamorphosis of intestinal worms into young Eels, goes on to tell us what he conceives to be the true mode of generation. "They are produced from what are called the entrails of the earth (εκ των καλουμενων γης εντερων), which exist spontaneously in mud and wet earth. Some have been observed to make their escape from these things, and others have been apparent in them on being dissected. Such things are produced in the sea, and in rivers where is much putrefaction, in such places in the sea which abound in sea-weed,

---

* *Historia Animalium*, viii. 4, § 5, ed. Schneider.

† *Halieutics*, iv. 559, Jones's translation. Ælian (*Nat. Hist.*, xiv. 8) has described a similar mode of catching Eels. The modern method of "bobbing with a bunch of grubs strung on worsted," if not so ingenious, is doubtless more successful.

‡ Nassis. "Nassa est piscatorii vasi genus, quo cum intravit piscis, εxire non potest."—Festus, s. v.

§ *Hist. Anim.* iv. 8. § 12.                          ∥ Aristoph., *Nub.*, 559.

and in rivers and lakes near the banks where the heat of the sun engenders putrefaction."＊ Aristotle believed that there was no difference of sex in the Eel, but that the so-called male and female were different species. He speaks correctly, however, of its migrating to the sea, of its nocturnal habits, of its dislike to very cold, and its love of pure fresh water.† Pliny's notion was as absurd as that of Aristotle as to the origin of Eels. "They rub themselves against rocks, and their scrapings come to life. Nor have they any other mode of propagation."‡

Other ancient writers were of opinion that Eels originated in the carcases of dead horses (as Virgil supposed bees were produced from the dead body of an ox). Curiously enough, Gesner sees no improbability in the above solution of the difficulty, but thinks that other carcases besides those of horses may engender Eels.§ And yet he does also give the true account when he says that the sexes are plainly to be distinguished.‖ It is remarkable, therefore, that Gesner should have had recourse to the "spontaneous production" theory; but we must remember that in his time this was a popular creed; and even this learned writer was not free from the fallacies of his age. Helmont gives the following recipe for obtaining young Eels:—"Cut up two turfs covered with May-dew, and lay one upon the other, the grassy sides inwards, and thus expose them to the heat of the sun; in a few hours there will spring from them an infinite quantity of Eels." Some writers, as Schwenckfeld and Schoneveld, appear to have mistaken parasitic leeches and Gordian worms for the young of the Eel. Chopped horse-hair, thrown into the water, was deemed a certain method of obtaining Eels; this opinion I have found to prevail amongst the uneducated classes to this day in some of the midland counties.¶ It is remarkable that even Walton seems to have imbibed contentedly the popular notions of his day, "That Eels may be bred as some worms, and some kind of bees and wasps are, seems to be made probable by the barnacles and young goslings bred by the sun's heat and the rotten planks of an old ship, and hatched of trees."＊＊—(P. 281.)

In another place Walton affirms his belief in the notion that Pike were sometimes produced from pickerel weed (p. 230). Such superstitions find a place in the "Piscatory Eclogues."

> "Say, canst thou tell how worms of moisture breed,
> Or pike are gendered of the pickrel-weed?
> How carp without the parent seed renew,
> Or slimy Eels are form'd of genial dew?"

The opinion that Eels are viviparous, though quite free from the absurdity that characterises the notions I have already mentioned, is unquestionably erroneous. It is not a little remarkable that the anatomy of the fish should not have been earlier ascertained. "Who can say," writes Dr. Badham as late as 1854, "that they have taken a female in roe, or tasted a male's milt?" If you ask a fishmonger whether he has ever seen the spawn of an Eel, he will think you are joking with him, and will probably consider "Eel's spawn" to be nearly analogous to "a mare's nest," or "pigeon's milk!"

---

＊ *Hist. Anim.* vi. 15, § 2.                     † *Hist. Anim.* vi. 13, § 7; viii. 4, § 5, 6.

‡ *Nat. Hist.* ix. 50. Oppian's theory will be found at Hal. i. 849.

§ "In putredine gignitur Anguilla ut vermes in terra, id quod experientia compertum fuit. Aliquando enim equo mortuo in Magalonæ stagnum injecto, paullo post innumerabiles Anguillæ illic visæ sunt, quod ego ita accipio ut non ex equi tantum, sed etiam ex aliorum animalium cadaveribus generentur."—*De Aquatilibus*, iii. p. 40, C.

‖ "Vidi equidem Anguillas mutuo corporum complexu coëuntes, neque puto partibus ad gignendum necessariis prorsus destitutas esse: inferiore enim ventris parte et vulva in fœminis et semen in maribus reperitur: sed pinguitudine multa circumfusæ hæ partes non apparent, quemadmodum neque ova pinguitudine permista."—*Ibid.*, p. 42, D.

¶ I have been informed that the same mode of accounting for the origin of Eels exists amongst the unlearned in Scotland.

＊＊ See the well-known plate of the goose tree, barnacle tree, or the tree bearing geese, in Gerard's *Herbal*, last plate.

C. U. Ekström says, "I have never found roe in the body of the Eel, but I nevertheless believe that it is through the deposit of eggs that the fish propagates its species." There can be little doubt that the belief in the viviparous nature of the Eel may be traced to the fact of the presence of intestinal worms in the stomach and intestines. These worms, several kinds of which are described by Diesing* as inhabiting the genus *Anguilla*, have been ignorantly taken for young Eels.

But although the oviparous nature of the Eel is established beyond a shadow of doubt, and the anatomy of the fish clearly ascertained, still we have by no means all the information we require on the general question. That Eels descend rivers to the sea for the sake of depositing their spawn in the brackish water of estuaries where the increased temperature of the water is favourable to their habits,† has been long known. Aristotle alludes to the fact, and divers observers in modern times have recorded it. But do these Eels ever again ascend the rivers, or do they remain in the sea and estuaries? At what season of the year are the eggs deposited? Is it *necessary* that Eels should descend to the sea for spawning, or do they propagate their species in ponds and fresh water?

Before I remark on these questions, I should state that there are two species of Eel indigenous to the British Isles, viz., the Common Eel (*Anguilla vulgaris*), and the Blunt-nosed (*A. latirostris*). The Blunt-nose is widely distributed, but does not appear to be nearly so abundant as the other species; it is probably the "Frog-mouthed Eel" "of the Severn fishermen; it is described as being a fiercer and more voracious fish than the other species, dashing at and seizing its prey as a terrier does a rat, and filthy in the extreme in the nature of its food."‡ It seldom exceeds five pounds in weight. Mr. Francis, whose name is well known in connection with the new Art of Pisciculture, describes the Blunt-nose as "a coarse worthless fish." Such is my own opinion. Surely it was Blunt-nose that fattened on the body of Asteropæus.

"When roll'd between the banks, it lay the food
Of curling Eels and fishes of the flood."—*Iliad*, xxi. 221.§

According to an authority quoted by Mr. Cholmondeley Pennell in his work (*The Angler Naturalist*), the Broad-nosed Eel does not migrate. The same writer states that the contractors for the fishery of the Toome "expressly stipulate that they will not take a single Broad-nosed Eel," but always throw them aside.

With regard to the question whether the Eels that have descended to the sea from the lakes and rivers return again, or whether they remain in the brackish estuaries, I cannot give any decided opinion. Many persons have witnessed the ascent of countless thousands of young Eels or elvers from the estuaries and the sea, and no one, I believe, has ever seen adult Eels accompanying the elvers, or journeying by themselves. Yarrell says that the return of adult Eels is shown by the habits and success of the basket-fishermen in rivers within the tide way, who place the mouths of their Eel-pots up stream in autumn, and down stream in the spring. The question must still be regarded as problematic. Another difficult matter to determine is the time of the deposition of the ova. From some notes kindly put into my hands by Mr. Jonathan Couch, some few years ago, it would appear that Eels breed almost throughout the year. Young Eels of very small size have been found on the sea-beach of Polperro, in Cornwall, so early in the year as the beginning of January. Early in March

---

\* *Systema Helminthum*, ii. p. 389.

† "The mixed water is shown by experiment to maintain a temperature two degrees higher than the pure sea or fresh water, from the combination of the fluids of different densities."

‡ The *Angler Naturalist*, p. 398.

§ See the *Ingoldsby Legends*—"The Knight and the Lady," p. 478, ed. 1862.

Mr. Couch has seen them migrating in immense numbers up the river near his house, and "from this date," he adds, "the passage is incessant during the summer, and continues during part of the autumn." Mr. Couch sent me a little elver, about two inches and a half long, on the 5th. of September, and' he told me that all that have passed upward from the beginning of the year are of the same size. "From microscopic examination of the ova embedded in the ovaria," the same writer observes, "I found the grains of very different size, as if the shedding them must require a long time, which is proved by the unremitting passage upwards of the young Eels for many months." The ova are scattered in the mud, and Mr. Couch concludes that the spawn for the most part is deposited in the harbour, near low-water mark, by Eels which lodge in the hollows of the stonework of the piers; but where there is no shelter, the Eels are sometimes known to enter rivulets.

That Eels breed in ponds from which there is no communication to the sea hardly admits of a doubt. The following remark of Mr. Young, published in the *Angler Naturalist*, clearly proves that Eels do not *always* deposit their spawn in tidal water:—"The rivers in Scotland," he says, "were very low in the month of July, and I watched the motions of the Eels in swarms (as I thought spawning) on the sand and gravel-banks in the river Shin. I should have mentioned this circumstance to you while here, had I not wished to be more certain; but in October last, I got a few men and made them dig out one of the gravel-banks where I had observed the Eels all together, and found it alive with young Eels, some of them scarcely hatched, at the depth of from six to fifteen inches."

Other observers have, from time to time, written in confirmation of this opinion; and I have examined a pond, the owner of which informed me that several years ago he mudded it, and then put a few Eels into it: that these Eels bred there is certain, for some years afterwards the pond was found to be pretty well stocked with Eels of different sizes; and the nature of the ground is such that it would have been impossible for any Eels—making all reasonable allowance for their powers of travelling over land—to have gained admission to it from streams which had no communication whatever with the pond itself.*

It is a most interesting spectacle to see the migration of the young Eels from the sea, and wonderful are the instinctive efforts of these little creatures to surmount obstacles that would at first view appear to present unconquerable difficulties. Mr. Anderson, upwards of a century ago, described the young Eels as ascending the upright posts and gates of the waterworks at Norwich until they came into the dam above. Ballyshannon is a very favourable place for the study of this curious subject, as we are informed by Dr. Davy, who makes the following interesting remarks on Eels ascending rocks:—

"AMICUS. This is indeed a curious sight. Here are some [Eels] wriggling up a perpendicular rock. How is it they accomplish this?

"PISCATOR. I believe they are able to accomplish it chiefly owing to two circumstances —their mucous glutinous surface favouring adhesion, and their form small and slender. None of these Eels, you perceive, are more than two or three inches long, and slender in proportion. Watch one that is now in progress, ascending that perpendicular rock. See how it makes its tail a support, adhering by that, whilst it projects itself upwards; and this done, now adhering by its trunk, it draws its tail after it. These are its steps, and the asperities of the surface of the rock are its stairs favouring its exertions."

Sir Humphry Davy, the celebrated author of *Salmonia*, and brother of the physiologist whose words I have just quoted, was a witness of the ascent of these elvers at Ballyshannon, at the end of July, 1823. He speaks of the mouth of the river under the fall being "blackened by millions of little Eels about as long as the finger, which were constantly

---

* I must, however, observe that I have never seen nor heard of the occurrence of elvers two or three inches long in a pond to which there was no communication to any rivers. As young elvers are diurnal in their habits, this is remarkable.

urging their way up the moist rock by the side of the fall." "Thousands," he adds, "died, but their bodies, remaining moist, served as a ladder for others to make their way; and I saw some ascending even perpendicular stones, making their road through wet moss, or adhering to some Eels that had died in the attempt. Such is the energy of these little animals that they continue to find their way in immense numbers to Loch Erne. The same thing happens at the fall of the Bann, and Loch Neagh is thus peopled by them. Even the mighty fall of Schaffhausen does not prevent them from making their way to the Lake of Constance, where I have seen many very large Eels."

That young Eels do ascend waterfalls in the manner described by so close an observer and philosopher as Dr. John Davy cannot be doubted: it is probable, however, that their ordinary method of climbing perpendicular obstructions is by *worming* themselves up through the overhanging dripping moss that covers the rocks. There would be no very great difficulty in "such a getting up stairs." Mr. Couch, who has repeatedly watched the ascent up a fall of four or five feet in a stream near his own house at Polperro, has never seen a young Eel successful in its efforts to climb a moderately dry rock: "if they advance on a dry portion, their course is arrested; and after many endeavours and frequent restings they were compelled to retreat and seek a moister spot."

After the little Eels have gained the summit of the fall, they rest for a while with their heads protruded into the stream. They then urge themselves forward, taking advantage of every projecting stone or slack water, and never get carried back by the current. Falls twenty feet high are not insuperable barriers to these persevering little creatures. Although, as we have already seen, this migration of young Eels continues throughout the greater portion of the year, yet it would appear that the spring and early summer are the seasons when they ascend in the greatest numbers. In some rivers, as in the Thames and Severn, this migration is termed Eel-fare, of which the word *elver* is, perhaps, a corruption. They often associate in the form of long ropes in their upward migration: at other times they proceed in a promiscuous manner; every now and then diving under the sand, or resting under the shelter of a stone; always, I have observed, keeping near the sides where the stream presents fewer difficulties of ascent. Young Eels have been observed at sea four or five leagues from the land: of the myriads that ascend our rivers, few, comparatively speaking, ever arrive at Eelhood: the young tender morsels are devoured by numerous enemies, the adult Eels being amongst the number. In some Salmon rivers, Mr. Francis states that he has seen the lower pools in a perfect boil with the constant rising of the fish as the small Eels wriggle along the top of the water; so that the Salmon, if the larger Eels be destructive to their fry, exact summary vengeance. But man, as usual, is their greatest enemy. Mr. Couch told me that one of the Cornish fishermen, when at Exeter some years ago, saw "four carts loaded with little Eels, not larger than a knitting-needle, for sale, and on making inquiry was informed that the people fried them into cakes!" Elver-cakes consist of a number of these young Eels, which, after being scoured and boiled, are pressed into flat masses: they are said to present a peculiar appearance, from the number of little black eyes that bespangle them, and to be delicious food. In France these little Eels are given to the ducks and poultry, and even share the same fate as Sticklebacks do on some parts of our coast, being carted away for manure.

Mr. Frank Buckland writes as follows in the *Field* newspaper of June 6th., 1863 :—"Some time since I received, through the kindness of a friend, four cakes composed entirely of young Eels. These Eels, or Eelvers, came to Langport (on the river Parrett) with the first flood-tide in March. They are about three or four inches long, and came in a continued shoal about eighteen inches wide, without cessation for some days, always against the stream, and close to the left bank. The women catch them at night by means of a canvass bag, attached to a hoop at the end of a long stick, to which a lantern is fixed. Occasionally a larger one is seen amongst them, of a dark colour, and almost black. They are thrown into a tub of salt, which cleanses them; they are then boiled, and pressed into cakes, which are cut into slices and fried, making the most delicious food. Sometimes they are so abundant that the people about get tired of eating them, and actually feed the pigs with them. Here there is a branch of fish-culture, which, I am sure, Mr. Francis will agree with me ought decidedly not to be neglected; and that these little Eels, which in a short time would increase their weight, and therefore their value a thousand-fold, should be looked after and not suffered to be lost to the resources of the country."

Eel-fare, once a striking and remarkable sight in the Thames, no longer exists on account of the filthy water about London, in which it has been proved that Eels cannot live any length of time. Mr. Francis has little doubt that when the Thames is once more purified "Eel-fare" will in time again recur to it.

I have occasionally taken small transparent specimens—the majority are dark olive, sometimes almost black—in which the action of the heart and gills is plainly visible. Mr. Couch thinks this transparent Eel may be a different species, and states he has never observed it in companies. According to my own experience, however, these light-coloured Eels are gregarious, and occur in company with the darker specimens. I have never succeeded in keeping young Eels of two or three inches long beyond the space of a few weeks in confinement; they are delicate little fellows, and, though they twist about with lively emotion, are doubtless not "as merry as grigs." It is impossible to obtain a better subject than a young transparent Eel for the examination of the lymphatic pulse at the end of the tail, first described by the late Dr. Marshall Hall.

Eels are pre-eminently nocturnal animals and fond of the dark. Towards evening the juvenile sniggler knows that he has the best chance of success. They always congregate at the darkest places of the stews in which they are kept, and invariably select the darkest nights for their autumnal migration to the sea. They will not start on their journey on moonlight nights; the darker and the more stormy the night, the better for a voyage. Millers are well aware of this fact, and take care to set their traps accordingly, when they are sure of a large catch. Eels are unable to endure very severe cold, unless there is plenty of mud or sand in which they can hide themselves; if kept in artificial stews without this necessary essential, they will, in frosty weather, grow quickly thin, and die in a few days. Eels generally lie buried in the mud during the winter, but, if the weather prove mild and there is abundance of rain, they will leave their holes and proceed with the floods on their migrations.* The mild winter of 1861, I was informed by a miller in my own neighbourhood, who takes many hundred-weight in the course of the twelve months, was favourable to the capture of Eels. In December of that year half a ton was taken after a flood, and continuously to March, 1862, captures were made each month. Eels will not start on their migrations unless after a flood, or at any rate without a flush of water. From November, 1862, to June, 1863, not an Eel was taken in the traps, the weather having been remarkably dry. The instinct of the Eels doubtless causes them to wait for a flush of water to carry them down quickly to the salt water. In that curious old work by Juliana Berners, the following notice of the Eel occurs:—"The Ele is a quaysy (quasi?) Fysshe. A ravenour and devourer of the brode of Fysshe, and the Pike also is a devourer of Fysshe. I put them bothe behinde al other for to angle. For this Ele ye shall finde an hole in the grounde of water, and it is blew and blackyshe. There put in your hooke till that it be a foote within the hole, and your bayte shall be a great anglet witch or a menowe."†

---

* As a contribution to Shropshire folk-lore I may mention the following couplet which I have heard in my neighbourhood:—

"When the wallow (willow) has leaves as big as mouse's ears,
Then sniggles, they'll run, they dunna care wheeres."

† *Treatyse on Fyssynge.*

As to the instinct and general intelligence of the Eel, I cannot regard M. Lacépède's notions as much exaggerated. Eels are capable of domestication, and if their affection is of the nature of cupboard love, the same is true of all other species of fish that have been tamed:—"In Otaheite," says Ellis,* "Eels are fed until they attain an enormous size. These pets are kept in large holes two or three feet deep, partially filled with water. On the sides of these pits they generally remained, excepting when called by the person who fed them. I have been several times with the young chief, when he has sat down by the side of the hole, and by giving a shrill sort of whistle, has brought out an enormous Eel, which has moved about the surface of the water and eaten with confidence out of his master's hand."

We have another account of some tame Eels given by Sir W. C. Trevelyan, of which the following is the substance:—"Some Eels had been kept for nine or ten years in a walled garden at Craigo, the seat of David Carnegie, Esq. During the cold of winter they lay torpid, unless on bright days, when they came out of their hiding-places; but they would not take food before the 26th. of April, and then they ate sparingly until the warm weather, when they became quite unsatiable. When they were first put into the pond and had no food given them they devoured one another. They generally kept quiet at the bottom of the pond, except when any of the family went to look into it, when they invariably rose to the surface, sometimes for food, and at others merely to play with the hand, or take the fingers into their mouths."

Eels have the power of living a long time out of the water, if the air is humid; this they are enabled to do on account of the smallness of the gill aperture, the membranous folds of which by closing the orifice when the Eel is out of the water prevent the desiccation of the branchiæ. Sometimes in their peregrinations overland they are overtaken by the rays of a warm sun, when they speedily die. They have been taken in gardens, on hooks baited for birds; and some authors have left it on record that they actually steal newly-sown peas !

Every sniggler knows that a sharp rap on the tail of an Eel is attended with satisfactory results to himself and with unpleasant consequences to the fish, which is immediately quieted by the operation. This, some say, is by reason of the injury done to the lymphatic heart or caudal pulse, as before referred to.† Eels, as everybody knows, are extremely tenacious of life. Yarrell states "that Eels exposed on the ground till frozen, then buried in snow, and at the end of four days put into water, and so thawed slowly, discovered gradually signs of life, and soon perfectly recovered." Such a power of endurance as this, however, must be exceptional; for, as a rule, Eels are not able to survive a hard frost unless they are embedded in their mud-holes. It may also be satisfactory to know that the stories which the shuddering cook can often tell of cut-up lengths of Eel jumping out of the "frying-pan into the fire" have in them only an appearance of horror. After the head is severed from the body, it is clear that there can be no sense of feeling properly so called; the life-like signs exhibited are accounted for by the high degree of irritability of the muscular fibre. Very curious stories have been told of the power of the Eel to survive under peculiar conditions.‡

Eels have many enemies: otters, polecats, rats, various water-birds, such as herons and swans, occasionally make them their prey, not to mention the rapacious Pike, the Salmon, and the Slob Trout, which are all very fond of elvers. The rats and polecats make their attacks in the winter when the Eels are dormant.§

* *Polynesian Researches,* ii. p. 286.

† But is it not more probable that the effect is due to concussion of the spine? The stoppage of the lymphatic heart could scarcely be followed by so immediate a result.

‡ Gesner says—"Phalacrocorax anguillas integras vorat, quod Anglus quidam nobis retulit; ille mox per intestina elapsæ, denuo devorantur, idque vel novies aliquando repetitur, prius quam debilitata tandem retineatur."—*De Aquat.,* p. 45, D. And see *Prose Halieutics,* p. 389.

§ See *The Angler Naturalist,* p. 381.

In a letter in the *Zoologist* for 1846 upon this subject, Mr. Banister says:—"We have polecats abundant in Pilling during the whole year; and in the winter season, when the water in the ditches in the main drains is chiefly congealed, and more especially when the ice is covered with snow, the footprints of the polecat may be traced on the ice, and the most indubitable evidence is thus afforded of its predilection for fish. Under such circumstances I have repeatedly ascertained that this animal is a most expert fisherman, for in severe and long-continued frosts many Eels ascend our open drains, and as these watercourses are most slightly frozen over near the springs, the polecats, either by instinct or experience, discover the retreat of the Eels. In tracing the footprints of the polecat it will soon be ascertained that he halts at every hole or opening he meets with in the ice, and at once commences fishing, by introducing a fore-foot into the water, and, no doubt, groping all around under the ice as far as he can reach in search of such Eels as may have come to the aperture for air. That he uses his fore-paws in this manner is distinctly proved by his dirty footprints afterwards in the snow. It is also an admitted fact in the natural history of the Eel, that it cannot exist without air. The polecats then, aware, either from instinct or habit, of this propensity of Eels to assemble round any aperture in the ice for the benefit of the air, invariably search for them at every opening they meet with; and in tracing their footprints in the snow, as above described, it will frequently be discovered that Eels have been dragged from under the ice by these wily fishermen, and either devoured on the surface or carried to their dens to satisfy their hunger at some future opportunity."

Every naturalist has observed the peculiar denticulation on the inside of the middle claw of the common heron: is it probable, as Lacépède observes, that the bird drives this claw into the body of the Eel, and so renders ineffectual all its efforts to slip from its grasp? The heron, doubtless, occasionally finds a large Eel an "awkward customer;" and he frequently has to come out of the water on to the land, so as to be able to deal his slippery friend stronger and better directed blows. Yarrell relates, and gives a spirited vignette of the circumstance, that a heron had once struck his sharp beak through the head of an Eel, piercing both eyes, and that the Eel—no doubt remembering that one good turn deserves another—had coiled itself so tightly round the neck of the heron as to stop the bird's respiration; both were dead.

That Eels are not devoid of sagacity is proved by many well-attested anecdotes: they are said to form themselves into companies for hunting, and by partly encircling a shoal of small fish, drive them to the shore, where they are more readily caught and devoured. Mr. Jesse states that he has observed this fact in the canal in Hampton Court Park. Eels are not particular in their choice of food: young water-fowl, fish of all kinds, worms, spawn, insects, crustacea, &c., form their staple articles of diet. They appear, however, to vary their dinners with occasional nibbles at fresh-water plants. In warm weather they are often to be seen coiled round an aquatic plant in a vertical position; for what purpose they do this I have been unable to discover. In the winter time Eels are often found knotted together in large masses. This fact was known to Pliny. Is it probable that they congregate for the sake of ensuring warmth?*

Eels are of great commercial value; and there seems to be no reason why Eel-culture, if attempted in the British Isles, should not be attended with satisfactory pecuniary results. Incalculable numbers are annually destroyed, as they ascend our rivers: it is a pity these young elvers are not protected. Of course, in rivers which are favourable to the increase of Salmon and Trout the presence of large quantities of devouring Eels is anything but desirable; but their multiplication in our sluggish rivers, which contain either such fish as are able to take care of themselves or such as are, comparatively speaking, worthless, is a matter worth consideration.

* See Lacépède, vi. p. 481.

The London market is principally supplied with Eels from Holland, a country where they abound. According to an estimate made by Mr. Mayhew, no fewer than nine millions seven hundred and ninety-seven thousand seven hundred and sixty Eels are annually sold in Billingsgate market, amounting to a weight of one million five hundred and five thousand two hundred and eighty pounds, one fourth of which is sold by the costermongers. Mr. Mayhew thus graphically describes a visit to the Dutch Eel-boats with their bulging polished oak sides:—"I went to the shore where the watermen ply for passengers to the Eel-boats; they were surrounded by skiffs that ply from the Surrey and Middlesex shores and wait whilst the fares buy their fish. The holds of these Eel-boats are fitted up with long tanks of muddy water, and the heads of the Eels are seen breathing on the surface, a thick brown bubble rising slowly and floating to the sides. Wooden sabots and large porcelain pipes are ranged round the ledges, and men in tall fur caps, with high cheek bones and rings in their ears, walk the decks. At the stern of one boat was moored a coffin-shaped barge pierced with holes, and hanging in the water were baskets shaped like olive-jars, both to keep the stock of fish alive and fresh. In the centre of the boat stood the scales, a tall, heavy apparatus, one side fitted up with the conical net-bag to hold the Eels, and the other with the weights, and pieces of stone to make up for the extra draught of the water hanging about the fish. When a skiff-load of purchasers arrives, the master Dutchman takes his hands from his pockets, lays down his pipe, and seizing a sort of long-handled landing-net, scoops from the tank a lot of Eels. The purchasers examine them, and try to beat down the price. 'You calls them Eels, do you?' said a man with his bag ready opened. 'Yeas,' answered the Dutchman, without any show of indignation. 'Certainly there is a few among them,' continued the customer; and after a little more of this kind of chaffering the bargain is struck."*

But although London is chiefly supplied with Eels from Holland, we must not suppose there are no valuable Eeleries in the British Isles. There is a large Eel-fishery at Toome, on the lower Bann, where from fifty to sixty tons of Eels are annually caught in the migrating season. "As many as seventy thousand Eels," we are told, have been taken at this place in one night, all of the Sharp-nosed species, with the slight exception of, perhaps, a dozen Broad-noses, that have been accidently mixed up with the shoal. "On one night in 1842," observes Mr. Pinkerton, "when I visited the Toome fishery, there were caught in round numbers, eleven thousand Eels. Now, as the persons who purchase the produce of a season's fishing by contract expressly stipulate that they will not take a single Broad-nosed Eel, every Eel—with a dexterity of eye and hand worthy of a Robin or a Frikel, and only acquired by long practice—is carefully counted, and all Broad-nosed ones thrown aside. And on this occasion there were only three Broad-noses in the whole number."†

There is also an extensive Eel-fishery on the Erne. That Eels were formerly in high repute in England seems clear from the fact that certain places take their names from them. Ely, according to one derivation, has its name from the Eel, the rents being formerly paid in this fish; the lords of the manors, it is said, being annually entitled to more than one hundred thousand. Elmore and Ellesmere are said to have the same derivation.

As to the question of the wholesomeness of Eel's flesh, there can be no doubt that, owing to the large amount of rich fatty matter which it contains, it is not a diet suited to the stomach of a man of weak digestion, unless eaten in very small quantities. I confine this observation to the flesh of a clean-fed Common Eel; drain-fed individuals, as well as the offensive Broad-nose, are likely to agree with none but very coarse feeders indeed. It was not the fault of the Lampreys that King Henry died, it was his own fault for eating too much. And although I cannot acquiesce in old Galen's expostulation with the gods for giving

* *London Labour and London Poor,* vol. i. p. 66.

† When I visited Toome in July, 1878, the Eel fishery was just commencing; and I saw great numbers packed in boxes which had been caught during the night in the large purse-shaped nets set across the stream of the Bann.

SHARP-NOSED EEL   BROAD-NOSED EEL

Eels so delicious a taste and so malignant and dangerous an operation, I must not forget the remark of Fuller, "Grant them never so good, excess is a venomous sting in the most wholesome flesh, fish and fowl." However, be this as it may, "the proof of the pudding is in the eating;" and it is certain that hot Eels are a most wholesome and nutritive food to the London poor. "Hot Eels" form an important street luxury; and Mr. Mayhew* has given a minute and interesting account of the trade.

The skin of the Eel is remarkably tough. In the times of the ancient Romans it was used to whip naughty boys, who were thus exempt from the infliction of any pecuniary fine, having been mulcted, not in coin, but in their own skin!† A similar use of Eel-skin prevailed in the sixteenth century, as appears from the following quotation from Rabelais:—"Whereupon his master gave him such a sound lash with an Eel-skin, that his own skin would have been worth nothing to make bag-pipe bags of."‡

Eel-skin is the object of a small trade in some cities. In Tartary it is used, after having being oiled, as a substitute for window-glass. It is supposed by the poor to be a good remedy for cramp or rheumatism, and I have often spoken with poor persons who attach great virtue to the skin of the Eel. "I amner quite sure, maister," said an old man to me once, "whether it be a sartain cure for the rheumatis; but for cromp, I knows there be nothing loike it."

Eel-skin must have inflicted severe punishment on boy-skin, not only on account of its toughness, but from the presence of innumerable numbers of concretions of carbonate of lime. A portion of Eel-skin mounted in Canada balsam, and viewed under the polariscope, is a beautiful object for the microscope. Eels vary much in colour; the silver Eel is generally the most highly prized. Silver Eels are certainly very delicious, but, according to my own experience, I find the green-bellied Eels equally good; nor have I any fault to find with yellow-bellied specimens. Prejudice, of course, is against both of these colours, but I can confidently recommend any Common Eel if he is taken out of clear water. I have seen a cream-coloured Broad-nose, which was doubtless an albino, and owed its whiteness to the absence of pigment cells. Sometimes piebald Eels have been met with, and a correspondent in the *Field* newspaper mentions his once having received an Eel of a rich golden colour like Gold-fish.

It is not common in this country to meet with an Eel above the weight of five pounds, though there are well authenticated instances of Eels attaining the weight of fifteen, or even twenty pounds.§

---

        * *London Labour and London Poor*, vol. i. p. 160.            † Pliny, N. H. ix. 23.

‡ Book ii. c. 30, translated by Mr. Ozell. Lond. 1737. The term *anguilla* was in later times applied to a whip made of leather thongs, which was used to flog boys. See Isidore's glosses quoted by Du Cange in his Latin Glossary. "Anguilla est quâ coercendi in Scholis pueri, quæ vulgo Scutica dicitur."

§ The substance of the above remarks on Eels was written by me a few years ago, and appeared in a number of the *Quarterly Review*. I have Mr. Murray's kind permission to make use of that article.

EEL BUCKS ON THE THAMES.

*Order IV.*
*PHYSOSTOMI.*

*Family*
*MURÆNIDÆ.*
*Group*—ANGUILLINA.

# SHARP-NOSED EEL.

### *(Anguilla vulgaris.)*

| | |
|---|---|
| *Anguilla omnium autorum, An Eel,* | WILLUGHBY, Hist. Pisc. p. 109, tab. G. 5. |
| *Muræna unicolor, maxilla inferiore longiore,* | ARTEDI, Gen. Pisc. p. 24, No. 1. |
| *Muræna anguilla,* | LIN., Sys. Nat. i. p. 426; BLOCH, Fisch. Deutschl. iii. p. 4, taf. 73. |
| *Common Eel,* | PENNANT, Brit. Zool. iii. p. 191. |
| *Anguilla vulgaris,* | FLEM., Brit. Anim. p. 199; SIEBOLD, Süsserwasserf. p. 342; GÜNTHER'S Cat. viii. p. 28. |
| *Anguilla acutirostris and mediorostris,* | YARRELL, Brit. Fish. ii. p. 381 and p. 399; COUCH, Fish. Brit. Isl. iv. p. 326, pl. 234 and 235. |
| *Anguilla hibernica,* | COUCH, p. 328, pl. 235. |

*Characters of the Genus* ANGUILLA.—"Small scales are imbedded in the skin. Upper jaw not projecting beyond the lower. Teeth small, forming bands. Gill openings narrow, at the base of the pectoral fins. The dorsal fin commences at a considerable distance from the occiput. Cosmopolitan, but not extending into the arctic regions."—GÜNTHER.

A S I think that I have already treated of most that can be said of interest in the natural history of the Eel, it will not be necessary for me to do more than to describe the species of Eels which occur in this country. There can be no doubt that Eels, like other fish, are subject to vary, not only in colour but in slight structural peculiarities. Any one who has seen the great numbers caught in the Eel traps, as, for instance, at Toome Bridge, County Antrim, and has had opportunities of noticing them, must have observed considerable difference amongst individuals in the form of the snout; in very many cases the snout is much pointed, in others less pointed, and not unfrequently the nose is almost obtuse. Hence some naturalists have regarded individuals with differently formed snouts as forming distinct species; which have been described as "Sharp-nosed Eels" (*A. acutirostris*), "Middle-nosed Eels" (*A. mediorostris*), and "Blunt-nosed Eels" (*A. latirostris*). This difference in the form of the nose, when existing as the *only* characteristic, is not regarded by the greatest authority on such matters, Dr. Günther, as being sufficient to constitute specific difference. It would appear, however, that there are two species of Eel, the *A. vulgaris* with its nasal varieties of form, and the *A. latirostris* which besides being generally possessed of a very obtuse snout, has other peculiarities which would entitle it to specific distinction. To these peculiarities as mentioned by Günther, I think I may add from personal experience that one of a disagreeable flavour. The varieties of the Common Eel are always, when taken from good waters, most delicious; and no difference in flavour can be detected from the Sharp-nosed variety, the Middle-nosed variety, and the Blunt-nosed variety of *A. vulgaris* when taken out of the same water; but my experience of *A. latirostris* would lead me to discard it altogether as food. In a large reservoir of excellent water which supplies a canal, at Knighton in Shropshire, there exist the varieties of the Common Eel and the Broad-nosed species. I have seen many taken on Eel-lines and trimmers of both species, and I have always found the flavour of the Broad-nosed species very bad eating.

The following is Dr. Günther's description of *Anguilla vulgaris;* the essential distinctive characters between this species and the other are printed in italics:—"The length of the head is contained once and one half, or once and a third in the distance of the gill opening from the origin of the dorsal fin, and twice and one third, or twice and two thirds in its distance from the vent. *Distance between the commencements of the dorsal and anal fins as long as or somewhat longer than the head. Lips narrow:* lower jaw prominent. Angle of the mouth below the eye, which is rather small or of moderate size, much shorter than the snout. Maxillary teeth equal and small. Tail considerably longer than the body."

---

*Order IV.*
*PHYSOSTOMI.*

*Family*
*MURÆNIDÆ.*
*Group*—ANGUILLINA.

# BROAD-NOSED EEL.

*(Anguilla latirostris.)*

| *Grigs or Gluts,* | PENNANT, Brit. Zool. iii. p. 194, ed. 1812. |
| *Anguilla latirostris,* | YARRELL, ii. p. 396; JENYNS' Man. p. 474; GÜNTHER'S Cat. viii. p. 32. |

PENNANT speaking of this Eel says, "Besides these" (Eels which vary in colour) "there is another variety of this fish, known in the Thames by the name of *grigs*, and about Oxford by that of *grigs* or *gluts*. They are scarcely ever seen near Oxford in the winter, but appear in spring, and bite readily at the hook, which Common Eels in that neighbourhood will not. They have a large head, a blunter nose, thicker skin, and are less fat than the common sort; neither are they so much esteemed; nor do they often exceed three or four pounds in weight." The term *grig* is also applied to any kind of Eel, especially to those individuals of small growth.

I have taken this Broad-nosed species, in company with Mr. Masefield, of Ellerton Hall, on several occasions, in Knighton Reservoir. Our plan is to set trimmers in the different parts of the pool baited with small Roach or other bright coloured fish, the bait being near the bottom; the bull-headed appearance and great thick lips, generally speaking, indicate the species. As already stated, as food it may be discarded; at least to the palate its flesh is very disappointing when one thinks of the deliciousness of the " white armed goddess," the Common Eel.

Dr. Günther describes this species as follows:—" The length of the head is contained once and a half, or once and three fourths in the distance of the gill opening from the origin of the dorsal fin, and twice and a half in its distance from the vent. *Distance between the commencements of the dorsal and anal fins shorter than the head. Lips broad and fleshy*, lower jaw prominent. Angle of the mouth below the hind margin of the eye, which is rather small, much shorter than the snout. Tail considerably longer than the body. Mandibulary teeth in a single band, without longitudinal groove."

This species occurs in Europe, the Nile, China, New Zealand, and the West Indies; it is the only form of all the varieties of the Common Eel, which is regarded by Günther as entitled to specific rank. " The width and length of the snout cannot be taken as a distinctive character, as there are found all intermediate forms between the extremes. I am more inclined to consider the situation of the origin of the dorsal fin, and the development of the lips, to indicate a distinct species."

Some years ago when I had been for some time occupied in dissecting a number of Common Eels and a couple of Congers, I observed the invariable presence of two sub-triangular openings in the fleshy portion of the head, just at its juncture with the spinal column. My first impression with regard to the use of these orifices was that they were connected with the auditory organs, and that they probably led to the vestibular cavity. Although so far, I believe, as has hitherto been observed, the existence of external auditory organs in the whole class of fishes is very exceptional—the Skates amongst the cartilaginous order, and a few of the members belonging to the *Gadidæ* and *Clupeidæ* amongst the osseous order alone possessing them—still I thought it not improbable that the Eel, which is commonly supposed to hear well, and which is occasionally an overland traveller, might prove another exception to the general rule. I may observe that Mr. Cholmondeley Pennell, in his work *The Angler Naturalist* (p. 397), asserts the presence of an " ear or auditory aperture" amongst the various mucus pores about the head, but from the most minute examination of a large number of Eels' heads I can confidently affirm that no such external auditory aperture exists. I have, therefore, no doubt that Mr. Pennell must have mistaken two of the mucus pores for ears.

Upon my inserting a bristle in each of these orifices, and on clearing away the flesh from the head, I found that each bristle traversed a closed-in duct or tube in the cranium, and came out just above the orbital bone (see fig. 1). On making a vertical section of the skull, and examining with great care the vestibular sacs, I became convinced that the tubular ducts had no connection with them nor with the auditory nerve (fig. 4). Each of these tubes, which in the Common Eel is just wide enough to admit a fine piece of silk-gut, terminates in a membranous fold or hollow in the subcutaneous tissue just above the eye (fig. 5), and contains a certain quantity of thin fluid or lymph, which, by the way, bears no resemblance to *mucus*. Are these cavities reservoirs for the supply of fluid to lubricate the surface, and may we conjecture that the lymph is drawn up the tubular ducts by capillary attraction?

There is little reason to doubt that the cranial ducts *are* connected with the so-called " mucus system," which is very complicated in the Eel tribe, but *in what manner* they are so I have hitherto been unable to satisfy myself, and leave the determination of the question to the investigation of more experienced anatomists.

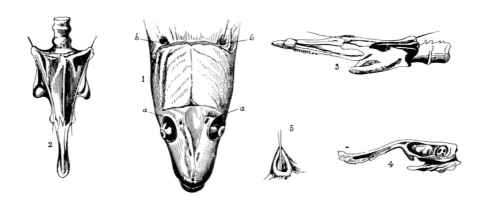

Fig. 1.—Head of *A. vulgaris*, showing the orifices of the canals.  *a*, Anterior orifice.  *b*, posterior ditto.
Fig. 2.—The same, with the soft parts removed, and with a bristle inserted into each canal.  Fig. 3.—Side view of same.
Fig. 4.—Vertical section of cranium of *A. vulgaris*.    Fig. 5.—Membranous fold or hollow in which the canal terminates.

# LAMPREYS.

THE Lampreys, Lamperns, or "nine-holes," as in some places they are termed, belong to a very remarkable family of fishes. From their habit of attaching themselves to stones or other submerged bodies, they have received the name of *Petromyzontidæ*, which in Greek signifies "stone-suckers," a term aptly proposed by Artedi. The body is worm-like, cylindrical, and limbless; the skeleton is imperfectly developed, being cartilaginous; the notochord is persistent through life; there are no ribs, and no real jaws; the skin is without scales and lubricous; the fin-fold of the tail is destitute of fin rays; the gills have no branchial arches, and are formed like little pockets or pouches. The mouth is of very peculiar

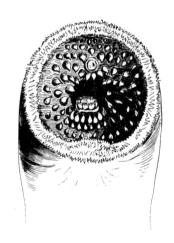

Sucker of Lamprey.

structure, of circular form in the adult fish, suctorial, and armed with either simple or many-pointed teeth of horny consistency. The nasal cavities do not communicate with the throat; the gill-pouches, with their external holes or openings, are seven in number, situated on each side of the neck, so that the popular name of "nine-holes" is an erroneous one. The respiratory apparatus is very peculiar; fishes as a rule admit water through the mouth and emit it through the branchial slit, or gill opening; the Lampreys fix themselves to submerged bodies by their suctorial mouth, so that when in such a position it is obvious that no water can be admitted through the mouth. How then is the water admitted so as to oxygenate the blood of the gill-pouches? The water is alternately received and expelled by the external openings of the gill-sacs. "If a Lamprey, while so attached to the side of a vessel, be held with one series of apertures out of the water, the respiratory currents are seen to enter by the submerged orifices, and after traversing the corresponding sacs and the pharynx, to pass through the opposite branchiæ, and to be forcibly ejected therefrom by the exposed orifices......The cyclostomous fishes thus present an obvious affinity to the *Cephalapoda*, inasmuch as the branchial currents are independent of the parts concerned in deglutition."— (Prof. Owen, *Catal. Phys. Scr. Mus. R.C.S.*, ii. p. 80.) The heart has an auricle and a ventricle, but no bulbus arteriosus. The alimentary canal is straight, simple, and without cæcal appendages; there is no swim-bladder. Probably all the species go through a metamorphosis.

The *Petromyzontidæ* are found in the fresh waters and around the sea-coasts of the temperate regions of both hemispheres. By means of their suctorial mouths they attach themselves to other fishes, and scrape off their flesh by their rasp-like teeth. The food consists also of worms and insect larvæ. The British species are three in number, and are all of them excellent food; but owing to the small size of one of the species, only two are of any commercial value.

1. SEA LAMPREY    2. LAMPERN    3. PLANER'S LAMPREY    4. PRIDE

Sub-class
*CYCLOSTOMATA.*

*Family*
*PETROMYZONTIDÆ.*

# Sea Lamprey.

*(Petromyzon marinus.)*

| | |
|---|---|
| *Lampetra major,* | Aldrov., iv. cap. 13. |
| *Mustela sive Lampetra,* | Bellon, De Aquatil. p. 76. |
| *A Lamprey* or *Lamprey Eel,* | Willughby, Hist. Pisc. p. 105. |
| *Petromyzon maculosus, ordinibus dentium circiter viginti,* | Artedi, Spec. Pisc. p. 90, No. 2. |
| *Petromyzon marinus,* | Lin., Sys. Nat. i. p. 394; Donovan, Brit. Fish. iv. pl. 81; Flem., Brit. An. p. 163; Yarrell, ii. p. 598; Siebold, Süsserwasserf. p. 368; Günther's Cat. viii. p. 501. |
| *Sea Lamprey,* | Pennant, Brit. Zool. iii. p. 102, ed. 1812; Couch, Fish. Brit. Isl. iv. p. 385, pl. 247, fig. 1. |

*Characters of the Genus* Petromyzon.—"Dorsal fins two, the posterior continuous with the caudal. The maxillary dentition consists of two teeth placed close together, or of a transverse bicuspid ridge; lingual teeth serrated. Coasts and fresh waters of the northern hemisphere."—Günther.

THE Sea Lamprey, which from its marbled appearance was called *Petromyzon maculosus* by Artedi, is an inhabitant of the rivers and coasts of Europe, North America, and West Africa, and specimens from all these parts are now in the British Museum. It occurs in

Scotland and Ireland. The Severn, in the neighbourhood of Gloucester and Worcester, has long been celebrated for this and another species, viz. the *P. fluviatilis*, which is considerably smaller than the *P. marinus*. In the neighbourhood of Worcester the term *Lamprey* is usually employed to designate the *P. marinus*, while the *P. fluviatilis* is known by the name of *Lampern*.

The species now under consideration is the one which brought King Henry the First to an untimely end; that monarch, it is said, having made a too full repast on this fish. Pennant states that it was an old custom for the city of Gloucester to present the kings with a Lamprey-pie, covered with a large raised crust. As the gift was made at Christmas, the corporation had great difficulty in procuring fresh Lampreys at that time, though they gave a guinea apiece for them so early in the season. At present, as I learned when I was at Worcester last October, the Sea Lamprey is taken only in the spring, when it is ascending the river from the sea for the purpose of spawning. They are caught both in nets and in large wicker weels. Pennant says that notwithstanding the accident which befel Henry I., Lampreys continued in high esteem. "Henry IV. granted protection to such ships as brought over Lampreys for the table of his royal consort. His successor issued out a warrant to William of Nantes, for supplying him and his army with Lampreys, wheresoever they happened to march."

The circular suctorial mouth of the Lamprey is made use of, at spawning time, for the purpose of forming furrows or holes in the gravel, by removing stones from the place where the fish wishes to deposit its spawn. Speaking of the Lampreys of Scotland, which make their appearance in the rivers there later than in southern rivers, Sir William Jardine says— "They ascend our rivers to breed about the end of June, and remain until the beginning of August. They are not furnished with any elongation of the jaw, to form the receiving furrows at this important season; but the want is supplied by their sucker-like mouth, by which they individually remove each stone. Their power is immense. Stones of a very large size are transported, and a large furrow is soon formed. The *P. marinus* remain in pairs; two on each spawning place; and while thus employed, they retain themselves affixed by the mouth to a large stone." From enquiries I made when at Worcester, the Lamprey spawning-bed consists of either furrows or holes made in the gravel in May;* the fish remain in the river a very short time after spawning; they seem much weakened after that process, and are quickly washed down by the river into the sea, where no doubt they recruit their exhausted condition.

I have never tasted the Sea Lamprey, but if the quality of its flesh is at all similar to that of the River Lampern, it must be most delicious eating.† According to Parnell the fishermen in the Forth, above Alloa, when they accidentally take Lampreys in their nets, "invariably return them again to the water, having a prejudice against them." Consequently they are never under any circumstances seen in the Edinburgh markets. The snake-like form and unpleasant look of the fish doubtless accounts for Scotch antipathy, as I have alluded to when speaking of Eels. Mr. Couch also, in his *Fauna of Cornwall*, says of this species that it is common, but rarely used as food.

The words *Lamprey* and *Lampern*, from *lambere*, "to lick," and *petra*, "a stone," answers to the Greek *petromyzon* already explained.

The characters of this species are thus given by Günther. "Two pointed maxillary teeth close together; mandibulatory tooth single, crescent shaped, with from seven to nine cusps. Two pairs of lunate, pectinate lingual teeth; the teeth of the anterior pair confluent. Suctorial

---

* Fishing for the Sea Lamprey in the Severn near Worcester begins in February and lasts till May.

† The mode of preparing the Lamprey, or Eel Lamprey as it is also called, at Worcester before cooking is by putting the fish in boiling water and then scraping them with a knife; this is done to get rid of their abundant mucus; they are then placed in cold water, and are ready for stewing or potting.

disc with numerous conical teeth, arranged in oblique series, those nearest to the buccal cavity being largest and partly bicuspid. First dorsal fin rather widely separated from the second. The distance of the last gill-opening from the extremity of the snout is one fifth, or in small individuals, one fourth of the total length. Body marbled with black."

---

*Sub-class*　　　　　　　　　　　　　　　　　　　　　　　　　　　　*Family*
CYCLOSTOMATA.　　　　　　　　　　　　　　　　　　　　　PETROMYZONTIDÆ.

# LAMPERN, OR RIVER LAMPREY.

(*Petromyzon fluviatilis.*)

| | |
|---|---|
| *Lampetræ medium genus,* | WILLUGHBY, Hist. Pisc. p. 106, tab. G. 3, fig. 2. |
| *Lampetra parva et fluviatilis,* | ROND., De Pisc. Fluv. p. 202. |
| *Petromyzon,* | ARTEDI, Spec. Pisc. p. 89, No. 1. |
| *Petromyzon fluviatilis,* | LIN., Sys. Nat. i. p. 394; DONOVAN, Brit. Fish. iii. pl. 54; YARRELL, ii. p. 604; SIEBOLD, Süsserwasserf. p. 372; GÜNTHER'S Cat. viii. p. 502. |
| *Lesser Lamprey,* | PENNANT, Brit. Zool. iii. p. 106, pl. x. fig. 2, ed. 1812. |
| *Lampern, Silver Lamprey,* | COUCH, Fish. Brit. Isl. iv. p. 395-400, pl. 247, figs. 2 & 3. |
| *Petromyzon pricka,* | LACÉP., i. p. 18. |

THE River Lamprey, or, to distinguish it from the Sea Lamprey, the Lampern, as it is more generally called, is a much smaller species than that already described. It occurs in the rivers and on the coasts of Europe, North America, and Japan, and has therefore a very wide geographical distribution. In this country it is abundant in many of the rivers of England, Scotland, and Ireland. It is probable that this species is not so generally migratory in its habits as *P. marinus*, and that it is sometimes, and perhaps frequently, a permanent inhabitant of fresh water. Yarrell's opinion is that it generally remains all the year in fresh water. "In the Thames," he says, "I am certain it is to be obtained every month in the year." From enquiries I made at Worcester, Lampern fishing begins, in the Severn and Teme, about the 1st. of October, and lasts till February or March; the fish then disappear. Lacépède states that the *P. fluviatilis* is an inhabitant rather of lakes than of rivers, that it ascends the latter only when about to spawn, that is to say, in the spring. Couch is, I think, correct when he says that some individuals have been found in the open sea, "to which it is probable they do not proceed at all seasons, as if in regular migration, and where they do not continue long."

In Pennant's time Lamperns were found in the Thames, Severn, and Dee; they were potted with the larger species, being preferred by some people to it, as being milder in flavour. He states that vast quantities were taken about Mortlake and sold to the Dutch as bait for their cod-fishing. "Above four hundred and fifty thousand have been sold in a season, at forty shillings a thousand." Owing to the present impure condition of the Thames, the numbers of these fish, I believe, have fallen off very considerably. The head-quarters for Lampern fishing is on the Severn, near Worcester and Gloucester, where great numbers are caught in wicker weels from October to March or April, about which time they spawn; nothing more is seen of them after that time. In order to get rid of the mucus the fish are placed in hot water in a vessel and whisked about with a bunch of straw; they are then put in cold water for a short time, and are ready for stewing or potting, under either of which happy conditions they are most delicious food, even rivalling the white-fleshed Eel in richness of flavour. The ordinary price for fresh Lamperns is about ten shillings a hundred.

The River Lampern lives on the larvæ of insects, worms, and according to Bloch the flesh of dead fish. The ordinary adult size of the Lampern is about a foot in length; when first out of the water the back and sides are of a pretty uniform brown, with a tinge of olive or green on the upper part of the head and back; the belly is pure white. "The maxillary tooth is single, forming a transverse ridge with a cusp at each end; mandibulary tooth single, crescent-shaped, with about seven cusps. Tongue with a broad, transverse, trenchant tooth, which is provided with a median cusp. Two or three bi- or tri-cuspid teeth on each side of the gullet; the other teeth of the suctorial disc are small and not numerous. First dorsal fin separated from the second by an interspace. Colouration immaculate; sides silvery."

---

*Sub-class*
CYCLOSTOMATA.

*Family*
PETROMYZONTIDÆ.

# SMALL LAMPREY, PRIDE, SANDPRIDE, PLANER'S LAMPREY.

### (*Petromyzon branchialis.*)

(1.) LARVAL FORM.

| | |
|---|---|
| *Lampetra cæca seu oculis carens,* | |
| *Einblinder, Neunogen,* | WILLUGHBY, Hist. Pisc. p. 107, tab. G. 3 fig. 1. |
| *Petromyzon corpore annuloso,* | ARTEDI, Spec. Pisc. p. 90, No. 3. |
| *Petromyzon branchialis,* | CUVIER, R. An. ii. p. 406; LIN., Syst. Nat. i. p. 394; LACÉP., i. p. 26, pl. 2, fig. 1; TURTON, Brit. Faun. p. 110. |
| *Pride Lamprey,* | PENNANT, Brit. Zool. iii. p. 107, pl. x. fig. 3, ed. 1812. |
| *Ammocœtes branchialis,* | FLEM., Brit. An. p. 164; JENYNS' Man. p. 522; YARRELL, ii. p. 609; PARNELL, Fish. Firth of Forth, Mem. Wern. Nat. Hist. Soc. vii. p. 447. |
| *Mud Lamprey,* | COUCH, Fish. Brit. Isl. iv. p. 404. |

(2.) MATURE FORM.

| | |
|---|---|
| *Petromyzon planeri,* | BLOCH, Fisch. Deutschl. iii. p. 47; LACÉP., i. p. 30, pl. 3, fig. 1; JENYNS' Man. p. 522; YARRELL, ii. p. 607; SIEBOLD, Süsserwasserf. p. 375 (Kleines Neunauge); COUCH, Fish. Brit. Isl. iv. p 402, pl. 248, fig. 1; GÜNTHER'S Cat. viii. p. 504. |
| *Petromyzon sanguisuga,* | LACÉP., ii. p. 101. |

ALTHOUGH this little Lampern is too small to be of any commercial value, it is peculiarly interesting in a zoological point of view, because it is the species in which Professor Aug. Müller first demonstrated that the individuals of this genus undergo a metamorphosis. The larval form, under the name of *Ammocœtes* (Duméril, Cuv., *R. An.*), was long considered to be a species distinct from the *Petromyzon planeri*, until Müller (Müller's *Archiv.*, 1856, p. 325) succeeded in tracing the development of *Ammocœtes branchialis* into *P. planeri*. It is probable, therefore, that not only the fishes of the genus *Petromyzon*, but also those of allied genera pass through a similar metamorphosis. In the larval form, the general shape of the body differs in no important respect from the mature individual; but the upper lip is semicircular, and the lower lip is very small; there are no teeth, and the mouth is furnished with numerous short membranous cirri. The eyes are very small, and are situated at the bottom of a small deep depression or groove. *Ammocœtes branchialis* is said to require three or four years for its complete development. The term *Ammocœtes*, or "sand-dweller," refers to the habits of this little larval form hiding itself in the sand or mud, for owing to the immature horse-shoe structure of the mouth, it is unable to adhere to stones or other submerged bodies, as in the case of the adult forms. The term *branchialis* was bestowed upon this fish by Linnæus, from a notion that it attached itself to the gills of fishes. As to size, it seldom exceeds six or seven inches in length, and is about as thick as a goose-quill. The fishermen use these fish as a bait in *whiffing* for Pollacks. "Buried in scattered companies in the soft soil," writes Couch, "it may be said to lead the life of the mole; and it is there it finds all it wants of food, in search of which, by taste or scent, it moves through its tracks as appetite or disposition prompts; and from observation it may be judged that, except in search of new feeding ground, it never willingly exposes itself to the dangers of a rapid stream, the strength of which it might scarcely be able to stem, or to the appetite of any prowling inhabitant of the river, from which its powers would not enable it to escape." Mr. Couch succeeded in keeping specimens of this larval form for months alive in stagnant water, with mud at the bottom, without injury to its health or activity. Dr. Plot, in his *History of Oxfordshire*, calls this Lampern the Pride of the Isis; the term *prid*, or *pride*, is probably a form of the fuller word Lam-*prey*, from which by a process of phonetic decay it appears to have been derived.*

In the mature form of this species the mouth is circular, and provided with numerous papillæ forming a fringe,—hence called "The Fringe-lipped Lampern" by some authors,—the two dorsal fins are in close connexion, but separated by a deep notch; the dentition differs from that of *P. fluviatilis* merely in having the cusps less prominent and more obtuse. It grows to the length of eight or nine inches. This species is widely distributed, occurring in the rivers of Europe and North America. The spawning time is in March and April. This species was named by Bloch after Planer, a Professor at Erfurt. In colour *P. branchialis* hardly differs from *P. fluviatilis*. I find this species common in the brooks and streams of various parts of Shropshire. Excepting as bait or food for other fish it has no value.

---

* "*Pride*, a Mud Lamprey. *West.* 'Lumbrici are littell fyshes taken in small ryvers, whiche are lyke to lampurnes, but they be muche lesse, and somewhat yeolowe, and are called in Wilshyre *prides*,' (Elyote's *Dictionarie*, fol. Lond. 1599."—Halliwell's *Arch. Dict.* p. 645.)

# Appendix

# PPENDIX.

---

## FRESHWATER FISHERIES ACT, 8TH. AUGUST, 1878.

BE it enacted by the Queen's Most Excellent Majesty, by and with the advice and consent of the Lords Spiritual and Temporal, and Commons, in this present Parliament assembled, and by the authority of the same, as follows:—

1. This Act may be cited as the Freshwater Fisheries Act, 1878.

2. This Act shall, so far as is consistent with the tenour thereof, be read as one with the Salmon Fishery Acts, 1861 to 1876.

3. This Act shall not extend to Scotland or Ireland, nor, except as regards sub-sections four and five of section eleven, and as regards section twelve, to the counties of Norfolk and Suffolk, and the county of the city of Norwich.

4. This Act shall come into operation from and immediately after the thirty-first day of December one thousand eight hundred and seventy-eight.

5. Sections eight and nine of the Salmon Fishery Act, 1861, (which relate to fishing with lights, spears, and other prohibited instruments, and to using roe as a bait,) and section sixty-four of the Salmon Fishery Act, 1865, (which provides a close time for trout and char), shall, as amended by the subsequent Salmon Fishery Acts, apply to trout and char in all waters within the limits of this Act; and the term "salmon river," as used in section sixty-four of the Salmon Fishery Act, 1865, shall include any such water.

6. The provisions of the Salmon Fishery Acts, 1865 and 1873, which relate to the formation, alteration, combination, and dissolution of fishery districts, and to the appointment, qualification, proceedings, and powers of conservators, shall extend and apply to all waters within the limits of this Act frequented by trout or char; and the term "salmon river" in the fourth and nineteenth sections of the Salmon Fishery Act, 1865, and in the twenty-sixth section of the Salmon Fishery Act, 1873, shall mean any river frequented by salmon, trout, or char.

7. In any fishery district subject to a board of conservators, the conservators shall have power to issue licences for the day, week, season, or any part thereof, to all persons fishing for trout or char, and, in the event of the power being exercised in any fishery district, the provisions of the thirty-third, thirty-fourth, thirty-fifth, thirty-sixth, and thirty-seventh sections of the Salmon Fishery Act, 1865, and of the twenty-first, twenty-second, twenty-fourth, and twenty-fifth sections of the Salmon Fishery Act, 1873, (relative to licences,) shall, with respect to such district, be construed as if the words "trout or char" were inserted throughout after the word "salmon."
Provided as follows:
(1.) A licence to fish for salmon shall have effect as a licence to fish for trout and char.
(2.) The fee payable for a licence to fish for trout or char exclusively of salmon in any district shall not exceed one third of the maximum amount chargeable for fishing for salmon under the provisions of the 21st. section of the Salmon Fishery Act, 1873.

8. The provisions of the thirty-first section of the Salmon Fishery Act, 1865, and of the thirty-sixth, thirty-seventh, and thirty-eighth sections of the Salmon Fishery Act, 1873, relative to the powers of water bailiffs, shall extend and apply to all waters within the limits of this Act, as if the words "salmon river," wherever they occur in such sections, included all waters frequented by salmon, trout, or char.

9. The provisions of the thirty-fourth section of the Salmon Fishery Act, 1861, which empower any justice of the peace upon information on oath to authorise the search of any premises, shall extend to all offences committed or alleged to have been committed under this Act, and that section shall be construed and have effect as if the word "salmon" included trout, char, and all freshwater fish.

10. The provisions of the Salmon Fishery Act, 1876, which empower a board of conservators to alter the period during which it shall be illegal to take or kill trout in any fishery district, shall extend to char, and the fourth section of that Act shall be construed and have effect as if the words "or char" followed the word "trout" in that section.

11.   (1.) In this section the term "freshwater fish" includes all kinds of fish (other than pollan, trout, and char) which live in fresh water, except those kinds which migrate to or from the open sea:

(2.) The period between the fifteenth day of March and the fifteenth day of June, both inclusive, shall be a close season for freshwater fish:

(3.) If any person during this close season fishes for, catches, or attempts to catch or kill any freshwater fish in any river, lake, tributary, stream, or other water connected or communicating with such river, he shall, on summary conviction before two justices, be liable to a fine not exceeding forty shillings:

Nothing in this sub-section shall apply—

(*a.*) To the owner of any several or private fishery where trout, char, or grayling are specially preserved destroying within such fishery any freshwater fish other than grayling;

(*b.*) To any person angling in any several fishery with the leave of the owner of such fishery or in any public fishery under the jurisdiction of a board of conservators with the leave of said board;

(*c.*) To any person taking freshwater fish for scientific purposes;

(*d.*) To any person taking freshwater fish for use as bait:

(4.) If any person during this close season buys, sells, or exposes for sale, or has in his possession for sale, any fresh-water fish, he shall, on summary conviction before two justices, be liable to a fine not exceeding forty shillings:

(5.) On a second or any subsequent conviction under this section the person convicted shall be liable to a fine not exceeding five pounds:

(6.) After every conviction under this section the person or persons convicted shall forfeit all fish so caught, bought, sold, exposed for sale, or in possession for sale, and shall be liable, at the discretion of the convicting justices, to the forfeiture of all instruments used in the taking of such fish:

(7.) A board of conservators appointed under the Salmon Fishery Acts, 1861 to 1876, or under this Act, may, as regards any or all kinds of freshwater fish, with the approval of the Secretary of State, exempt the whole or any part of their district from the operation of the first, second, and third sub-sections of this section. The exemptions shall be advertised in such manner as the Secretary of State shall direct:

(8.) The provisions of the Salmon Fishery Acts, 1861 to 1876, as to legal proceedings, offences, and penalties under those Acts, shall apply to legal proceedings, offences, and penalties under this section.

12. The Fisheries (Dynamite) Act, 1877, which prohibits the use of dynamite or other explosive substance for the catching or destruction of fish in a public fishery, shall apply to the use of any such substance for the catching or destruction of fish in any water, whether public or private, within the limits of this Act.

13. So much of the Act of Parliament made and passed in the eighteenth year of the reign of King George the Third, chapter thirty-three, intituled "An Act for the better preservation of fish and regulating the fisheries in the River Severn and Verniew," as prohibits any person or persons in the months of June or July laying, drawing, making use of, or fishing within the said rivers, or either of them, with any net the meshes whereof shall be under two inches and a half square by the standard, and not extended, or ten inches round, allowing to each mesh four knots, is hereby repealed.

## SLOB, OR TIDAL TROUT.

THROUGH the kind exertions of Mr. William Haynes, I have an opportunity of examining one of these fish. Owing to the severity of the weather few had as yet (February 25th., 1879) made their appearance in the river, and Mr. Haynes was able to send me one specimen only. From an examination of a single individual I am not able to speak at all with certainty as to what these Slob Trout really are. The general appearance is that of a well-fed Common Trout (*S. fario*), from which, however, it seems to me to differ in a few structural characters. The maxillary in the specimen before me—a fish twelve inches in length, three in depth, and weighing nearly twelve ounces—is not so strong as that organ is in *fario*, nor does it extend perceptibly beyond the posterior orbit of the eye, as is the case in the Brown Trout. The tail is very decidedly forked, while in Trout of this size the caudal fin is almost always truncate; the sides and belly below the lateral line are more silvery, and appear to be covered with smaller and more deciduous scales than in *fario*. The dentition in the Slob Trout is rather feeble; the head of the vomer is without teeth; on the body of this bone there is a single series of teeth, fourteen or fifteen in number, arranged in a zigzag line; the dentition in *fario* is strong. In these particulars, therefore, the Slob Trout bears some resemblance to *S. trutta*, although in general appearance it is more like *S. fario*.

The following is a description of this specimen:—Total length twelve inches; greatest depth three inches; length of the head two inches and five eighths; maxillary one inch long, rather feeble, extending very slightly beyond the posterior orbit of the eye; prœoperculum crescent-shaped, with an indistinct lower limb; suboperculum extending beyond the operculum; fins rather short. Dorsal fin pale brown, with pale purplish spots; adipose fin edged with red; the caudal fin forked, the lateral margins edged with red; fins without black and white outer edge; gill-cover with five or six purplish round spots; back and sides light purplish brown, with numerous large dark purple or red reticulated spots; several of these spots are surrounded with a whitish ring; there are some red or vermilion spots on the lateral line and below it; scales small and rather deciduous; belly and sides silvery, but in some lights this part is somewhat cream-coloured.

The specimen sent, which came in excellent condition, was amazingly fat; the stomach, œsophagus, and mouth were absolutely crammed with elvers, or young Eels, about two inches long; it had also been feeding on some crustacea allied to the fresh-water shrimp. The stomach and pyloric appendages were thickly spread over with fat. This specimen appears to be a sterile male. Mr. Haynes's account of the habits of the Tidal Trout will be found at page 114. They ascend the rivers with the flow of the tide, descending with the ebb; they are to be caught from January to May. In the summer they disappear, probably migrating to the sea, where they remain till the beginning of another year Nothing is known about their spawning. In very cold weather in January and February they remain in the slob, and do not ascend with the tide.

I am inclined to believe that these Tidal Trout are hybrids between the *S. fario* and *S. trutta*, both of which species they appear to resemble in some particulars. It may be that the sexual organs do not develope; consequently there is no spawning time. Did they spawn in the rivers, such an occurrence would have been noticed by so patient and painstaking an observer as Mr. Haynes. Is it possible that they spawn in the salt water of the sea? Such a phenomenon would be an exception to what is known to occur in the *Salmonidæ*. Moreover, did these fish spawn in the sea, say in November or December, could they possibly appear in the rivers, as early as January, in such splendid condition as they are known to show at that time? They could not have "mended" themselves in so short a time.

In general appearance the Slob Trout looks like the Common Trout, as I have said, but in certain structural characters it reminds one of the Salmon Trout. In its migratory habits it more closely resembles this latter fish, although the Common Trout is known occasionally to adopt migratory habits, and to descend to the sea.

The word *slob*, of which *slab* and *slop* are only other forms, denotes wet and loose mud, such as is usually abundant at the estuaries of rivers. The Trout descend with the tide to the slob, where they remain till the return of the tide.

# TITLES OF WORKS

## AND EDITIONS QUOTED IN THIS VOLUME.

Aristotelis, De Animalibus Historiæ, Libri x. ed. Schneider, 1811.

Ælian, De Animalium Naturæ, ed. Jacobs, 2 vols. 8vo., Jenæ 1832.

Plinius (C. Secundus) Historia Naturalis, Lugd. Batav. et Roterod. apud Hackios 1669.

Athenæus, Deipnosophistæ (Lib. vii.) ed. Dindorf, Leipsic 1827.

Oppianus, Halieutica, ed. Schneider, Argentorati 1776.

Ausonius, Id. x. Carmen de Mosella; Corpus Poet. Latin.

Bellonius (Petrus) De Aquatilibus, Paris 1553.

Rondeletius, Universæ Aquatilium Historiæ pars altera (de Piscibus, Lib. iv.—vii.), 1560.

Aldrovandus, De Piscibus, 1638.

Willughby (Franciscus) De Historia Piscium libri quatuor, recognovit Johannes Ray, 1686.

Artedi (Petri) Ichthyologia sive opera omnia de Piscibus, recognovit Carolus Linnæus, 1738.

Barrington on the Gillaroo Trout, also Hunter and Watson in Philosophical Transactions for 1774.

Linnæus (Carolus) Systema Naturæ, Holmiæ, ed. 1766.

Pennant, British Zoology, 4to., Warrington, printed by William Eyres, 4 vols., 1776—1777; and 8vo., 4 vols., ed. 1812.

Walton (Izaak) and Cotton, Complete Angler, ed. Sir J. Hawkins, 1760.

Bloch, Naturgeschichte der Fische Deutschlands, 4to. ed. Berlin 1782.

Lacépède, Histoire des Poissons, Paris 1798—1803, 4to.

Cuvier, Le Règne Animal, 8vo., Paris 1800—1805.

Donovan (Edw.) The Natural History of British Fishes, 5 vols. 8vo., London 1802—1808.

Turton, The British Fauna, Swansea 1807.

Fleming (John, D.D.) History of British Animals, 2nd. ed., London 1842.

Cuvier et Valenciennes, Histoire Naturelle des Poissons, Paris 1828.

Richardson (Sir John) Fauna Boreali-Americana, Part iii., London, 4to., 1836.

Parnell, The Natural History of the Fishes of the Firth of Forth, in vol. vii. of the Memoirs of the Wernerian Natural History Society, Edinburgh 1838.

Yarrell (William) A History of British Fishes, 2nd. edition, London, Van Voorst, 1841.

Jenyns'(Rev. Leonard) A Manual of British Vertebrate Animals, Cambridge, 1835.

Jardine (Sir William) and Selby, Edinburgh New Philosophical Journal for 1835.

Jardine (Sir William) Illustrations of Scotch Salmonidæ, folio.

Owen (R.) Descriptive Catalogue of the Physiological Series contained in the Collection of the Royal College of Surgeons, vol. i. Fishes, London, 4to., 1853.

Owen (R.) On the Anatomy of Vertebrates, vol. i. Fishes, London 1866.

Gaimard (P.) Voyage en Islande et en Grönland, exécuté pendant les années 1835 et 1836 sur la Corvette 'La Recherche,' Paris 1851.

Davy (Sir Humphry) Salmonia, London, J. Murray, 1869.

Davy (Dr. John) Physiological Researches, London 1863.

Couch, Fishes of the British Isles, 4 vols. 8vo., 1862—1865.

Siebold, Die Süsserwasserfische von Mittel-Europa, Leipzig 1863.

Thompson (William) The Natural History of Ireland, 4 vols., vol. iv., 1856, 8vo.

Günther's Catalogue of the Fishes in the British Museum, 8vo., 8 vols., London 1859—1870.

Buckland (F.) Familiar History of British Fishes, 8vo., S. P. C. K. 1873.

# INDEX.